Gridiron Glory Days: Football at Mercer 1892-1942

Gridiron Glory Days

Football at Mercer 1892-1942

by

Robert E. Wilder

Mercer University Press

MUP/P439

1400 Coleman Avenue
Macon, Georgia 31207

First Paperback Edition

Originally published in 1982.

Books published by Mercer University Press are printed on acid-free paper that meets the requirements of American National Standard for Information Sciences—Permanence of Paper for Printed Library Materials.

Mercer University Press is a member of Green Press Initiative (greenpressinitiative.org), a nonprofit organization working to help publishers and printers increase their use of recycled paper and decrease their use of fiber derived from endangered forests. This book is printed on recycled paper.

Library of Congress Cataloging-in-Publication Data

Wilder, Robert E. 1931–
Gridiron glory days

1. Mercer University—Football—History. I. Title.
GV958.M47W54 796.332'63'09758552 82-6366
ISBN: 978-0-88146-267-8 AACR2

Table of Contents

Foreword

by Leslie H. Peek ix

Chapter 1

Rah! Rah! Mercer! 1

Chapter 2

Football Revived 15

Chapter 3

Second Kickoff 29

Chapter 4

First Down 41

Chapter 5

Second Down 59

Chapter 6

Third and Long Yardage 79

Chapter 7

Last Down 171

Extra Points

An Afterword 191

Appendixes

A. Mercer Gridiron Record, 1892-1941 195
B. Mercer Gridiron Record, by Opponents 203
C. Football Scoring Leaders for the Mercer Bears 208
D. Mercer University Athletic Hall of Fame 212

Preface

Following a long period of hibernation, it is back to the future for Mercer football and the new gigantic bear mascot. World War II gave the last pause of 70 years, 1941-2013.

On November 19, 2010 the Board of Trustees unanimously voted to bring the Bear out of his cave and continue the quest for status in collegiate football at a called press conference of the trustees, students, members of the Mercer community, alumni, government officials, and members of the press. The process began.

Judge Homer Drake, Trustee Chairman, passed the baton to President Bill Underwood in the form of a new shiny football helmet with Mercer's colors and logo. President Underwood assured the audience the student athletes and program would have the necessities of a stellar program.

The men of yesteryear would tell the new recruits to "gear up," "achieve gridiron glory and make proud all those hearty players who have come before." Show the opponents in fine and aggressive form, "whence cometh that Bear!"

Bobby Wilder, Author
Spring, 2011

Foreword

Those of us who love football (what a crowd!) read eagerly the sports pages, magazines, team brochures, and numerous books available on every phase of the game. Here is an exciting addition to the lore of American football. It is an amazing chronicle of a team from a small Baptist school in Middle Georgia fielding a team against the likes of Georgia, Georgia Tech, Auburn, and Tennessee.

From the days when the ball was round and no padding was thought necessary to the heady splendor of the late Thirties, one can follow how the game has changed. Some of the early rules might surprise you (who remembers when a touchdown counted four points while a field goal was worth five?) and some of the game accounts owe much to the writers' imagination.

As you read, many of the names will be recognizable as early heroes and innovators who made their indelible marks on the history of the game. But most of the participants were ordinary men who played because of the exhilaration of running, tackling, blocking, and catching a ball in the air. I think you will find some of the same feelings as you read about the game of football as played by the Mercer Bears beginning back in 1892.

Leslie H. Peek

Chapter 1 RAH! RAH! MERCER!

The ball was round, the equipment was homemade, and the rules were uncertain, but that game the boys were playing on the lawn at Mercer University in 1892 was football. It resembled the modern day game in name only, as the "Battling Bears" made up in spirit what they lacked in know-how. During the next fifty years Mercer played more than 300 games against opponents such as Georgia, Georgia Tech, Florida, Army and Navy.

Those early games must have been an amazing spectacle for the Macon citizenry. Playing with no padding, the boys piled into each other with abandon in the rough-and-tumble style of the day. This apparently disorganized free-for-all was the beginning of football for Mercer and the rest of Georgia. It was a beginning that was a far cry from the organized splendor that is known today.

Class football started at Mercer in 1888, but the first intercollegiate meeting between Rutgers and Princeton took place back in 1869. The game moved slowly to the South from the Northeast as professors who were educated in northern schools provided instruction and demonstrated the plays to local students. Also, books and pamphlets were being written about the art of playing football, and many readers took up the game without any other source of information.

The students at Mercer, after reading Spalding's dime book on how to play football, gathered together to have a go at it. Very few, if any, had ever seen a game.

This activity was on an informal basis, and after the beginning in 1888 football continued on the campus with play between classes. The players developed skill and understanding of the game until they had enough confidence to accept a challenge for a match. A Thanksgiving Day meeting with the University of Georgia was arranged. The year was 1891, but getting the team organized caused a delay until January of the following year.

Preparation for the game was serious after the date was finalized. Regular practice sessions were held and plans were made to outfit the team. The uniforms consisted of white canvas jackets, white cannon knee pants, black stockings, and caps of orange and black, Mercer's school colors.

There was no padding or protective devices worn, so the uniforms offered little protection. However, the canvas pants and jackets were difficult to grasp and one former player related that grabbing an opponent's clothing often resulted in raw or sandpapered fingers.

Although there were no pads or helments, the players grew their hair long for padding against blows to the head. Needless to say, this gave very little protection. There was a leather noseguard developed later and boots of some fashion completed the outfit. A well-dressed football player of the era was not very well insulated against the knocks and jolts which were sure to come his way.

Daily accounts of practice were reported in the *Macon Telegraph*. Dave Beggs, a local citizen, was elected coach and captain. Beggs was not one of Mercer's 179 registered students at that time, but since there were no formal eligibility rules as we know them today, anyone could play for any team. Members of that first team were Beggs, Walter Turpin, J. V. Brown, R. E. Anderson, S. L. Chapman, Will Connor, D. R. Poteet, Reid Combs Nash, E. S. Atkinson, James M. Madden, and George Offerman, Jr. Brown was the largest boy on the team, and Madden, at five feet, six inches and 125 pounds, was the quarterback.

Of this 1892 team, Chapman and Offerman were students in the University High School. Beggs was from Macon, while Walter H. Turpin was a student enrolled at Washington and Lee. Home on vacation, Turpin was drafted for the team, since he knew something about the game. It is very interesting to note that through this experience with the Mercer boys and other experiences, Turpin became very fond of Mercer. On his death he bequeathed $5,000 to the University.

In addition to the varsity, the substitutes for the game were Felton Hatcher, Claud Poteet, Denny Poteet, C. B. Brown, Y. E. Bargeron and J. Grier. Following weeks of practice, the team was ready for the battle with the "varsities."

Since the game was to be played in Athens, most of the students, faculty, and many local citizens took the train for Athens. The fans who attended this game would actually witness the first college football game in Georgia, and one of the first in the deep South. Records indicate that Mercer was the initial opponent not only for Georgia, but for Georgia Tech and the University of Florida as well. The Bears also appeared on the schedule the first year that the University of Miami had a team.

The Mercer team, all decked out in their new, unsoiled uniforms, arrived, and after extensive welcoming ceremonies and good treatment by the Georgia students and Athens citizens, the game began. It might be noted here that touchdowns were four points, extra points were two, safeties were two, and field goals were five points.

Mercer got the ball first. There was no kickoff. They kept control for six minutes but could not score. Georgia took over; and Frank Herty, nephew of the Georgia coach, Charles Herty, promptly scored a touchdown. This score was followed by a touchdown by Kimball and an extra point by Brown to give Georgia a 10-0 lead. Shackleford caught a Mercer runner and carried him back over the goal for a safety. Kimball and Herty added touchdowns and Brown hit two more extra points. The first half lasted forty-five minutes, and when the referee called time, the score stood 28-0 in favor of Georgia.

After a five minute rest, Herty and Kimball ran over two touchdowns and Brown added the extra points to give Georgia a 38-0 lead. The newspaper account stated: "Herty got in another touchdown by a magnificent run, dodging his opponents after his blocking had been left, broke through the excited crowd, ran under a flight of steps, and scored with a Mercer man at his heels." Shackleford scored on a long run, and Herty scored the final touchdown to run his total to five for the day. The Mercer men drew praises for their hard fought battle, but they were no match for the "varsities" as the game ended 50-0.

As stated previously, the players wore no helmets and let their hair grow very long. One story has it that players began in June letting their hair grow for the football season, but that long hair was just a feature of an era and offered no protection for the head when it was used as a battering ram. As any Mercer alumnus knows, the school colors are orange and black and the nickname is "Bears." Supposedly, this nickname resulted from the Georgia game when one of the Mercer runners burst through the line and a Georgia player, looking up and seeing a bushy-headed runner coming toward him, remarked, "Whence Cometh That Bear?" Dr. S. V. Sanford, former president of Georgia and Mercer alumnus, told this story to a group of Mercer alumni in 1926. Whether true or not, this gives an interesting beginning to the athletic nickname.

Mercer offered to meet Georgia in another contest that season, but the match was never played. However, Georgia did play another game on 22 February 1892 against Auburn in Atlanta before 8,000 fans. Georgia lost this contest 10-0.

Mercer was able to schedule a second game for the 1892 season by accepting a challenge from the Savannah Catholic Library Association. Despite threats of rain, the Savannah team, fifty strong, arrived for the game on 26 March 1892. Since this was the first football contest the people of Macon were to see, great preparations were made, and the city had football fever. The Wesleyan girls came in great numbers. Banners and team colors were displayed by a throng of 2,000 which crowded the sidelines at the playing field in Central City Park.

The battle at Georgia had proved costly for the Bears, as some players dropped off the team, forcing inexperienced players to start against the invaders from the Forest City. Mercer players mentioned in this game were Nash, Bargeron, Burkhalter, J. V. Brown, Smith, McCall, Atkinson, and Chapman. The first half ended with Savannah leading 16-0, and after a ten-minute rest, the second half began. Since the first half provided experience for the Mercer players, they were able to hold Savannah to a lone touchdown while scoring a safety in the second half. The final score stood 20-2. The fans were very excited with the game, and they anticipated great things from the Mercer boys.

The rules for football had to be written as the game progressed through the years. Originally, a combination of rugby and soccer rules was used. When Mercer began to play in 1892, the field was 110 yards long and fifty-three yards wide, marked off in five-yard stripes, but there were no line sticks, and only two officials were used. The referee had to judge the distance of each play and used a handkerchief to mark the spot where the play began. He had to spend most of his time watching the handkerchief, to see that it did not get moved forward or backward by one of the teams. A team was composed of eleven players, which number had been reduced from twenty-two to fifteen, and there were usually four substitutes. The game was divided into playing halves of forty-five minutes, and a player could not leave the game unless he was injured. If he did, he couldn't return.

If on three consecutive downs a team did not advance five yards, the ball was awarded to the other side. Scoring values were: touchdowns, four points; extra points, two; field goals, five; and safeties, two points. Football was a rough sport, with strange rules and herculean expectations of players and officials. Since it was so rough, there were numerous injuries and many schools began to place restraining measures on their teams. Rules had to be amended and revised for the protection of the players if the game was to survive.

Mercer had now engaged the enemy twice, losing to Georgia 50-0 and to the Savannah Catholic Library Association 20-2. The opening of the following season in the fall of 1892 brought a victory over Georgia Tech by a 12-6 score. Following is the exact account of the game of 5 November 1892, as reported by the *Macon Telegraph*. This was the first football victory for Mercer and was also the first football game that Georgia Tech played.

Rah! Rah! Rah!
Mercer Does the Tech Up In
Great Shape
A FINE GAME OF FOOTBALL
An Exciting and Interesting Game
The Mercer Boys Were Too Heavy
for the Techs
Rah! Rah! Rah!
U-n-i
Sis, Bum, Rah,
Ver-Si-Ty-
Mercer!!!

Techs-
Tech-i-ty-Tech-
Who Rex-Who Rex-
Tech-i-ty-Tech-
Who Rex-Who Rex-
Boom, Rah!
Georgia!!!

Mercer has at last scored a touchdown and a triumph in football. She was twice defeated last season, but the present victory more than compensates for the last year's "walloping."

The Techs reached Macon at 10:30 by the E. T. V. and G. and marched to the Hotel Lanier, where they remained during the morning. The Mercers paraded the streets and gave their yell at frequent intervals.

The two teams left the Lanier in the band-wagon and reached the grounds at 2:15 p.m. After a little promiscuous kicking, the Techs took the ball and did a little steady practicing, afterwards running around the field. They seemed confident of victory, and certainly were a fine and formidable-looking set of men, although not quite so heavy as the home boys. They were active and looked in good wind and condition. By 2:45 the bleachers were packed and the grand stand was fairly filled. The opposing crowds were filling the air with their alternate and sometimes commingled yells and things were getting interesting. At 3 o'clock sharp referee Lane blew his whistle, and the ball was carried to the center of the field. Capt. West won choice, and took the ball. The Techs stood with their backs to the grand stand. A wedge was formed and the ball passed to West, who made a good attempt, but was downed by Small before he gained much ground. First down: Tech's ball, ball passed to Hunter; Atkinson breaks through and throws him hard. Second down: Forrest fumbled the ball in passing it back, and Nash had to cry down. Third down: a repetition of number two. The Techs seemed rather nervous. The fourth down failing to make their five yards, the ball went to Mercer, with wild cheers from the bleachers.

Mercer's ball, first down: ball passed to Small, who is downed by West. Second down: passed to McCall, who gains his five, round left end.

Mercer's ball, first down: passed to Small, who gains slightly round right end. Second down: centre forced and five yards gained. First down: ball passed to McCall, who fumbles and cries down. Second down: centre forced by Chapman; ball passed to Brown, who gains about six yards. First down: passed to Small, who goes through by tackle and gains his distance. First down: centre forced by Chapman and distance gained; but owing to a foul by the quarter, the ball went to the Techs, and Mercer was for the time checked.

Tech's ball, first down: passed to left half, who gains by a run round McRae, guarded by West and Miles. Second down: passed to West, who failed to advance. Third down: ball thrown to Niles, who, in trying to punt, misses and loses the ball. Ball goes to Mercer on Orr's downing it. First down: attempt on centre fails, second down: Small fails to advance and an attack on the centre failing, the ball goes to the Techs. First down: ball passed to full back, who is slow in punting and is downed by Atkinson. Second down: passed to West, who, guarded by Hunter, Niles and Nash, gains thirty-five yards. Failing to advance further by their next downs, the ball goes to Mercer. First down: double pass from Small to S. Kinnall, who goes round right end and gains his distance. First down: passed to McCall, who runs entirely across the field, but fails to gain a foot. Second down: Small makes a lovely run and downs the ball within eight yards of goal. First down: attack on centre fails. Techs fighting like good fellows. Second down: S. Kinnall fails to advance. Third down: centre forced by Chapman who carries the ball and, seemingly the whole Atlanta team over the line and makes the first score of the game. McCall failed to kick at goal, and the Techs took the ball again at 3:20.

The kick off by Niles was quickly followed, and McRae downed S. Kinnall immediately on his touching the ball. Mercer's ball, first down: attempt on centre fails. Third down: ball passed to Chapman who gains the distance. First down: Small fails, and successive attempts on centre failing, the ball goes to Tech. First down: the centre attempts to kick the ball past Brown, but it is stopped and downed. Mercer's ball, first down: Small gains slightly by guard of Sanford. Second down: Centre forced by Chapman and distance gained. First down: passed to McCall, who is not guarded and fails to advance. Second down: McCall makes a beautiful punt and Brown breaks through and downs the ball by placing fullback Niles out of the way. Gain: twenty yards. First down: Chapman forces centre and gains five yards. First down. S. Kinnall is beautifully guarded and advances his distance without being touched. At last downed by Whitney. First down: S. Kinnall fumbled and Warner breaks through and downs him. Second down and ten yards to make. An attempt on centre and attempted punt by McCall failing to materialize, the Techs take the ball. First down: Bargeron goes through and downs West. Second down: punt by Niles and fair catch by McCall. Mercer's ball, first down: Little comes through and downs S. Kinnall. Second down: Ball dropped in passing from Small to S. Kinnall and McCall downs it. Ball passed to McCall, who makes a lovely run, but loses it from foul by Small striking West in the face.

Tech's ball, first down: fumble by quarter and downed. Second down: West takes the ball and by means of splendid warding off, advances about ten yards. First down: foul tackle by Orr and West gives Techs five yards more. First down: ball passed back and fumbled. Secured by Atkinson, who completely ran over Whitney and carried the ball behind the post, running half the length of the field. He was well guarded by Sanford, Brown, and Stetson. McCall missed goal. Five minutes of first half remained. Techs formed a V, which gained but little, owing to the half being downed by Sanford. First down: West fails to advance. Second down: Niles makes a low bouncing punt which McCall fails to return, fumbles in picking up, attempts to kick, and misses. McRae and Nash come charging down. McRae blocks McCall and Nash carries the ball in touch, scoring the only point made by the Techs. Good kick by Nash. Mercer took the ball but failed to advance far before time was called, and the first half ended.

Mercer - Touchdowns 2; Points 8

Tech - Touchdowns 1; Points 6

The crowd made a desperate attempt to cross the field and reach the spot where the players were resting and eating, but owing to the skillful blocking of the police, were prevented, and had to return to the bleachers, where they greatly enjoyed a pugilistic contest that was held in spite of the police.

At 4:05 p.m. the second half began. Mercer gained ground by her wedge, but the ball was started again by command of referee, on Brown's passing it back with his hand and not by means of his foot. Second wedge did not advance far, and the half was downed. First down: centre forced and gain of two yards. Second down: centre forced and gain. From this point on the Mercer boys had the Techs completely at their mercy, and by means of a twisting motion by the entire team pushed the Atlantans at will. First down: Small goes through centre by Chapman, again gains. Second down: S. Kinnall goes by Green and gains. First down: Small gains on centre by Chapman. Second down: Small goes with Chapman again and the Techs are forced over another five-yard line. First down: pass to Brown and gain through centre. Second down: S. Kinnall goes by Green and gains on centre. First down: ball given to Chapman who carries everyone before him, and makes a big gain, which is lost on a claim of forward pass. Tech's ball. Ball passed to full back Niles, who punts. McCall catches and runs, doing some pretty dodging and brings the ball almost to the starting point before West downs him. Mercer's ball. Pass to S. Kinnall who loses the ball to West's tackle. Tech's ball.

Pass to West, who runs ten yards, and is thrown in touch. Second down: punt by Niles and failure to return by McCall makes fifteen yards for the Tech. An attempt was here made to substitute Hammond for S. Kinnall, but West objects and the game continues. Mercer's ball, first down: S. Kinnall goes through centre by Green and gains. First down: Small goes through an opening in the line and gains. First down: attempt on centre fails. Second down: centre by Chapman is forced by Small and touchdown made. McCall fails to kick goal. Time. 4:44.

Tech's ball. West runs with ball, but is downed by Atkinson. First down: Hunter is thrown by Bargeron. Second down: West gains ground by left end. Does good dodging. Techs gain five yards by Stetson's foul tackle. Techs gain five yards by Orr's foul on halfback. Mercer gets the ball on fumble of quarterback. First down: McCall makes a long run across the field and gains four yards. Second down: Small gains on the centre being forced, S. Kinnall gains on centre by Green and Bargeron. First down: McCall gains round left end. Second down: McCall gains on centre forced by Chapman. First down: McCall goes through a break in centre made by the great "J. V." but is called back on claim of held previous to forcing through. Five minutes left for play was called by referee. Centre forced by McCall aided by Small and results in a big gain. Mercer takes five yards on West's foul tackle. Mercer loses ball on foul pass. Tech's ball. Techs take five yards on Orr's foul tackle of West. First down: Bargeron throws Hunter hard. Time called.

Julian Lane, Referee. J. H. Brown, Atlanta, Umpire. Average weight of Mercer, 164 pounds; of the Techs, 160 pounds.

The game, while not brilliant, was full of earnest and determined effort, and this sort of playing is after all, the most enjoyable to watch. The frequent fumbles, which so frequently marred the beauty of the game, were caused by the quarterbacks passing the ball too high, and compelling the half backs to reach for it and lose time. Mercer has scored one more triumph for Macon over Atlanta.

Following are the names of the players and their positions:

Mercer	**Position**	**Techs**
Brown	Centre	Forrest
Green	Rt. Guard	Holmes
Chapman	Lt. Guard	Spain
Toole	Rt. Tackle	Little

Mercer	Position	Techs
Stetson	Lt. Tackle	Warner
Atkinson (Prep)	Rt. End	McRae
Sanford	Lt. End	Whitney
Small (Capt)	Rt. Half	Hunter
S. Kinnall	Full back	Niles

Substitutes for Mercer: Wright, Greer, Poteet.
Substitutes for Techs: Nally, Long, Black.

Football at Mercer did not have the sanction of the entire university, and the boys played on an unofficial basis. There were many faculty members who were opposed to the boys spending their time engaging in such a wasteful pastime when they should be mastering their lessons. The students felt otherwise and pushed for a recognized program. On 24 September 1893, Claude Gray and Polhill Wheeler, both students, requested permission from the faculty to be allowed to play football. Records are scarce, but they do indicate that George T. Stallings became football trainer on 3 December 1893.

One game was scheduled with Tech for the 1894 season, and Mercer lost 10-6. Since there were no eligibility rules at this time, coaches, faculty members, graduate students, and non-students played for Mercer and Captain Leonard Wood played for Tech. Captain Wood was an army surgeon who was stationed in Atlanta. He eventually reached the rank of major general and was recognized as one of the most outstanding military men of all time.

Some years later, Stallings reminisced about how tough Wood was and how he made life miserable for the Mercer team in that game against Tech. Wood's playing against Georgia in 1893 may have resulted in the first accusation of player ineligibility in the South. It was also found that Georgia used their trainer in that game.

Stallings only worked with the Mercer boys during the football season, since his major interest was baseball. He lived in Augusta and came to Macon on the weekends, so the Mercer boys actually got little training during the week. Stallings, originally from Haddock, Georgia, managed the Boston Braves, the Detroit Tigers, and the New York Yankees. He led Boston over the Philadelphia Athletics in the 1914 World Series. It is interesting to note that his wife visited the campus during the 1940s when efforts were made to start the football program again.

In 1895 Mercer's Athletic Association was reorganized, but no games were played during that season. This was still a very difficult time for football. Many colleges were requiring their students to discontinue the sport, and the Mercer administration was not very enthusiastic about endorsing a team.

Mercer did have a talented football player on the campus in T. J. Cochran, and his services were in demand. He was reported to have played center for Georgia against North Carolina, Auburn and Vanderbilt. The story goes that he was wired from Athens to come play for Georgia, after which he returned to his law studies at Mercer.

In 1896 J. D. Winston was retained as trainer and H. L. D. Hughes was manager. In October of that year, a request was presented to the faculty by the athletic committee for permission to play Georgia and Tech. Permission was granted to play Georgia, but permission to play Tech was contingent upon good behavior in Athens. The game with Georgia did not materialize, but two games were played with Tech. The first game Tech won 6-4, and the second resulted in a 4-4 tie.

Manager Hughes secured a game with Auburn, since the Georgia game was not played, but Auburn proved too tough, and romped 46-0. K. C. Moore, of the class of '89, described some of the action to this writer. "In a game with Auburn, Alabama, they were really beating us. I was substitute quarterback, weighing 148 pounds, and was put in at the start of the second half. Our fullback kicked one very high, and I sped down the field. Just as the Auburn man caught the ball, I picked him up and ran back five yards with him. The referee O.K.'d it."

The students at Mercer began to take more positive steps toward intercollegiate athletics with a formal petition on 15 February 1896. "The student body, believing that intercollegiate sport, properly and judiciously conducted, serves to promote the interest of the institution in that it will bring it more prominently before the public and will render it more popular to young men who are contemplating entering college, and also believing that the encouragement of such exercises contributes to the physical development of the students, respectfully petition you to permit the students to play a few intercollegiate games of football during the present season, on condition that the athletic association confer with the faculty before arranging any games." This petition was signed by A. Y. Napier, J. T. Arnall, and J. M. Heard.

In 1897 one game was played with Auburn, and Auburn won 26-0. Gordon Saussy was coach and T. O. Lee was captain and manager. Saussy coached the University of Georgia in 1899. Mercer entered the Southern Intercollegiate Athletic Conference, known as the SIAC, in 1897. This conference had been formed in 1894 and was composed of most of the colleges in the southern states. (Later, the Conference became an Association—SIAA.)

It was in 1897 that football in Georgia suffered a nearly fatal blow. Richard "Von" Gammon, a member of the Georgia team, died of injuries sustained in a game. As a result of his death, the faculty at Mercer forbade the students to play football. The state government was even pondering legislation making football illegal. Had it not been for the intervention of Gammon's mother, football would have probably been banned from the campuses of Georgia. She intervened by writing a letter to her representative asking that football not be declared illegal. This letter was published in the newspapers.

On 14 November 1898, the Mercer faculty reacted with a regulation stating that "no game of football shall be allowed off the campus, nor with any outside team on the campus, and further that no individual student be allowed to play on an outside team without first filing with the President a written request from parent or guardian." The playing of football was thus curtailed for a period of time. Class football was allowed in 1901 and the faculty athletic committee, which had been formed in 1899, recommended that football be encouraged for 1903.

W. K. Young, the football manager, got permission from the faculty to schedule three games with minor schools. The faculty consented but stipulated that team members could not have as many as two unexcused absences from classes, that the manager couldn't have ten in a term, and that players and manager must have a seventy average. The manager in this era was a very important person. It was his task to schedule games, handle all aspects of equipment, transportation, and meals. He was also very often responsible for the hiring of a trainer. Generally, the trainer was not a faculty member and would work with the team only during the sports seasons.

The Mercer Athletic Association was now actively trying to get Mercer involved in a broader athletic program. The Association, operating independently of the University, provided the money and facilities for all contests. In 1903 the Athletic Association agreed to buy, for an athletic park, four and one-half acres of land between Boundary Street and Tindall Old Field for $2,800. The Association paid $1,000 cash and borrowed the remainder from Mercer. This was to be repaid in six notes of $300 each bearing six percent interest. Practice had been held on the campus and in Tattnall Square Park, but the park was being renovated as a public park, so a new area was needed.

The students returned to school in 1903 and found that a contract with Georgia Tech for a game in Atlanta had to be met. Actually no team had been planned and Coach Harvey, who had been hired for the season, did not report at the beginning of school. A meeting was held and a team was selected for the game against the "Blacksmiths" in Atlanta. The men chosen were Ellison, Brown, Todd, McWhorter, Roberts, Quarles, Stovall, Lewis, Lowe, Munday, and Redding.

The plan for the season was to continue playing if the game against Tech was won and to discontinue playing if the team lost. Mercer lost 46-0 in a game in which the last half was reduced ten minutes. It was reported that Mercer's trouble was "ignorance of the game." The second game of the season was supposed to have been with Georgia but it was canceled.

O. C. Griner in one of his "Robin Trot" letters wrote about this game in 1955 and stated:

Sometime during the year 1903 the Mercer Athletic Association signed a contract to play Georgia Tech a game of football on Grant Field. The contract provided for the forfeit of $1,000 in case either team failed to show up for the game. I was a member of the athletic council at Mercer for the year and soon after the opening of school in September the many problems connected with putting out a football team were discussed. I do not think the college had a team the year before, so the hiring of a coach, arranging more games, buying equipment, etc. were discussed; but as there was no money in the Association treasury our dilemma grew bigger from week to week. No coach could be hired without our promise to pay him a salary and that we could not do—the till was empty.

The big forfeiture specified in the contract stared us in the face at every meeting so that we were all in a state of near desperation. One member of the faculty was on the council. He was the chairman. At one meeting early in October he asked if we just had to have a coach, if we could not fill the engagement, maybe win it, and especially save the $1,000 by playing the game with an uncoached team. He made an impassioned appeal and the student members of the council thought the idea wonderful.

Our problem was put before the student body next morning at chapel by the chairman. Volunteers were called for, and that afternoon the most disreputable looking bunch of would-be footballers imaginable showed up on Tattnall Square for practice. It was mostly a Brick Hall crowd—men like W. H. Daniel, Paul Ellison, and myself; some eighteen or twenty reporting for practice daily until selections were made for the squad of fifteen to go to Atlanta and play the game; yes, win it, our chairman told us; save the institution a thousand dollars. A man named Harris, Charley Harris, living in Macon, had attended some northern school and played football there, and perhaps it was the chairman who persuaded him to arrange and diagram a number of plays for us. It was these we had been using and working on during practice.

We went to Atlanta Friday afternoon. Tech representatives met us and took us to the Windsor Hotel, a pretty good hotel then, situated across Pryor Street from the present Candler Building.

Saturday was cold. At game time a stiff wind swept across Grant Field. Our men were poorly and thinly clad and our teeth were chattering when the whistle blew; but soon were steaming hot from the furious play. At half time Tech had scored two touchdowns, each, I think, then counted only five points, and they had scored once on the "dropkick," a play not used now, counting them as the "goal from field" does at present—three points.

Our little band had given its all in the first half. We had stood off the great Tech team time and time again from our goal. Hands, faces, noses, nearly all were bruised, skinned, and some were limping from near-breaks; but there was no second team to put in nor did we have but the four substitutes. Every man gave his best. Tech scored often, especially in the last quarter. Georgia Tech had at that time one of the great coaches of the day. He came on the field at the finish of the game and congratulated us every one, holding the hand of our captain, Paul Ellison, while he praised our spirit and courage, particularly our cooperative spirit. There had been no fight, no slugging, no flaring of tempers. He said it was a good, clean, hardfought game, a better game really than they expected us to give them; that he was sure the big crowd had enjoyed it.

The squad returned to Macon by train Saturday night. Not a Mercer man at the station to meet us. No Rah-Rahs could be heard. Suitcases in hand, we caught streetcars to the campus. The majority of us lived in cottages on the campus and in Brick Hall. The write-up of the game in Sunday's paper praised Tech highly for the big score and commended Mercer for its stamina and fine spirit.

Following the devotional and announcements at Chapel Monday morning, lightning struck as from a clear sky. Our athletic council chairman told of this, one of the most loyal and courageous groups of men ever to represent Mercer anywhere. He said he thought Mercer, on Friday before, sent a load of bears to Atlanta; but from reports they must have been rabbits; swift of foot to get out of the way. For several minutes that little band of volunteers who had saved the institution one thousand dollars, and also had brought back a check for more than a thousand dollars for the athletic treasury, this council chairman belittled our effort, and with apparent great glee held us up to derision before the student body.

Everyone of us took it good-naturedly, but it was harder for me to absorb than any bump or bruise I had brought home from Grant Field.

Chapter 2
FOOTBALL REVIVED

Football returned to the Mercer scene in a much larger way in 1906 as six games were played. E. E. Tarr, probably the first paid coach at Mercer, had thirty-five men out for the team. The new rule allowing the use of the stiff arm caused much excitement among the players.

The "Tarros" of Coach Tarr opened up the season with a 28-5 victory over Gordon in a practice game. Gordon was a prep school, now Gordon Military, which had a notable football team during these early years and played a number of colleges.

Mercer took on Georgia once again in Central City Park on 4 November 1906. Georgia was smarting from a losing streak of thirteen games and romped over Mercer 55-0. It was customary in that day for the winning team to get the ball, but the Bears were having none of that. Georgia won the game and Mercer won the battle following the game and kept the ball. This quite naturally strained the Mercer-Georgia relationship, but the ball was finally mailed to Georgia after the boys from Mercer were prevailed upon by Professor E. T. Holmes to show good sportsmanship. Todd Connor captained the team and had Adamson, Samms, McCathern, Scoggin, Westberry, Dyar, Melton, Hogg, Shaw, Loftin, Sutton, Farmer, Mosley, and Bussell as teammates.

The Citadel defeated Mercer 10-0, but the Bears then defeated Florida 12-0. The final game of the season saw Tech pour it on Mercer in Central City Park by a score of 61-0. One of the Tech guards stated, "These Mercer fellows are a d---ed gentlemanly set of fellows if they can't play football."

In 1907 H. R. Shencker, a Yale graduate, was retained as coach and fifteen new uniforms were bought. Harry Shaw was the captain. The season opened with a 6-0 victory over Florida when a punt was blocked on the Florida ten-yard line. J. A. Scoggin recovered and ran it over for the touchdown. A. C. Knight added the extra point. This was the second year for Florida in football, and Mercer had defeated the school both years. The 1906 game was the first intercollegiate game for Florida.

On 16 November 1907 Mercer edged Gordon 5-0 in Macon. The win was a difficult one, for Mercer had to hold a determined Gordon eleven at the five-yard line three times during the game.

Auburn once again proved superior to Mercer in a 63-0 rout in Auburn. Mercer bounced back, however, with an 11-6 win over Howard College as Baylor Landrum and N. D. Mallary scored for the Bears.

On 19 October Mercer entertained Georgia before an enthusiastic overflow crowd, with Georgia winning once again 26-6. In the first half the defensive line of John Underwood, Ed Poole, Rowe Hicks, George Spurlin, J. A. Scoggin, and Hub Dowis, along with Shaw and Melton, held the mighty varsities to a lone touchdown. An extra point and a field goal were added to make the score 10-0 at the half. In the second period Mercer fumbled and Georgia got a quick touchdown. Then Georgia got an unusual touchdown when a Georgia man ran outside the boundary line for a touchdown with no Mercer player attempting to stop him. Mercer's only score came when J. A. Scoggin intercepted a pass and ran it back for five points. Landrum added the point after, to account for Mercer's sixth point. Although the defeat was bitter, the team was jubilant with the touchdown, and J. A. Scoggin was particularly proud of scoring the first touchdown against Georgia for Mercer.

The final game of the 1907 season matched Mercer with Mississippi A&M in Columbus, Mississippi. This game followed a night and day train ride which left the gallant band of seventeen too tired to fight. A&M won 75-0. In addition to the players mentioned earlier, others on the 1907 squad were J. M. Gillespie, John Underwood, Bob Poole, Tutt Dunaway, Tom Farmer, Dean Newman, Willie Suddeth, Parker, and Malone.

In 1906 the forward pass had been introduced and it eventually revolutionized the game. The original intent was for the pass to be thrown underhanded, but enterprising players mastered the art of tossing it overhand. The early ball, more round than oval, was difficult to throw and to control. As the shape of the ball was gradually changed, the passers became more proficient. The number of officials was also changed, to include a referee, two umpires, and a linesman. The length of the game was reduced to sixty minutes and divided into thirty-minute halves. The distance to gain on downs for a first down was increased to ten yards.

The 1908 season brought Frank Blake, a Vanderbilt graduate, to Mercer as coach. Blake had received some fame as a prep coach at Bowen Institute in Nashville and at Gordon. His Gordon team was narrowly defeated by the Bears in 1907 by a score of 5-0. H. C. Miller, from Richmond College, was assistant coach and was probably the first assistant coach that Mercer ever hired.

The season opened with a 56-0 romp over Locust Grove Institute in a practice game. Auburn once again proved too tough and won for the fourth consecutive time, by a score of 23-0. The halftime score was 6-0 and Mercer's biggest threat was an intercepted pass early in the first half, which Poole returned to the Auburn eight. Florida once again fell under the spell of the Bears and suffered a 24-0 loss.

On 22 November Mercer faced the "Golden Tornadoes" of Georgia Tech. Mercer was primed for the fight as Clay Binion unlimbered his arm with passes to ends Poole and Salter. Mercer got on the board first by punting to the Tech ten-yard line, where the ball was promptly fumbled. Gillespie recovered, and he was dragged across the goal by Poole for the Mercer touchdown. Binion made the extra point to give Mercer a 6-0 lead. Tech scored to make it 6-6 at the half and added two more touchdowns for a 16-6 victory.

Once again the Georgia Bulldogs had to fight hard for an 11-0 victory over the Bears. Coach Blake had really drilled the boys well, and their defense proved it as Georgia was held scoreless during the first half. In the second half Georgia got a touchdown on a fumble and a blocked punt deep in Mercer's territory.

Captain Scoggin and his teammates really got fired up on Thanksgiving Day and walloped Howard 45-0 for the largest score in the United States that day. The passing game was really clicking as three passes from beyond the twenty went for touchdowns. Salter got an assisted touchdown when he returned a punt to Howard's ten-yard line and then was dragged across by his teammates as the Howard defenders tried to pull him back. The final game of the season was lost to the Citadel 10-0.

The 1909 season ended with a record of three victories and four defeats. Frank Blake returned as coach and brought R. E. Blake to serve as his assistant. Bob Blake, a former end at Vanderbilt, remained at Mercer only until 15 October, when he left to resume studies at Oxford on a Rhodes scholarship.

The first game of the season matched Mercer and Vanderbilt in Nashville. The half score was 11-5 in favor of Vanderbilt. Mercer scored when Bob Poole intercepted a Neely pass and returned it sixty yards for a touchdown. Tutt Dunaway threw the key block for the touchdown. The Mercer team fought hard and McGugin, the famous Vandy coach, said, "Barring Sewanee and Tennessee, Mercer is the only team which has played on Dudley Field for several years that fought as hard the last down as they did the first." The final score was 28-5.

Auburn came to Mercer on 15 October with a team that outweighed the Mercer boys twelve pounds per man. The visit to Macon marked one of the few times that the game was held on Mercer's home field. Auburn scored first with a field goal by Reynolds. Mercer recovered with Clay Binion, left halfback, making a spectacular dash to the Auburn twenty-yard line. Bob Poole was on the receiving end of a ten-yard pass and was dragged the remaining ten yards by Scoggin as three Auburn players tried to stop him. Auburn scored another field goal for a 6-5 halftime lead. The final score was 23-5 in favor of Auburn, with Clay Binion playing the most outstanding game of his career for Mercer.

In a rough affair, in which Mercer was penalized over one hundred yards, Georgia Tech defeated Mercer 35-0 in Atlanta. Although Tech won, Scoggins and Poole gained yardage every time they were given the ball. J. M. Gillespie and Captain R. C. Griffith "got away with several splendid tackles, while Zellars covered himself with glory by making some of the most sensational open field tackles ever seen here."

The Chattanooga Moccasins fell 10-2 before the touchdowns of J. W. Jacobs and Binion. Jacobs went forty yards after the kickoff, but Mercer was stopped at the Chattanooga fifteen-yard line. A Chattanooga runner broke away but was stopped short of a touchdown with a dazzling tackle by Bob Poole. Mercer got the ball again and drove to the Chattanooga ten where Jacobs went over for the touchdown. The goal was not kicked "owing to interference of the electric wires used for lighting the park." In the second half Binion returned a punt thirty yards for a touchdown. Chattanooga's only score came on a safety. Bob Poole, Binion, Scoggin, Dunaway, Brown, and Jacobs were outstanding in this game.

In a game with South Carolina, Mercer came from behind in the final ninety seconds to overcome a 3-0 deficit. South Carolina arrived late for the game and called time out nine times in the second half, stalling for darkness. In the first half Mercer went to the Carolina seven-yard line three times but lost the ball twice on fumbles and was held for downs once. With two minutes to play, Binion hit H. L. Grice with a thirty-yard aerial from the South Carolina thirty-eight. Jacobs scored a touchdown on third down for a 5-3 win. "Scoggin, Jacobs, Grice, and Dunaway were outstanding. Capt. Griffith made a spectacular return of a punt while Zellars' broken field running was of the highest order."

On 23 October 1909, in Macon, Mercer battled Howard College. It resembled the War Between the States as a number of Howard's troops and a coach came from Pennsylvania. This was one of the earliest instances of recruiting from the North. "During the game, Denny and Williams of Howard were ordered from the field for cursing a Mercer player, but Howard had brought only one substitute, so the two boys stayed in the game." Scoggin got Mercer's only touchdown in the second half when he recovered 6-5 as the extra point was missed.

The season ended with a 26-0 scrimmage victory over Norman Park. Members of the 1909 team were Bradley Hogg, Abe Conger, Tutt Dunaway, Bob Poole, Ed Poole, J. A. Scoggin, E. P. Mosley, Jake Zellars, R. C. Griffith, Clay Binion, J. M. Gillespie, J. W. Jacobs, H. L. Grice, S. R. McDaniel, R. N. Burns, and H. G. Howell. J. A. "Cap" Scoggin played football at Mercer for five years, captained the team twice, and was a standout performer during his playing days.

There were some significant changes evident at the beginning of the 1910 season. The University hired Dr. C. C. Stroud, a graduate of Tufts Medical College, as director of physical culture, coach, and history professor. He had formerly been at the University of Rochester where his teams won three championships. The football schedule was increased to nine games, and the team fashioned an enviable 6-3 record.

Rule changes for 1910 season saw the game divided into quarters of fifteen minutes each instead of thirty-minute halves. The reports of the games indicate that rarely was a half actually thirty minutes. The unreliable method of keeping time caused halves to be from twenty to forty minutes in length. There was also a possibility of variations occurring on opponents' fields, especially in the thick of battle, or when it would be advantageous to the home team. Time out between quarters was limited to one minute with a thirty-minute rest at the half. Other rules beginning in 1910 were:

1. Forward pass may not be executed out of a twenty-yard zone.
2. Onside kick may not be made within a twenty-yard zone.
3. Forward passer or kicker must be five yards back of the line.
4. Quarterback may advance ball without five-yard restriction.
5. Tackler in the open must have one foot on the ground.
6. Ends may not be interfered with within twenty-yard zone.
7. Pushing or pulling of the runner is strictly forbidden.
8. Forward passes may cross the line of scrimmage at any point.

9. Interference with the man receiving the forward pass is forbidden.

10. Player may return to the game once in any subsequent quarter.

11. Crawling, after the ball is dead, is penalized.

The season opened on 24 September with a 32-0 romp over Locust Grove with S. R. McDaniel, Jake Zellars, and Clay Binion getting two touchdowns each. Binion also added two extra points. Officials for the game were Coach Stroud of Mercer and Coach Turner of L. G. I.

On 1 October Mercer traveled to Clemson and earned a 3-0 victory on Binion's thirty-yard field goal. After having great difficulty with transportation, the team arrived just two hours before the game. In addition to this frustrating situation, the team was penalized a record 160 yards during the game.

The Bears' third consecutive victory saw Mercer defeat the Medical Department of Georgia 22-0. Binion led the scoring with two touchdowns and two extra points. McDaniel and Bill Foxworth scored touchdowns. Other outstanding players in this game were Bradley Hogg, Tutt Dunaway, Abe Conger, and Jake Zellars.

Georgia Tech, fast becoming a football power, raced past Mercer 46-0 in Atlanta. Old foe Florida fell for the fourth straight time to Mercer 13-0. The home crowd roared with delight as Mercer held the Gators in check. Florida took the ball and recorded four quick first downs, but the Mercer warriors quickly put an end to the threat. Binion with a field goal and McDaniel and Bob Poole with touchdowns paced the Mercer scoring.

Georgia proved too much once again and recorded a 21-0 win. The score at the half stood 6-0, but the superior strength and manpower of the Bulldogs stopped the Bears in the second half. Outstanding in that game for Mercer were Bradley Hogg, Captain Dunaway, Grice, Conger, R. N. Burns, Poole, Hal Davidson, Binion, McDaniel, Zellars, and Foxworth.

Following the Georgia loss, Mercer journeyed to Chattanooga and suffered a 6-0 loss in cold and rainy weather. The next weekend found the Mercer Bears in Savannah for a battle with the Citadel. This wet and rainy day proved more to their liking and a 21-0 victory was recorded over the Cadets. "The Citadel tried the Carlisle Indian stunt by bunching the backfield and having one man put the pigskin behind him, under his sweater, then another player, faking with a headgear, ran down the field." The trick failed and Mercer won with Frank Norman, Zellars, Foxworth, and Binion scoring touchdowns.

The final game of the season was played in Macon where Howard was defeated 28-0. Mercer didn't get on the scoreboard until the third quarter when Zellars scored from twenty yards out. The highlight was Binion's seventy-five-yard run in the fourth quarter. Touchdowns were scored by Binion, Zellars, and McDaniel who got one each, and by Foxworth who scored twice. Foxworth added two extra points and McDaniel, one.

Members of the 1910 team not mentioned previously were Lionel West, Hugh Mills, John "Mugs" Lawrence, Fred Herndon, Sam Granade, R. N. Salter, Ray Cook, C. W. Coleman, O. S. Marett, and G. F. Kelley. Bill Joy served as assistant coach.

Lionel West, a lineman on the 1910 team, was a very interesting individual. At age twenty he had been a fireman and an engineer for the railroad, but entered school to play football. After leaving Mercer he went to Georgia to study farming, then to Tech, and finally to the University of California where he was one of 287 out for the football team. He once boxed a twenty-round exhibition bout with Jack Dempsey and eventually worked in the movies where he was known as the "The Dramatic Giant," and "screendom's greatest athlete."

Bradley Hogg received more fame for his baseball ability than for football, as did many of the players in that day. Hogg was an outstanding pitcher for Mercer and eventually played for the Philadelphia Athletics.

Following the 1910 season, the SIAA passed a one-year rule regarding transfers. This meant that the practice of recruiting players off other campuses would be curtailed since a player was no longer immediately eligible for play.

Thirty-five men reported for practice in Tattnall Square Park for the 1911 season. Dr. Stroud returned as coach and Jake Zellars was elected captain. Members of the team were W. W. Granade, G. F. Kelley, Hugh Mills, Fred Bloom, J. W. Bradford, H. L. Grice, J. W. Foxworth, Herschel Forrester, J. Frank Norman, J. T. Edwards, Roy Cook, Donald Powell, Harry Irwin, J. T. Zellars, Leon McKnight, C. E. Doyle, B. Y. Jameson, W. J. Stribling, Charles Huguley, Abe Conger, Kellog, Pirkle, Brown, Hudson, Morris, and Chapman.

The season opener with Locust Grove was a 25-0 win for Mercer with Howell getting one touchdown and "Dutch" Irwin and Frank Norman getting two each. Gordon proved tough, as usual, and Mercer won 12-0 with Irwin getting two touchdowns for ten points, and a safety accounting for the other two.

The Georgia Bulldogs, expecting an easy victory over the Bears, ran into trouble and had to fight for an 8-5 victory. Jake Zellars became the second Mercer man in history to score on the mighty "Dogs." The game was played amid cries of "ringers," "unfair coaching," and "poor sportsmanship." Following the game, and for several days after, the papers were thick with charges and counter-charges. Two charges made by Georgia were that H. L. Grice was a ringer along with Irwin, and that Dr. Stroud used unfair coaching techniques during the game. It was not legal to yell encouragement from the sidelines or make coaching suggestions to the players, and the Georgia fans thought Stroud was guilty of this infraction.

Grice was a rough, tough, former railroad man, who had entered college late to study for the ministry. He was fully capable of handling any man around and really enjoyed his work. Morgan Blake, a sportswriter of considerable note for a number of years in Georgia, told a story about Grice in his book, *A Sports Editor Finds Christ*. He wrote:

> It was en route to Thomaston with Harvey Hardy, Tech's first all-America, and Randall Gann in the car with us, that Coach W. A. Alexander cut loose with this one:
>
> The meanest and toughest guy I ever ran across on a gridiron was a fellow by the name of Grice, who is now a Baptist preacher. He was on a Mercer team we were playing. I was doing a little scrubbing at different places in the line, and when we had a comfortable lead on Mercer, Coach Heisman took out our regular center, Al Loeb, and sent me in to take his place. Every time I snapped the ball, this Baptist preacher-to-be would come charging in and hit me like a ton of bricks, growling imprecations as he did so. I would be hurled back at such speed that I often arrived in the quarterback's arms shortly after the ball got there. Our backs were nevertheless gaining pretty steadily because this fiend, the Mercer center, didn't seem to be interested in anything but bruising me. By the time we had reached their 20-yard line on the drive, I was in a woeful physical condition. So I called time out. I said to my teammates, "Let's punt, I can't take any more."
>
> They replied: "What? Punt when we've reached their 20-yard line and first down?"
>
> "Yes," I said, "I don't care if we've reached the two-yard line. Let's punt. Let's let them have the ball a while."
>
> "So," concluded Alex, "we punted over the goal and Mercer took over—which may have saved my life.

In the fourth game of the season, Columbia College of Lakeland, Florida edged Mercer 6-5 as Zellars came up with the Mercer touchdown. The big win of the season came over Clemson in Columbus, Georgia, by a score of 20-6. Irwin and McKnight got touchdowns while Irwin added three field goals and one extra point. The final victory of the season was over Howard as the Bears romped 29-0. Frank Norman scored three touchdowns while McKnight and Foxworth added one each. Irwin had four extra points.

Other losses that year were to Auburn 29-0, Tech 17-0, Mississippi 34-0, and Citadel 5-0. The final game of the season resulted in a 6-6 tie with Columbia as Zellars scored and Irwin added the extra point. Homer Grice, the Mercer "bad boy," as far as the opponents were concerned, made all-Georgia and second team all-Southern. He also wrote and delivered the senior class poem at graduation exercises.

J. Frank Norman captained the 1912 team which recorded five wins, three defeats, and one tie. New schools on the schedule which suffered defeat at the hands of the Bears were Stetson, 6-0, and Tennessee, 27-14. Mercer also defeated Columbia 71-0, Gordon 29-6, and Howard 36-0. Losses were to Auburn 56-0, Clemson 21-13, Tech 16-0, and Florida was tied 0-0.

The 1912 season opened with the Bears battling Gordon in Central City Park. Touchdowns now counted six points. A highlight of the game was when Col. Teddy Roosevelt attended the game for a few minutes while traveling through the city on a political visit. Touchdowns were scored by Holman, Irwin, Norman, and Forrester. Irwin had a field goal and two extra points.

The Bears blasted the Howard Bulldogs in Birmingham for one of the rare victories in the Steel City. Touchdowns were made by McKnight, Norman, and Sams, who got one each and "Skipper" Cochran who had two. Irwin added one extra point and one field goal while Norman kicked two extra points.

The Tennessee Vols came to Central City Park for a battle on 9 November and were soundly defeated as Bo Phillips and Skipper Cochran got one score each and Frank Norman added two. Bill Foxworth booted three extra points. Although the Bears won, there was a loss of $200 at the gate. The final score was 27-14.

The final game of the season saw Clemson beat Mercer 21-13 as Phillips scored on a seventy-yard pass from Carson. Norman scored the other touchdown and Foxworth added the extra point.

Following the 1912 season Dr. Stroud left Mercer and became track coach at Louisiana State University. He had worked hard at Mercer, serving as football, basketball, and baseball coach during his entire tenure. One of his former players stated: "Dr. Stroud was a very excellent coach and well-liked by the boys. He was probably more famous as a basketball coach than anything else. On many occasions when a player would get hurt and require stitches he would open his bag, get out the needle, and sew him up on the spot." Stroud once stated that he had endeavored to have a well-balanced sports program while other schools had winter football leagues to develop talent. When he left to go to LSU, he had been coach at Mercer longer than any other person, having been at Mercer since early in 1910.

Fred Kelley was elected captain of the 1913 team at the close of the 1912 season, but he did not return to school. The new coach, Lewie Hardage, found the going rough and posted a 2-5-1 record during his one-year stay. Hardage was a former Vanderbilt player. Three standout performers of the 1912 team, Norman, Kelley, and Foxworth, failed to return to school. Men out for the team were: F. A. Sams, McKibben Lane, W. C. Parker, J. M. Lanier, Herschel Forrester, Hugh Mills, Charles Huguley, G. H. "Skipper" Cochran, John Westmoreland, C. E. Dewberry, J. W. Holman, E. P. Lee, Charles Hertwig, Charles Wills, Williams, Sammons, Dunn, Fort, Sharpe, and Levie.

The season opened with a 44-0 victory over the Tenth District Aggies from Granite Hill. Pat Hogan, a former Mercer player, was the opposing coach. Hugh Mills served as Mercer's captain as Sams scored three times, Westmoreland twice, and Parker twice. Westmoreland booted two extra points.

Auburn blistered the Bears 52-0, and Tech followed with a 33-0 victory. Against the Citadel, Mercer scored in the first three minutes as Sams went over for the touchdown and then booted the extra point for a 7-0 lead. The Cadets came back and scored for a 7-7 tie. Skipper Cochran and Big Boy Forrester led the Bears. The game ended in a 7-7 tie.

The second win of the season came over the Alabama Presbyterians by a score of 33-0. Cochran ran over four touchdowns and Sams scored a touchdown and added three extra points. Forrester scored the only touchdown in a 13-6 loss to Stetson on 7 November 1913. The last two games of the season were losses. Professor R. W. Edenfield sent out one thousand letters seeking support for the Clemson game, which was won by the Tigers 52-0. Florida finished off the Bears for the disappointing 1913 season with a 24-0 victory.

In 1914 Fred A. "Rabbit" Robins became coach and George C. Gibson was the manager. Nine games were scheduled in this rebuilding year. The seventeen-man squad was captained by Herschel Forrester.

The season opened with a 44-0 romp over Gordon with A. J. Swann and Skipper Cochran getting two touchdowns each while Dick Hawes, Willie Parker, and Red Welch scored one each. Parker kicked two extra points.

The team suffered when Forrester got injured in the Chattanooga game the following weekend. Chattanooga won 16-0. The next weekend, Georgia Tech, with a team that outweighed the Bears twenty-five pounds per man, blasted to a record 105-0 win as the Tech team, coached by John Heisman, ran up thirty-three points in the first quarter.

The following Saturday Mercer faced a high scoring machine in Kings College which had defeated Washington College 127-7 while Tech was trouncing Mercer. The Bears bounced back, however, and took Kings 27-7 as Frank Sammons starred for Mercer by getting three touchdowns. Swann added one score and Parker booted three extra points. Mercer completely outclassed Kings, rolling up fifteen first downs to only five for the visitors.

Another win was posted in a practice game with Gordon Military College by a score of 26-0. Losses were to Florida 14-0 and to Mississippi State 73-0 as the season ended. Cochran was an honorable mention SIAA by Coach Heisman of Tech. Cochran and Forrester made the all-Georgia teams.

The final victory of the 1914 campaign came over Furman 39-0 as Charlie Dewberry, substituting for the injured Cochran, ran wild. Swann scored four touchdowns, picked up 179 yards rushing, and caught a pass for thirty yards. Dewberry passed to Hawes for a touchdown, and Parker booted three extra points and scored one touchdown.

Some rule changes that had taken place in recent years resulted in larger scores and a more interesting game for the spectators. In 1910 a player withdrawn from a game for any reason was permitted to return to play in the next period. Prior to this, a player who was removed from the game in one half could not return until the next half. This lack of substitution actually created the iron-man atmosphere of football. It was detrimental to remove a starter from the game unless he was unable to play. Substitutes usually didn't get to play much. Thus, a starter missing from the lineup meant the loss of considerable game experience for the team.

In 1912 teams were allowed four downs instead of three to cover ten yards. It was also made legal for a forward pass to be caught across the goal line. Previously the ball had to be carried across. The higher scores were due to the fact that touchdowns now counted six points instead of five. The spectators got a treat when the players began to be numbered; now they could distinguish their favorites. The lack of numbers on the players had caused quite a concern for newspaper reporters. Morgan Blake wrote that as a young reporter he would often run out on the field and stop the play to see who had done what. He felt that the sportswriters were in better shape than the players in that era. They were never able to stop running during the game. Accounts of the games of this early era did not show complete statistics as do reports of games today. As a result, the exploits, yardage gained, touchdowns, and other features of many games often existed only in the minds of the men who played.

John Zellars, the former Mercer star, became coach in 1915 after a tenure as coach at Lanier High School. J. D. Carlisle served as manager and A. J. Swann was captain of the team. Other men on the sixteen-man squad were W. S. Florence, C. D. Hollingsworth, C. E. Vinson, J. F. Mayo, Mose Gordon, H. W. Drane, L. U. Bloodworth, J. S. Weekly, E. R. Welch, T. A. Fuss, B. F. Sammons, R. C. Dorsey, R. L. Cochran, W. H. Dowis, and Ralph Newton.

Mercer opened with Gordon in Central City Park and got a 6-0 win, when Newton went around right end in the fourth quarter for thirty yards to the one-yard line. Sammons rammed the ball across for the only touchdown. With big Seth Weekly anchoring the line, the stubborn Bear defense held the Gordon team scoreless. Although there were few bright spots on offense in this first game, Swann showed great form on punt returns.

The journey to Atlanta for the annual battle with Tech saw Mercer shut out 52-0. Everett Strupper, a Tech All-America and later coach at Mercer, scored three touchdowns.

On 11 October Mercer returned to Central City Park and recorded a 13-6 win over Wofford College. The game was delayed a number of times by coaches charging on the field disputing calls the officials made. Wofford scored in the first quarter, but Mercer, with Dorsey and Sammons getting touchdowns and Weekly adding one extra point, roared from behind to clinch the game. Dorsey and Cochran were lauded for hitting the line hard while Swann and Sammons also had outstanding games. Both teams scrambled for the victory. On several occasions penalties for slugging were administered.

A scheduled game with South Carolina was called off because President Griggs of the SIAA reported that nine of the eleven players for South Carolina were ineligible. This week of rest for the Bears was followed by a game in Chattanooga. Although Mercer outplayed Chattanooga in the first half, the final score stood 20-6 in favor of the Moccasins. Drane got the only score for Mercer after a long run by Swann set the ball up.

The rough game with Chattanooga weakened Mercer for the October 30 game with Howard as six starters were hurt. A. J. Swann was the offensive star of the day as he went sixty-five yards for the first score and returned a punt forty yards for the second in a 14-7 victory. Weekly added the two extra points. Dorsey made the key block as Swann raced down the sidelines for the final touchdown. Mercer's defense, led by Hollingsworth, Gordon, Mayo, Bloodworth, Drane, Weekly, and Welch, repulsed the Bulldogs three times near the Mercer goal line.

Mercer once again failed to score on Auburn, marking the eighth shutout. The score of this game was 45-0 as the sixteen-man Mercer squad could manage only three first downs. Throughout all the games with Auburn, Mercer had scored only one touchdown. It had come in 1909 when Cap Scoggin dragged Bob Poole across the goal line with Auburn defenders hanging on.

The Mercer team pulled a super feat the next weekend, playing and winning two games in two days. The Douglas Aggies and Columbia College both fell before the rampaging Bears. On 12 November Mercer romped over Douglas before 2,500 fans by a 20-0 score on a field that had recently been plowed. All the members of the twenty-man squad saw action. The following day in Valdosta, Mercer defeated Columbia College 32-0. In this game the last two quarters were reduced by mutual consent to five minutes in length. Both Douglas and Columbia were small schools, and the experience the Mercer team had gained against tougher opponents proved valuable.

F. A. Sams, a former Mercer star, was the coach of Columbia and played for his team that day. Sams suffered a broken leg and a dislocated ankle in the game. Jake Zellars, the Mercer coach, scampered around right end thirty yards for a touchdown.

The final tilt of the season brought Florida to Macon and resulted in a 34-7 victory for the Gators. Swann broke seven tackles as he went eighty yards for the only Mercer touchdown and Weekly added the extra point. The 1915 season ended with a 5-4 record, and 15 men earned letters.

In 1916 Jake Zellars returned for his second year as coach and the team posted a 1-6 record. The opening game against Georgia Military College saw Mercer gain a tough 7-0 victory. The action started when Harvey Henderson picked up a fumble and ran fifty yards. Doc Bass then ran for ten yards over tackle, and Captain J. R. Newton punched over for the score. W. H. Drane added the extra point.

On 7 October 1916 Chattanooga romped over Mercer 49-0 in Chattanooga. Coach Zellars, a member of the Macon unit of the Army Reserves, was called to active duty, and D. R. Peacock took over the team. Peacock was a former assistant at Michigan and Georgia. Auburn was the first foe for Coach "Imp" Peacock, and the game was a 93-0 runaway in Auburn's favor. This depressing score was followed by a 26-7 loss to Howard and a 7-0 loss to little Columbia.

The game with Florida was canceled when it was discovered that Mercer had five ineligible players. The two final games were shutouts as South Carolina won 47-0 and Tech stormed to a 61-0 victory before a crowd of 2,000 in Atlanta.

At the end of the 1916 season the football activity at Mercer stopped for the duration of World War I. Mercer had participated in 93 games since the first one in 1892. The record for the fifteen years of play was thirty-nine won, fifty-one lost, and three tied. During this time there were ten different coaches, with Dr. C. C. Stroud holding the record for the longest tenure as coach at Mercer with three years.

The success of football at Mercer during this period was not great, due to a variety of problems. Mercer was yet to get into the subsidization business. The student body, being small in number, didn't actually have enough personnel to field a football team equal to such powerful opponents as scheduled. But the battling Baptists were determined to succeed, and greater emphasis and determination went into the program following the war.

Chapter 3
SECOND KICKOFF

Football was resumed in 1919 after a two-yard break for World War I. Robert Maxwell James, a former Howard player, was hired as coach and E. G. Jackson was selected as the manager. There was a great deal of uncertainty regarding the team for 1919, but two games were scheduled. Practice began on a new field on Gray's Hill, which had been developed under the leadership of Dr. W. G. Lee. Charles O'Quinn, a big 185-pounder, captained the team. Mercer then had 275 students enrolled and other members of the squad were: J. R. Newton, R. B. Davis, Robert Lane, E. O. Sinclair, Harvey Cutts, J. E. Rackley, O. W. Burnett, George P. Oslin, L. D. Clark, Morris, Freeman, McWilliams, Luke, and Peyton.

The first game of the season matched Mercer against the Florida "Alligators" in Gainesville. The game was played in three inches of water and the light Mercer backs found no footing as the team was defeated 48-0.

The second game of the season resulted in a 73-0 loss to Oglethorpe in Atlanta. It was a rough affair, and quarterback Burnett was knocked out after five minutes of play. Newton was knocked out in the second quarter and did not return to action. The team continued to practice and games with Tech, Furman, and Chattanooga were scheduled, but then canceled. After the two demoralizing losses, interest in football waned considerably. Football was dropped on 13 November 1919 for the remainder of the season.

1920

Mercer's football fortunes were stimulated in 1920 with the hiring of Josh Cody, a well-known former All-American at Vanderbilt, as coach. The alumni actively began to support the program, and steps were taken to strengthen it. More money was pledged as the team got ready for the first full season since the war.

The line that season averaged 186 pounds, making it one of the heaviest in history, while the backs averaged 163 pounds. A number of former players who had been in the service returned, and Coach Cody did some recruiting to bolster the squad. Members of the 1920 squad were: D. J. Stokes, J. S. Weekly, P. E. Garrison, S. H. Ellison, Ike Cowart, Mike Herndon, Sid Johnson, Carl Lancaster, B. G. Gaines, E. R. Welch, E. S. Whitehead, H. I. Scott, E. S. Parker, W. B. Barron, Ed "Smoky" Harper, and Capt. Tom "Slap" Rentz. Ike Cowart, weighing in at over 220 pounds, was the biggest man to suit up for Mercer in years.

The first game of the season matched the Bears against a strong Gordon team, which was coached by E. P. Mosley, a former Mercer player. Gordon proved too tough in the opener, winning 14-0.

Mercer 59, Lanier University 0

On 9 October Mercer journeyed to Atlanta for a game with Lanier University. Fifteen men made the trip. The Bears enjoyed one of their biggest romps in years with a 59-0 win. Weekly started things off with a touchdown from the five, and Cowart kicked the extra point. F. M. White galloped twenty-five yards around left end for a touchdown, then Weekly passed to Whitehead for two touchdowns as the first quarter came to a close. In the third quarter White scored again with a seventy-five-yard jaunt while Weekly crossed the goal line in the third and fourth quarters to end the rout.

Mercer 13, Howard 33

Returning to Macon for a game with Howard College on 16 October at Central City Park, the Bears fell by a score of 33-13. Howard got on the scoreboard after some stubborn defense by both teams when Stokes of

Mercer touched a punt, and Head of Howard picked it up and went thirty yards for a touchdown. Mercer fought back with runs and punts by Welch, but Howard kept forcing Mercer back and scored again after receiving a short punt on the Mercer twelve-yard line. The Bears began moving, following the kickoff, with Weekly and Garrison carrying the ball. Garrison finally scored from the seventeen-yard line, and Mercer trailed 13-6.

In the second half Howard got two quick scores and led 27-6. Garrison scored from the ten to make the score 27-13 as Tommy Rentz added the extra point. A final touchdown by Howard in the last quarter brought the score to 33-13. Mercer's record with Howard now stood at six wins and at three losses.

Mercer 0, Chattanooga 20

Up in Chattanooga Mercer fumbled often, and the Moccasins cashed in on two of these for touchdowns. Mercer got to the Chattanooga three-yard line twice but couldn't score. Chattanooga exhibited a successful passing attack, getting the final score with ten seconds remaining on the clock.

Mercer 0, Florida 30

Playing once again in Valdosta, Georgia, the Bears outplayed the Gators the first half but trailed 9-0. The Gators got Mercer for a safety and the Bears drove back to the Florida fifteen-yard line but couldn't score. With just fifteen seconds to go in the first half, Florida scored the first touchdown. Carlton scored three times for Florida, and Welch was outstanding for Mercer.

Mercer 19, Stetson 6

The team traveled to Deland for a game with the Hatters and earned a surprising 19-6 victory. Within the first four minutes Garrison went around left end thirty yards for a touchdown. Stetson scored before the half to make it 6-6. In the fourth quarter Weekly scored a touchdown and a Stokes-to-Rentz pass for twenty-five yards accounted for the last touchdown. Rentz added the extra point in the 19-6 win.

Mercer 6, Erskine 20

The final tilt of the season was played in Macon against Erskine College, with Erskine winning 20-6. Mercer scored in the first quarter when 220-pound Ike Cowart ran forty yards with a recovered fumble for a touchdown. The great Phillips of Erskine was impossible to stop as he scored all the winners' points. Most of his scores came on long runs.

Following the season the Macon alumni met again to consider the football situation. Pledges were made to create greater support and enthusiasm for the 1921 season. Plans were made to hire an assistant coach and for more extensive recruiting.

1921

Mercer 0, Georgia 28

Mercer opened the 1921 season with a game against Georgia in Athens, resuming athletic relations between the two colleges after a lapse of ten years. This was the seventh time that the Bears and the Bulldogs battled.

The game lasted two hours and twenty-five minutes with Georgia getting three touchdowns in the marathon third quarter which lasted one hour and twenty minutes. Georgia, sporting a new backfield shift, fooled the Mercer ends repeatedly, causing many penalties. The biggest offensive opportunity for Mercer came when Kid Cecil recovered the ball on the Georgia thirty-yard line. But Mercer was unable to take advantage of this opportunity for a score. Georgia added a final touchdown in the fourth quarter and finished with a 28-0 win. Byron L. "Crook" Smith, playing with a sprained shoulder, was the star of the day for Mercer. Carl Lancaster broke through often to spill the hard-running Georgia backs, while Mike Herndon and Sid Johnson spearheaded a tough Mercer line.

Cody had spent the summer rounding up a team and had brought a number of boys to Mercer from Tennessee. Many of the men who played on the 1920 team did not play during Cody's second season at Mercer.

Mercer 0, Vanderbilt 42

Big Josh took his band of warriors to Nashville for a game with his alma mater the following weekend, and the team was thrashed 42-0. Vandy got four touchdowns in the second quarter while gaining 173 yards. Ninety-one of these yards came on two passes. Mercer started strong by driving to the Vanderbilt six-yard line before losing the ball. Vandy was held in check the first quarter and did not get a first down. Mercer drove again within scoring territory but was unable to move the outstanding Commodore defense.

Mercer 0, Florida 7

The third consecutive out-of-town game resulted in a loss to Florida in Gainesville 7-0. The contest proved rough, and Welch was banished from the game for his aggressive play. Norman Felder made a great run for Mercer in the third quarter but was caught short of the goal. Crook Smith was outstanding for Mercer, along with Mike Herndon, George Harmon, Beverly Gaines, and Red Simmons. Others on the squad making the trip were Carl Lancaster, Sid Johnson, Eldridge Rhea, Richard Dasher, Dave Rice, Shorty Poore, Irwin, and Cone.

Mercer 20, Birmingham Southern 0

Finally, after three losses to larger schools, the Bears returned to Macon and played Birmingham Southern on the new Alumni Field, located on the campus. Before a home crowd of 2,500 the Panthers were defeated 20-0 for a much-needed victory. The game started as Mercer kicked off and then refused to let the Southerners advance. After receiving the ball, Poore, Cecil, and Welch advanced the ball twenty-three yards before running out of gas. Irwin then boomed a punt fifty-eight yards.

After another exchange of the ball, Mercer recovered a fumble on the Panther twenty-five-yard line. Harmon hit the line for two yards; Poore then added four yards on two carries. Harmon scored on a seven-yard pass from Cecil for a 6-0 lead with 8:46 gone in the first quarter. The touchdown by Harmon was the first of the 1921 season for the Bears and also the first on the new field.

In the second quarter Poore added a touchdown, and Irwin booted the extra point for a 13-0 lead. Jim Harbin, playing with an unprotected broken jaw, added the final touchdown in the 20-0 game. Mercer finished with twenty-two first downs, cheered on by Wayne Hagan, Frey Caylor, and Guy Cheeney. Red Welch provided offensive fireworks with a sixty-three-yard run during the game, while Irwin thrilled the crowd with his booming punts that averaged fifty yards.

Mercer 41, Stetson 0

Getting used to winning and again playing equitable competition, the Bears raced past Stetson 41-0 on Alumni Field. Red Welch was the outstanding player of the day for Mercer as he gained yardage on every play but one. He scored three touchdowns, and Shorty Poore had one six-pointer. Irwin had a great day kicking extra points, booting five of six.

In this fine offensive show Mercer drove for twenty-five first downs while holding Stetson to only four. "Broken Jaw" Harbin had the prettiest run of the day, a twenty-five yarder. Captain Sid Johnson, Coach Josh Cody, Assistant Coach Russ Cohen, and twelve iron men were jubilant with the victory.

Mercer 0, Furman 37

Furman proved to be too formidable an opponent on 5 November and copped a 37-0 victory. It was just not a good day for the orange and black. Cowart, Dasher, and Smith were the stalwarts in the line while Welch, Harbin, and Cecil provided the major offensive thrust.

Mercer 6, Oglethorpe 7

In a bitterly contested game the following weekend, Oglethorpe edged by Mercer 7-6. Mercer amassed a total of 268 yards and seven first downs while Oglethorpe, held in check most of the day, gained only 104 yards. The Petrels recovered a Harmon fumble on the Mercer seventeen-yard line and subsequently made a first down at the Mercer four-yard line. The resulting touchdown gave Oglethorpe a 7-0 lead.

Before a crowd of 2,000, Crook Smith raced down the field and took a high arching pass that had been thrown by Kid Cecil. He then streaked sixty-five yards for the only Mercer touchdown. The important point after the touchdown was missed, and Oglethorpe led 7-6. The remainder of the game was played in Oglethorpe territory, but the Bears lost the chance to go ahead when the Petrels' defense held on the three-yard line.

Mercer 18, Chattanooga 0

In one of the rare trips to Macon for Chattanooga, the Bears atoned for several defeats with an 18-0 shutout. Before a crowd of 1,000 rain-drenched fans, Mercer rolled up 451 yards and twenty-four first downs for the biggest offensive show of the year. Harbin, Welch, and Cecil scored touchdowns while Carl Lancaster was described as the outstanding defensive player of the day.

The initial Mercer score came after the first exchange of the ball when Harbin, Welch, Smith, and Cecil accounted for thirty yards. Felder then sprinted around end for thirty-eight yards to the Chattanooga ten-yard line. Harbin, behind superior blocking, sped the final ten yards for the touchdown. Felder's thirty-eight-yard run in this drive was the longest of the day.

After another exchange of the ball, Welch put together runs of twenty-five, ten, and eight yards on the way to another touchdown. In this drive Harbin added thirteen yards and Smith nine more. Cecil scored the final touchdown of the day after recovering a Welch fumble over the goal line.

In the final quarter Mercer was content to punt the ball back to Chattanooga every time the ball was received. This marked the second victory over Chattanooga, with the first coming in 1909 by a score of 10-2. The leading ground gainers for Mercer were Welch with 115 yards, Cecil with seventy-five, and Harbin with sixty-three.

Mercer 7, Ft. Benning 24

On 24 November 1921 Mercer journeyed to Ft. Benning for a scrimmage with the doughboys, losing 24-7. The only score for Mercer came on a twenty-five-yard pass from Irwin to Smith. After this final game, Everett Strupper signed as assistant coach at Mercer for the 1922 season. Strupper had been All-Southern at Tech in 1915, 1916, 1917 and had been All-America in 1917.

1922

In 1922 Josh Cody returned for his third year as head coach, Everett Strupper was backfield coach, and E. Parker Mosley was freshman coach. Mosley was a former Mercer player who had been successful with his team at Gordon in Barnesville. The hiring of Mosley marked the first time that an assistant was hired primarily as freshman coach.

Mercer 24, Piedmont College 3

The season began against Piedmont College on 23 September 1922 in Macon. Mercer now had an enrollment of 500 students. Neufville "Shorty" Poore and Houston "Kid" Cecil scored the four touchdowns for the Bears in a 24-3 win.

Poore started things off when he returned a punt twenty yards. Norman Felder added twenty yards on an end run, Rice ran for eight yards, and then Poore drove over for the touchdown. Harmon missed the dropkick for the extra point.

Some minutes later Poore went on the rampage again. Dave Rice made three yards. Skinny Woolwine ran for ten yards, George Harmon added ten more yards, then Shorty Poore took over. He inched forward two yards, then burst loose on the next play for twenty-five yards and a touchdown. The Piedmont score came on a twenty-five-yard field goal by Exline.

After the intermission, Woolwine returned the second half kickoff ten yards. Cecil and Woolwine added twenty-five yards together, then Rice bulled forward for three yards and a first down. Rice then hit Harmon with a twenty-yard pass. Woolwine, Rice, and Harmon combined to take the ball to the Piedmont ten-yard line. Cecil got the touchdown after Harmon had carried the ball to the five-yard line. Cecil added the final touchdown in the last quarter just before the freshmen came into the game.

Mercer 0, Georgia 41

The 1922 season for Mercer had opened with sixty candidates out for the team. Fifteen of these were lettermen. This was one of the finest turnouts ever for the football team. Following the easy win over Piedmont, the Bears faced Georgia in Athens. Mercer was not at full strength because Carl Lancaster, "Bubber" Pope, and Ike Cowart were out with injuries.

Red Simmons kicked off forty-five yards for Mercer, and Georgia had a two-yard return. Mercer got the ball on the second play when Georgia fumbled. Poore earned two first downs, and Georgia was penalized to the fourteen-yard line. On the next play Harmon pushed forward for two yards, but the ball was fumbled to Georgia at the ten-yard line. Once again the Bears were denied the opportunity to get a touchdown.

After two exchanges of the ball and some stellar defense by both teams, the Bears were guilty of pass interference on their own one-yard line. Randall skipped over for the score and then booted the extra point for a 7-0 advantage. Rogers then ran the ball three times for Mercer and picked up eight yards, but Poore lost four yards as the first quarter ended.

In the second quarter Randall intercepted a Mercer pass and galloped ninety yards for a touchdown. He then added the extra point to make the score 14-0. Mercer chose to kick off, and Simmons boomed it sixty-seven yards down the field. The half ended with Poore intercepting a Georgia pass.

In the second half it was all Georgia as Bennett grabbed a blocked punt and ran twenty-three yards for a touchdown. Randall scored his third touchdown of the day, receiving a twenty-four-yard pass from Mulvihill. He once again booted the extra point to personally account for twenty-one of Georgia's points.

Simmons again kicked off to the Georgia goal line and Mulvihill ran it back twenty yards. Two plays later Mulvihill raced seventy-five yards for a touchdown to make the score 41-0, notching Georgia's eighth victory over Mercer.

Mercer 31, North Georgia A&M 0

The Bears bounced back into the win column with a 31-0 victory over the North Georgia Aggies, now called North Georgia College. Crook Smith opened the scoring with a touchdown from the fifteen-yard line. Norman Felder and Bubber Pope added quick touchdowns. Dave Rice got into the act by picking off an errant Aggie pass and racing fifty-five yards for a touchdown. S. T. "Little" Reese added the final score with a twenty-yard end run. George Harmon, following a penalty, kicked one extra point from the fifteen-yard line. Nineteen men saw action as Sid Johnson and Jarred "Red" Simmons anchored the defensive line which held the Aggies scoreless.

Mercer 17, Birmingham Southern 13

On October 13 Mercer traveled to Birmingham for a hard-fought victory over the Panthers by the score of 17-13. Howard Pill reporting in the *Macon Telegraph* wrote:

> As the shades of night were closing down upon Rickwood Park Friday afternoon with one minute left to play, a long, lanky Mercer end, Irwin by name, standing on his own twenty-yard line, tossed a long pass to another long, lanky Mercer end, "Consuello" Smith. Smith raced fifty-five yards, half the length of the field, for a touchdown and the points that gave Mercer a hard-earned victory over Birmingham Southern today, the final score being 17-13.
>
> A few moments before, another pass between the same parties mentioned above had paved the way for the first Mercer touchdown. This time the oval traveled twenty-five yards in the air. Harmon went over for the counter in two plays from the fifteen-yard line. A perfect dropkick by "Little" Reese early in the first quarter had accounted for the first three points.
>
> The two Mercer ends, Irwin and Smith, were fifty per cent of the Mercer team Friday. Both of these huskies smeared play after play, refused to be boxed, and were in every scrimmage from whistle to whistle. Simmons, a roving tackle, was another particularly bright light in the play of the Georgians, while Poore and Harmon, together with Reese and Rogers, were the leaders of the Baptist attack.

The game started with Mercer kicking off and the Panthers moved for two first downs. Mercer's defense tightened, and an exchange of punts followed. A fumbled pass then set up a thirty-yard dropkick by Reese of Mercer. Birmingham Southern continued with a thirty-seven-yard scoring pass. A few minutes later Irwin was forced to punt from behind the goal line, and the Panthers scored their second touchdown after getting the ball at the fifteen-yard line. Then "Miller kicked the goal by a drop kick, but a Birmingham Southern man was holding and the point was not allowed."

Mercer chose to punt following the touchdown, and the strategy worked well as the ball was returned to Mercer on the Panther thirty-five line. It was from there that Irwin passed to Smith for the first touchdown. Harmon later scored the winning points with a fifteen-yard run. Cecil and Harmon added the important extra points. Others who made more than a normal contribution in that game were "Coot" Lynch, Mike Herndon, and Beverly Gaines.

Mercer 7, Auburn 50

Mercer went into the 21 October battle with Auburn in Auburn with six regulars out of action. Using the reserves as much as the varsity, the Plainsmen scored at will and defeated the outmanned Baptists 50-7. Auburn made sixteen first downs and Mercer got three, although Auburn never did have over six regulars in the game at one time. Norman Felder scored the only Mercer touchdown on a three-yard run in the second quarter. The extra point was missed, but Auburn was offside and the point counted.

Mercer 0, Vanderbilt 25

Mercer traveled to Nashville on 28 October and came up on the short end of a 25-0 score against Vanderbilt. After a scoreless first quarter, Vandy cut loose for two touchdowns in the second quarter and two in the fourth. The Vandy substitutes were used throughout the game because many of the regulars were injured and unable to play. Although Mercer outweighed the Commodores more than twenty pounds per man, the Bears still were unable to contain this determined team. Quarterback Roundtree and his subs gained 241 yards on Mercer.

McLain saw action in place of the injured Cowart; Lancaster had not returned since being injured in the game with the Aggies; and Harmon, Rogers, Ellison, and Dasher were also out of action. The small number of men on the squad was indeed a handicap when key people were injured.

Mercer 12, Maryville College 0

Maryville College of Tennessee became a victim of the win-hungry Bears in Macon the following weekend, by a score of 12-0. Sid Ellison, returning to action after being injured earlier in the year, broke his jaw in the early moments of the game. After a few minutes' rest he returned to the field and played the most outstanding game of his career.

The first Mercer touchdown came after an exchange of punts, when Mercer got the ball on the Maryville forty-two yard line. Dave Rice hit S. T. Reese with a thirty-four yard pass. Felder then went off right tackle for eight yards and a touchdown. Reese's attempted drop kick for the extra point was blocked.

After the ball had changed hands again several times, Mercer was on the Maryville twenty-five. Rice went for twelve yards off tackle; Poore added five more; Reese ran for another five and a first down; then Rice bulled in for the touchdown. Mercer got twelve first downs while holding Maryville to only five. Crook Smith and Red Simmons were outstanding, along with Coot Lynch and Dave Rice.

Mercer 6, Chattanooga 13

Chattanooga defeated Mercer again in Chattanooga by a score of 13-6 on two fourth-quarter touchdowns. Just before the moon came up over the mountain, Anderson returned a punt forty yards for the winning touchdown. The touchdown for Mercer had come as Irwin passed to Red Simmons for the six points.

Mercer 18, Oglethorpe 16

The first win over Oglethorpe after three consecutive defeats was registered in Macon on 17 November 1922, before a crowd of 2,500 fans.

The game opened with Felder returning the ball fifteen yards to the twenty-two-yard line. Mercer promptly fumbled and on the third down David of Oglethorpe split the uprights from the twenty-five-yard line for three points. Mercer received, and Irwin was forced to punt after two short gains. Morris of Oglethorpe then boomed a punt to the Mercer twenty-three-yard line, and once again the ball was fumbled by a Mercer man. Oglethorpe recovered the fumble and rushed for a touchdown and a 10-0 lead.

Following two punts by each team, Felder and Cecil alternated running the ball from the fifty-yard line to the twenty-five. From here Irwin passed to Smith on the goal line for a touchdown. The extra point was missed and Oglethorpe still led 10-6. Mercer, with a taste of success, began to move again. After taking the ball on the twenty, the team steadily marched the eighty yards for a 12-10 lead. Irwin missed the second of two extra point attempts. An Irwin-to-Smith pass had accounted for twenty-six yards and the advancing touchdown.

Carl Lancaster, returning to action after missing a number of games, intercepted a pass at the beginning of the second half to set up a touchdown by Felder, which gave Mercer an 18-10 lead. But after a series of punts, Mercer fumbled again. Maurer picked up the ball and ran forty-five yards for an Oglethorpe touchdown. In the last few minutes, with the ball on the forty-five, Oglethorpe attempted a game-winning field goal, but it was blocked. Smith recovered for Mercer on the twenty-five-yard line as the game ended.

Mercer 7, Carson-Newman 12

A new foe, Carson-Newman, edged Mercer in Knoxville on November 26. The score was 12-7 in a game which Mercer reportedly should have won. Mercer ran up a total of fourteen first downs to only five for the Eagles. On top of all the problems of the day for the Bears, the sure-handed Smith dropped two passes on the Carson-Newman goal line.

Mercer got the seven points with Felder and Coot Lynch carrying the mail. A Smith-to-Irwin pass ate up six yards on the touchdown drive. Felder finally ran the ball across from the two-yard line, and Irwin proved true on the extra point.

Carson-Newman got on the scoreboard with a sixty-yard punt return by John Hutchins, and a sixty-yard Hutchins-to-Higgins pass. The pass was the only completion out of thirteen attempts for Carson-Newman that day. Mercer attempted 19 passes and completed four for ninety-five yards. Jarred "Red" Simmons played an outstanding game for the Bears.

Mercer 13, Ft. Benning 27

The final game of the 1922 season was a 27-13 loss to Ft. Benning. The game lasted two hours and forty minutes with the moon coming up before the game was over. Mercer came from behind to knot the score at 6-6 with a forty-five-yard pass from Irwin to Smith. Benning scored twice to lead 20-6 at the half. Reese scored for Mercer after Benning had scored another touchdown and the game ended 27-13.

At the end of the school year Josh Cody resigned to accept a position as line coach at Vanderbilt under Dan McGugin. Everett Strupper also resigned after a one-year tour at Mercer.

From Vanderbilt, Cody went to Clemson as coach, but he went back to Vanderbilt as an assistant. He was almost selected as head coach of his alma mater when McGugin retired. He then moved to the University of Florida and from Florida to Temple University, where he stayed until his death in 1961. As a tribute to Joshua Crittenden Cody, the Atlanta Chapter of the Mercer Alumni Association, under the leadership of Hugh Carney, H. H. Ware, and Winston E. Burdine, prepared the following resolution:

> Whereas, it has come to our attention through the medium of the Associated Press and the *Atlanta Constitution* that our beloved Josh Cody, head coach and athletic director at Mercer University from 1920-1923, where he served with great ability, distinction, and honor as coach of three major sports (football, basketball, and baseball) has passed to his reward at age 69;
>
> And whereas, the death of Coach Cody brought back fond memories of his great services to Mercer University as well as the deepest of sorrow to his thousands of friends and followers in this section who recall that he was the first coach to put Mercer in the forefront of intercollegiate athletics, as well as serving honorably at Vanderbilt, his alma mater, Clemson, and University of Florida, we the members of the Mercer University Alumni Chapter of Greater Atlanta, Georgia, do hereby extend our heartfelt sympathy to you, Mrs. Cody, and to all the members of your family. Dated 23 June 1961.

Chapter 4
FIRST DOWN

Stanley L. Robinson, a former All-American at Colgate University and successful coach at Mississippi College, became the fourteenth football coach at Mercer in 1923. Great plans were made to strengthen the football program. The first step was to hire an experienced and successful coach. Alumni Field was also resodded and leveled. It was reported that during the 1922 season the field was six feet lower at one end than at the other.

1923

The University enrollment had now increased to 863 students, and great preparations were made for the first game of the season. Forty men reported for practice under new coach Robinson. Assisting him were Tink Gillam and E. Parker Mosley. Although there were eleven lettermen back, Ed Irwin, a standout on the 1922 team, did not return to school. Also Lynch, Pope, Cowart, and Jack Bate did not report in time to play in the opener with Georgia.

Mercer 0, Georgia 7

The Bears played well in the opening game in Athens. Twenty-two men made the trip, and fifteen saw action. The rúgged Mercer defense led by Poore, Rice, Cecil, Bowling, and Eli McDonald held the Bulldogs scoreless the first half.

Georgia scored in the third quarter when Son Sammons' punt from behind the goal line was blocked by Bennett and Taylor. Bennett fell on the ball for the only touchdown of the day.

Mercer 6, Furman 3

The outstanding showing against Georgia stimulated the students, and fifty-two reported for practice the following Monday. Lynch, Pope, Cowart, and Bate suited up and began to practice. Coach Robinson put his men through their paces preparing for the strong Furman eleven. On one occasion, after practicing in the rain, the team had to take the day off because the suits were still too wet to use.

The game started as Furman kicked off, and Tarzan Bowling returned it twenty yards. Dave Rice ran off right tackle for five yards, and Norman Felder got two yards at right end. Bowling then made a first down after gaining six yards. But Felder lost four yards and Crook Smith punted to Furman.

After an exchange of punts, Furman drove to the Mercer one-yard line. Here the Mercer defense bowed their necks and refused to let the Paladins score. Smith quickly punted fifty-six yards to get the Bears out of trouble. Rice intercepted moments later, but the ball was fumbled back to Furman. On the first play Furman fumbled, and Kid Cecil recovered. This Mercer drive started and ended when Rice's pass was kicked off by an alert Furman defender as the half ended 0-0.

Furman received the kickoff, ran twelve plays and punted to Mercer. The ball was promptly fumbled back to Furman on the Mercer eighteen-yard line. Furman fought for a first down in four plays at the Mercer ten-yard line. After three plays and only a two-yard gain against the stubborn Bear defense, Tilghman booted a fifteen-yard field goal for Furman.

Mercer started strong after receiving the kickoff, only to lose the ball as a Rice pass fell into the hands of a Furman defender. Furman could not advance against the hard-charging Mercer defense and punted.

Mercer returned the favor only to have Furman give the ball back on a pass interception by Cecil. He ran it sixty-three yards to the Furman seven-yard line. Mercer couldn't score but subsequently got the ball again on a short punt on the Furman twenty-yard line. Rice went for three yards, then Simmons raced seventeen yards around left end with a fake play for the 6-3 victory.

Mercer 7, Ft. Benning 0

After two successive defeats at the hands of the Army, Mercer finally defeated Ft. Benning by a narrow 7-0 score. One reason the score was low was that the Mercer substitutes played much of the game. In the first half, Rice, Poore, and Bowling carried the ball steadily toward the goal but were unable to score. After blocking a Benning punt, Rice attempted a field goal, only to have it hit the crossbar and bounce out to the thirty, where Benning recovered.

In the second half, Selby Buck, former coach for Lanier High School, played for Benning. The Bears finally got on the scoreboard when Felder went into the game and ripped off forty-five yards to the Benning twenty-yard line. Shorty Poore added four yards, then Felder hit for sixteen yards and the touchdown. Crook Smith booted the extra point.

Mercer threatened again in the final minutes of play when Felder intercepted a pass and returned it twenty yards to the Ft. Benning thirteen-yard line. On the second play Poore was knocked out as he hit the line for no gain. Tarzan Bowling came in and got three yards, but Cecil had a pass intercepted, and the threat ended. Poore, Rice, and Bowling were the main ball carriers, although Cecil carried three times for sixty-three yards and the touchdown. Poore had seventy-five yards in fifteen tries, Bowling thirty-three in eleven runs, and Rice got eighteen in nine attempts.

Mercer 18, Chattanooga 3

Mercer bested Chattanooga 18-3 for the third victory in a row and for the third time in nine games. The teams fought evenly until Poore recovered a fumble on the Chattanooga twenty-four yard line. Lynch and Poore picked up seven yards, and a Cecil-to-Sammons pass accounted for seven more and a first down. Poore hit fight tackle for two yards to the ten-yard line. Two plays later Poore scored from the six-yard line and Mercer took a 6-0 lead.

After several punt exchanges in the second half, Givens hit a twenty-five-yard field goal for Chattanooga and made the score 6-3. After the kickoff, Mercer started a goalward drive from the twenty-yard line with Cecil, Reese, and Lynch earning consecutive first downs. Cecil and Lynch ran for five yards and Reese added twenty-four to the Moccasin ten-yard line. On the next play Reese dived into the end zone to make the score 12-3.

The final quarter shaped up as a punting duel with each team trying to back the other to the goal. Finally, Crook Smith punted one for forty yards that fell dead on the Chattanooga nine-yard line. Givens then booted a short one that Cecil returned to the Chattanooga twenty-yard line.

Lynch carried the ball two times and earned four yards. Kid Cecil passed to Son Sammons for five yards, then Poore ran the remaining eleven yards for the touchdown. The Mercer team played superior defense in the 18-3 victory. One of the bright spots on offense was Crook Smith's punting as he kicked eleven times, the longest being fifty yards.

Mercer 12, Birmingham Southern 0

The victory streak was stretched to four in a row on October 26 with a win over Birmingham Southern in Macon. This was the longest winning streak in Mercer's football history up to this time. The game started as Jack Bate returned the kickoff twenty yards for Mercer. Smith got ten yards with an end-around, then Bate got thirteen on two carries to place the ball on the fifty-yard line. Cecil passed to Simmons for twenty yards to the Southern thirty, and Bate got ten yards on a reverse. Two plays later the drive stopped when Cecil's pass was intercepted.

The remainder of the first half was a battle between the punters as each team had the ball six times and couldn't score. In the fourth quarter Mercer got the ball on the forty-four-yard line and started a drive that ended in a touchdown. Seven plays after receiving the ball, Cecil passed to Smith for fifteen yards and a 6-0 lead. Following the kickoff, Smith intercepted a Panther pass on the thirty-yard line. Reese ran for six yards, then Tarzan Bowling sped twenty-two yards to the Southern two-yard line. On the next play he bulled over for the touchdown and a 12-0 victory.

Mercer 7, Florida 19

Before the largest crowd in Florida history, 5,000 fans, Mercer fell to the Gators 19-7. The Bears were held to two first downs while Florida amassed eighteen. The strong Florida defense limited the Bears to only short gains around end while Florida scored on a twenty-yard pass play and two short runs.

Mercer scored in the first period as Smith blocked a punt and Dick Carson fell on it for the Mercer touchdown. Smith and Sammons had outstanding games at end, and Cecil thrilled the crowd with his dramatic touchdown-saving tackles.

Mercer 6, Oglethorpe 7

Kid Cecil made the third longest run in southern football history on 11 November 1923 in a game with Oglethorpe in Atlanta. Since that time there have been many individuals who duplicated or bettered his feat. In this game he went 85 yards for a touchdown in a 7-6 loss.

Oglethorpe proved far superior offensively in the first half, getting ten first downs to just two for Mercer. For the game the Petrels had 213 yards while the Bears got 105. Although Oglethorpe was able to get only one touchdown, they won the game when the extra point sailed through the uprights.

Maurer was outstanding again for Oglethorpe, while Poore and Cecil were the offensive leaders for Mercer. Crook Smith, although playing with a separated shoulder, had a good day defensively and recovered a second half fumble.

Mercer 0, Mississippi College 15

Playing in Clinton, Mississippi, for the first time, Mercer lost 15-0 to Coach Robinson's former team. Mercer fumbled six times during the game, losing the ball twice. Scotty Young, who could kick the ball with either foot, ran the ball well for the Bears. He may have been the forerunner of present day soccer-style kickers. Cecil and Poore played their usual game in the offensive backfield. The Bears were still not up to full strength as Sid Ellison missed the third game in a row.

Mercer 0, Carson-Newman 12

Mercer was now at a low ebb. Many players had been injured during the season. The team was not at full strength for the final game of the season. The coaches attempted to bolster the offense with a spread formation but made little progress. The final score was 12-0 in favor of Carson-Newman. Once again Cecil and Poore played well for the Bears on offense.

Lettermen for the 1923 season were Kid Cecil, Shorty Poore, Dave Rice, Lewis Reese, Bela Lancaster, Red Simmons, Son Sammons, Eli McDonald, B. L. Smith, Dewey Jowers, Marion Roberts, Beverly Gaines, Mike Herndon, Norman Felder, Jack Bate, Dick Carson, Bill Barron, Tarzan Bowling, Scotty Young, Baxter Coke, Coot Lynch, and Manager Henry Shell. All-SIAA honors went to Crook Smith and Mike Herndon.

1924

Football was beginning to be *the* college sport in 1924 as more fans than ever were attending the games. The football squads and the coaching staffs grew larger. Recruiting became an important factor in having winning teams. Also, rules were being introduced which greatly changed the game.

A significant rule change for the 1922 season was placement of the ball on the five-yard line to try for the extra point. Before, it had to be kicked where the runner crossed the goal line, or a kickback could be called. In this case the ball was kicked back up field, and if the ball was caught the extra point could be tried from there.

In 1924 the kickoff was made from the middle of the field. Players were required to come to a full stop on shift plays. This eliminated some of the quick plays and offside situations.

Mercer began preseason practice at Glen Cove Springs, Florida, on September 2, preparing for a game with Georgia on September 27 in Athens. Stanley Robinson was assisted by E. Parker Mosley, Tink Gillam, and Carey Robinson. Carey Robinson was a former Auburn star. Twenty-seven men made the trip for the football camp.

Mercer 7, Georgia 26

The season opened on schedule before 8,000 fans in the rain at Athens. This was the largest crowd to see a Mercer team play up to this time. New faces in the 1924 squad were Rusty Lawrence, quarterback from Gordon; John Parks, 164-pound halfback from Richland High School; and Slew Dunn, a 177-pound tackle from Georgia Military College. The Bear squad averaged 175 pounds in the line while the backs weighed in at a 165-pound average.

In the opening game the battling Baptists fought gallantly against overwhelming odds. Although Mercer played well, Georgia recovered two Mercer fumbles and intercepted one pass. Once again the Bears failed in the bid for a victory over the mighty "varsities." The game began, and the Mercer team quickly had their backs to the wall. Parks stopped an early Georgia threat with a timely pass interception.

Following limited gains and a thirty-five-yard Lawrence punt, Georgia got the ball on the thirty-six. Three plays later Kilpatrick broke loose from would-be tacklers and spurted around end for fifty yards and a touchdown. Georgia led 6-0. Mercer chose to kick off, and Georgia lost eight yards on two attempts as the fired-up Bears pushed them back. After receiving the Georgia punt, Lawrence kicked the ball back to Georgia at the twenty-two-yard stripe.

Nelson picked up twenty yards at left end, but Red Simmons broke through on the next play to throw the great Randall for an eight-yard loss. Several plays later John Parks intercepted another pass at the Georgia forty-eight-yard line to stop another threat. The Bulldog defense was just too tough for the Bears to make progress. Later Randall and Nelson drove from the Mercer forty-six to the end zone and gave Georgia a 13-0 lead.

Mercer got a touchdown in the second quarter when Rice pushed over from the two-yard line. Lawrence added the extra point. Minutes before, Mercer had driven to the Georgia one-foot line, only to lose the ball on downs. Georgia got two more touchdowns and an extra point to make the final score 26-7.

The team had left Macon for the trip to Athens on Thursday evening. They planned to stop over in Madison for a workout on Friday. The boys were jubilant as they boarded the train. One distinguishing feature of the team was the parting of the hair in the middle, for all except Captain Red Simmons. His hair didn't part.

Although the Bears lost, there was still talk about the exploits of Lawrence, Simmons, and Smith the following Tuesday. Jesse O. Irvin, sports editor of the *Macon Telegraph* wrote, "Rusty Lawrence gave Georgia the hardest battle in the history of the annual classic between the two institutions." Simmons drew praise for his great defensive work and fine sportsmanship. In the fourth quarter, after being knocked out, he was removed from the field and received a tremendous ovation.

The score on Georgia marked the first time since 1910 that Mercer was able to cross the Bulldog goal line. For the day Georgia gained 128 yards and made seven first downs. Mercer had 106 yards and six first downs. Mercer also connected on five of eleven passes for sixty-nine yards.

Mercer 0, Syracuse 26

The Bears left Macon without practicing after the Georgia game for a two-week trip. On October 4 the team was to participate in the first intersectional contest for Mercer against Syracuse University. An elated group of players boarded the train on Wednesday, October 1, and arrived in Buffalo on October 2. Coach Robinson, originally from New York, made arrangements for the team to stay in the Buffalo Athletic Club.

Before a crowd of 6,500 people who had come out to see the Georgia "crackers," the expected battle of the North against the South began. The Mercer boys, really showing their mettle, played superb defense the first half, and the game was tied at 0-0.

Following the halftime activities, Bowman, an Olympic sprinter, went ninety-five yards on the kickoff for a touchdown. Syracuse kicked off, and Parks returned the ball fifteen yards to the Mercer twenty-five-yard line. The ball was fumbled and a new series of plays began for Syracuse. Jimmy Glover got the ball back by recovering a fumble on the Mercer ten-yard line.

Lawrence attempted to punt out of trouble but had the ball blocked and was caught for a safety. Later Syracuse scored from the twenty-yard line, kicked a field goal, and ran back a pass interception to make the final score 26-0.

The superior depth of Syracuse took a heavy toll, but the Bears played well. They drew great praise from the fans, sportswriters, and coaches. Smith and Lawrence drew applause for their defensive work. Rice also proved particularly outstanding by intercepting passes and recovering a fumble.

The team traveled back through New York City and watched the Giants and Senators play baseball. Following additional sightseeing trips, the team headed south.

Mercer 23, Furman 0

Mercer arrived for a game with Furman in Greenville, South Carolina. The Paladins had lost two games but were expected to take the measure of the Mercer team. Alabama had beaten Furman 20-0 and Georgia had won 23-0.

The game opened in a fierce fashion with strong tackling and great blocking. Kid Cecil, playing an outstanding game, was injured in the first quarter. Dick Carson was also injured in the game. In the first quarter both teams were feeling each other out, and Mercer's biggest threat was an eleven-yard pass from Lawrence to Kay Tipton.

In the second quarter Mercer went to the Furman fifteen-yard line , but the drive stalled and Lawrence booted a field goal for a 3-0 lead. Minutes later Crook Smith and Denver Fleming blocked a Chewning punt. Fleming picked it up and sprinted fifty-five yards for the touchdown. Fleming was a new addition to the Mercer squad from Hartwell, Georgia. The touchdown thrilled his family, who had driven the 160 miles to see him play.

In the third quarter Lawrence attempted a thirty-yard field goal but missed. Mercer got possession of the ball again when Dave Rice pounced on a Furman fumble. Jimmy Glover, from Eastman, went over for the touchdown in two plays. Lawrence kicked the extra point from the twenty-yard line following a penalty.

In the final quarter Smith caught a pass from Rusty Lawrence and raced forty-seven yards for the final touchdown of the game. The entire team saw action as Red Simmons spearheaded the defense.

Mercer 33, Chattanooga 0

A jubilant band of bootball players returned to Macon following their two-week absence and honed up their attack for the mighty Chattanooga Moccasins. The overall record against Chattanooga was now 6-3, in favor of Chattanooga. Mercer had won the 1923 game, and the players hoped to make it two wins in a row.

In the first few minutes Red Adams, Lawrence, and Rice carried the team to the Chattanooga twelve-yard line, where Lawrence attempted a field goal. The kick was wide, but the Bears got the ball back again on the Moccasin twenty-nine yard line.

Rice ran up the middle for eleven yards, and Adams hit guard for three more yards. Rice then ran the ball twice for six yards and a touchdown. The extra point was missed but the 6-0 lead was more than Chattanooga could overcome in the first quarter.

In the second quarter, Chattanooga drove to the Mercer three-yard line, but on fourth and a yard to go Rice intercepted to end the threat. After two punt exchanges, Mercer started again from the thirteen-yard line. Rusty Lawrence started the fireworks with a scamper around left end for forty yards. Adams added five, Rice fifteen, and Parks got thirteen yards, but then the team lost fifteen yards on a holding penalty.

This was only a temporary setback as Lawrence quickly got the fifteen yards back. Rice, running from fullback, hit the middle for six yards on two plunges. Jimmy Glover then went into the end zone from the six-yard line for 12-0 lead.

Minutes later, Red Simmons, playing his usually aggressive game, jarred the ball loose from Barnes of Chattanooga and recovered on the twenty-yard line. On the next play Parks gave it back to Chattanooga on a fumble. Chattanooga got nothing and punted to Lawrence, who returned twenty-nine yards. Shorty Poore drove for a five-yard gain. A pass from Lawrence to Smith accounted for twenty yards, then big Dave Rice ran two plays and crossed the goal line again. Lawrence added the extra point for a 19-0 lead.

Sid Ellison came in and kicked off. The Moccasins were unable to gain and were forced to turn the ball over to Mercer on the forty-three-yard line. Red Adams went to work and made three yards at right end. After being held for no gain, Rice broke through tackle for twenty-nine yards. Glover slipped around end for three yards, then Adams scored the fourth touchdown from the eleven-yard line. Ellison split the uprights to bring the total to 26-0.

The Chattanooga offense could not advance because of the outstanding Mercer defense. The Mercer offense was having one of its greatest days, and once again the Bears were goalward bound. Gerald Teasley, Rice, Glover, and Poore carried the ball in this series. Jewdy Stein, a 200-pound fullback, came in and got two yards, then Shorty Poore went the final three yards for the touchdown. Ellison was true once again on the extra point, and Mercer led 33-0.

The taste of victory was sweet as the team played before an estimated 4,500 fans, even though gate receipts for the day only accounted for 944 paid admissions. Those present were treated to a great show as Dave Rice, with 108 yards and two touchdowns, was outstanding once again. Adams also ran well, as did Glover, Poore, and Lawrence. With Red Simmons knocking down runners and Crook Smith batting down passes, the Mercer defense was too much. The 33-0 score proved to be the largest score and most decisive victory ever earned over Chattanooga.

Mercer 14, Howard 5

The next week Howard came to Georgia's "Central City" to engage the Bears. Once again 5,000 people were estimated to be in attendance, but less than 500 actually paid. Evidently quite a few passes were given out. The fans were not disappointed as the Bears roared to victory again. While the offense was providing the scoring punch, the defense did not allow a touchdown. Howard only got three first downs and completed one pass in six attempts.

Lawrence's kickoff was over the goal line and Howard put the ball in play at the twenty-yard line. The Bulldogs ran one play, then decided to punt. Lawrence brought the ball back five yards to the forty-five-yard line. The defense tightened up here, and Glover and Cecil got five yards. After another run for a one-yard loss, Lawrence was unsuccessful with a twenty-six yard field goal attempt.

The remainder of the first half was a punting duel between Lawrence and Stevens of Howard. Howard scored when Stevens was successful on a twenty-five-yard drop kick. Mercer started to drive again, but a Lawrence fumble gave the ball back to Howard as the half ended.

The Bears returned to the field in the second half determined to score. From the Howard forty-eight, Rice ran the ball five times in a row to advance the team to the twenty-seven-yard line. Following a five-yard penalty on Howard, Glover sped twenty-two yards to the one-foot line. Glover carried the ball again and scored the touchdown. Lawrence booted the extra point, and Mercer led 7-3.

The gate was open now, and the Mercer defense took over, making life miserable for the visitors from Alabama. The first time that Howard attempted to punt after the Mercer touchdown, Smith blocked the ball. Howard recovered on the twelve-yard line, but the punter Stevens fumbled after two plays, and the ever-present Smith recovered on the Howard fifteen-yard line. After offsetting penalties of fifteen yards, Glover blasted through a hole at left guard and raced for his second touchdown of the afternoon. Lawrence once again kicked true for a 14-3 advantage.

Some plays later a Lawrence punt was blocked and Howard got a safety to bring the score to 14-5. The Mercer defense was far superior to the Howard offense for the remainder of the game. Simmons recovered a fumble, Smith blocked another punt, and Lawrence tried two more field goals. Rice picked up fifty-three yards as the principal runner while Glover added fifty-four yards on five carries, scoring two touchdowns.

Mercer 0, Loyola 0

The team traveled west to New Orleans for a game with Loyola on November 1. According to Coach Robinson, it was played in "weather that was too hot and among mosquitoes that nearly ate us up." The backfield consisted of Lawrence at quarterback, Glover and Cecil at halfbacks, and Rice at fullback. Up front were Smith and Ellison at ends, Simmons and Jowers at tackle, Bela Lancaster and Slew Dunn at guard, and Carson at center. Others seeing action in the Bayou City were Barnes, McDonald, Denver, Fleming and Adams.

It was a defensive game all the way, and a scoreless tie resulted. Lawrence attempted three field goals, but the Loyola defense put too much pressure on him. Kid Cecil had a thirty-yard run as a bright spot, and Simmons continued to shine on defense.

Mercer 16, Wofford 0

The team made it five games in a row with no losses when they bested Wofford 16-0 on 8 November in Macon. Mercer had an outstanding day with forty-five running plays and 201 yards gained. Lawrence ran for sixty-seven yards while Cecil accounted for another sixty. The hard-charging offensive line cleared the way for twelve first downs, and the defense recovered four Terrier fumbles.

Rusty Lawrence put Mercer on the scoreboard first with a field goal. Then Ellison blocked a punt and recovered it for a touchdown. The final touchdown was scored by hard-charging Dave Rice on a forty-yard jaunt. Once again Lawrence kicked the ball over the bar, making the final score 16-0. During the next week Jewdy Stein was lost from the squad due to grades, and Eli McDonald was placed on the injured list with two broken bones in his foot.

Mercer 10, Florida 0

On 14 November Florida was the victim before a crowd of 6,000 in Macon. Florida, a three-touchdown favorite over the Bears, had been beaten by Army 14-7 and had tied Georgia Tech 7-7.

Florida kicked off, and Dunn returned the ball five yards. After two plays Lawrence punted forty-five yards, and the ball was returned to the Mercer thirty-five. Florida charged, picking up two first downs, but on the crucial third down Pittman was dropped by Crook Smith. A fourth-down pass failed for Florida, and the Mercer men started anew from their own twenty-yard line.

After no significant gains by either team, Florida attempted a forty-yard field goal, and Mercer got the ball on the twenty-yard line. Kid Cecil, on the next play, ran for thirty-nine yards to the Florida forty-one-yard line. Rice then ran for sixteen and another first down. Bate added one, but Rice was stopped for no gain. On the next play Lawrence threw a jump pass for twenty-two yards and Cecil, fighting with a Gator defender, pulled it out of the air for a Mercer touchdown. Lawrence booted the extra point for a 7-0 advantage.

Florida chose to kick off and Cecil returned it twenty-seven yards. Mercer then drove goalward with Rice personally accounting for forty-one yards. Others made short yardage, and the ball was carried to the twenty-yard line. From here Lawrence booted a field goal on fourth down.

Florida kicked off again, but Mercer couldn't gain, and Lawrence punted—one of thirteen punts for him during the afternoon. Florida's drive this time was halted by an interception by Rice on the Mercer twenty-eight-yard line.

Mercer picked up a first down but was forced to punt. Florida moved to the Mercer thirty in eight plays, but two plays later Dunn intercepted to stop this threat. The remainder of the first half found neither team able to get an advantage.

In the second half Lawrence was knocked out as he returned Florida's first punt, but Mercer had the ball on the thirty-yard line. Glover went around right end for forty yards on the next play. Three plays later Lawrence returned to action and missed on a twenty-five-yard field goal attempt.

Two series later Smith put a real scare into the Gators by blocking a punt on the four-yard line, but Florida recovered. The remainder of the quarter was a punting duel between Newton and Lawrence.

In the final quarter Rice once again intercepted deep in Mercer's territory and returned the ball thirty yards to midfield. Mercer's defensive secondary really had a great day as Florida attempted twenty-four passes and completed only two for thirty-five yards. For the afternoon, Florida had 106 yards on thirty-seven attempts. Cecil had ninety-five yards gained, Glover seventy-eight, and Lawrence forty-eight as Mercer showed a balanced running attack.

According to sports writer Morgan Blake, this was the greatest upset of the southern football season. Although the entire team drew praise, Dunn, for his outstanding play, was rated as one of the best in the South.

Mercer 0, Oglethorpe 25

The bubble burst the following weekend as Oglethorpe took the measure of Mercer by a 25-0 count. It was all Oglethorpe as they gained 202 yards while holding the Bears to a total of ninety-five yards. Mercer's passing attack went zero for thirteen. They were intercepted four times by the Petrels.

The game began with Mercer on the twenty-yard line following the kickoff. The Bears could make no headway during the first quarter as Lawrence was forced to punt six times. Oglethorpe finally scored when Campbell dropkicked a forty-five yard field goal for a 3-0 lead.

Oglethorpe kicked off again, but Mercer was forced to punt. Oglethorpe then drove from the forty-seven-yard line for a touchdown, with Maurer getting twenty yards on one run. Two intercepted passes by Oglethorpe led to the final scores. The Oglethorpe defense was so stingy that in the fourth quarter Mercer did not gain a yard while Oglethorpe earned eighty-four yards and two touchdowns. The final victory of the season was a great one for Oglethorpe, bringing them the SIAA championship.

Mercer 7, Mississippi College 7

The 1924 season ended in Macon as Mississippi College tied the Bears 7-7. Mercer took the lead with a great catch of a thirty-yard pass by Kay Tipton from Lawrence. The point was added by Rusty Lawrence.

1925

The 1925 season began with fourteen lettermen reporting for preseason practice at the Colaparchee Club. Stanley Robinson, John King, and Sid Johnson were coaches. Tink Gillam had resigned following the 1924 season to become an assistant coach at Clemson.

The feature attraction for the 1925 team was the new Centennial Stadium, now Porter Stadium, which had been built at a cost of $100,000. The dedication game pitted Mercer against Georgia in the season opener.

The 1925 edition of the "Orange and Black" listed John Parks and Kay Tipton at end, Slew Dunn and Eli McDonald at tackle, Bela Lancaster and John Herndon at guard, Captain Dick Carson at center, Gerald Teasley at quarterback, Phoney Smith and Red Skelton at halfback. The 1925 season marked the beginning of the career of Joseph Farrar "Phoney" Smith who was destined to become one of the most outstanding football players in Mercer's history.

Mercer 0, Georgia 32

"Glory, Glory to Old Georgia" was the only song sung following the opening of the new stadium in Macon. The Bears were just not able to contain the Bulldogs on that bleak September day. Georgia got a 19-0 lead before Wally Butts, Smith, and Skelton drove to the Georgia thirty-five-yard line for the best Mercer attack of the day. The loss was the eleventh consecutive loss to Georgia for Mercer since the series began in 1892.

Mercer 0, Florida 21

The Bears did little better the next week in Gainesville as Florida scored three touchdowns and kicked a field goal while holding Mercer scoreless.

This defeat reduced Mercer's advantage over Florida to seven wins, five losses, and one tie, in the series dating back to 1906. Dunn, Davis, Charlton "Bit" Pierce, and Prentiss Neal were outstanding in the Mercer line, while Teasley performed well at quarterback.

Mercer 14, Rollins 0

Playing in Macon on October 10, the Bears won their first game in Centennial Stadium. The first half was scoreless, with Mercer moving to the Rollins five-yard line three times without cashing in. Jack Bate, Ralph Skelton, and Wally Butts gained most of the ground on these drives.

In the second half Phoney Smith returned a punt for thirty-three yards and then carried the ball for twelve yards and a first down. Gerald Teasley got a yard, Smith was caught for a four-yard loss, but he then made runs of ten, forty-one, and two yards. From the Rollins twenty-seven-yard line Smith went to the three and then over for the touchdown. Skelton scored later in the half, and Smith added both extra points.

This determined second half offensive effort gave the Bears a 1-2 record. The Mercer defense also returned to form with help from substitutes Beddingfield, Bennett, and Redmon.

Mercer 7, Chattanooga 12

The winning ways did not last long, as the third loss of the 1925 season was to Chattanooga by a score of 12-7. The Bears were not able to put it all together. When the defense was going good, the offense couldn't get started. After a scoreless first half in the rain, Chattanooga scored in the third quarter. Dale Viers recovered a Mercer fumble on the twenty-five and ran for a touchdown. The final touchdown for Chattanooga came in the last quarter on a pass play.

Mercer registered a touchdown in the final minutes of the contest when Phoney Smith crossed the goal and then added the extra point. One factor influencing the game was the fact that the game started late. The freshman game lasted quite a long time, and the final ten minutes of the varsity game were played in near darkness.

The Bears lost a good opportunity to tie the game when Smith broke loose for twenty yards to the Chattanooga seven-yard line. On the next play the ball was fumbled and the Moccasins recovered. Smith on offense and Carson on defense were outstanding for Mercer.

Mercer 0, North Carolina 3

One of the reasons that the Bears were having a rough season was the presence of inexperienced players. There were only two juniors on the team and the others were sophomores. The North Carolina Tar Heels provided more experience for the former Cubs before pinning a 3-0 loss on them in Centennial Stadium. Underwood of Carolina hit on a field goal in the first few minutes. Neither team was able to generate an offense for the remainder of the game.

Mercer 0, Citadel 16

The Citadel made it five losses for the Bears in Augusta on 30 October 1925. Touchdowns were scored in the first and fourth quarters, and a field goal was added in the final quarter. The game began as Skelton kicked off, and the Citadel was held for downs. Mercer couldn't advance, and Skelton punted to Berry, who took the ball to the Mercer thirty-six-yard line in two plays. Berry was then thrown for a twenty-yard loss, but Weinberg recovered the yardage with a fifty-yard run. Following a two- yard run, Berry passed to Reeder for thirty yards and a Citadel touchdown.

In the second quarter Smith picked up twenty-five yards, Glover added thirteen, and Bate got four yards, but the Citadel defense held the Bears off. A pass from Smith to Bate for twenty yards brought Mercer to the Citadel ten-yard line as the half ended. In the second half the Citadel had thirty-six plays while Mercer ran only twenty-three. The longest effort for Mercer was a thirty-yard run by Smith midway in the second half. A Smith-to-Parks pass for fourteen yards closed out the Mercer offense that day.

The battle in Augusta saw a revised starting lineup with Butts and Parks at end, McDonald and Pierce at tackle, Lancaster and Herndon at guard, Fleming at center, Prentiss Neal at quarterback, Skelton and B. F. Cliatt at halfback, and Marion Roberts at fullback. The fact that the Mercer team was very inexperienced, particularly at quarterback, hurt the offense greatly. Injuries also took a heavy toll during the season.

Mercer 17, Furman 0

The losing streak was finally broken with Furman's visit to Macon as the Bears were victorious by a 17-0 count. The first touchdown came on a Skelton-to-Parks pass for forty yards with Smith hitting the extra point. "Bit" Pierce got into the scoring column, a lineman's dream, by recovering a fumbled Smith punt and scoring from the ten-yard line. Smith added the extra point and a field goal from the fifteen-yard line to make the score 17-0.

Smith made the longest run of the day, forty-four yards, as he accumulated 146 yards in twenty-three attempts. This was his best effort since coming up from the freshman team. Ralph Skelton added eighty yards in twenty-nine runs.

At halftime the fans were treated to a cross country race between runners from Mercer and Furman. Charley Walker of Mercer won first place in the 2½ mile run in the time of 13:37.

Mercer 21, Oglethorpe 6

Rejuvenated and gaining experience, the Bears went into the game with Oglethorpe as a two-touchdown underdog. The Bears avenged the trouncing they received in 1924 by ruining the Petrels' perfect SIAA record. Mercer scored quickly as John Parks recovered a Campbell fumble following Glover's long kickoff. Parks carried the ball back thirty yards for a touchdown and Smith booted the extra point.

Following Glover's second kickoff, Maurer got five yards on two plays, then Parks—the battler from Richland—roared through on defense and smacked Kilgore for ten-yard loss. Mercer took over on the Oglethorpe thirty-seven line. Ralph Skelton ran seven plays for twenty-two yards, then Smith made fifteen on three attempts, the last being a counter for six points. Smith once again hit the extra point and Mercer's devastating rookies led the amazed Petrels 14-0, after only five minutes of play. Oglethorpe got their touchdown with Maurer running twelve yards following a long series of plays. The point was missed and the score stood at 14-6.

In the second half, the game was a defensive struggle. Skelton stopped one Oglethorpe threat by intercepting a pass and returning it twenty-five yards. In the fourth quarter Mercer scored again. Skelton passed to Smith for thirty-five yards to the seven-yard line. Skelton went into the end zone on the next play for the final touchdown. Phoney Smith booted his third extra point, and Mercer had beaten the fierce Oglethorpe eleven. Skelton, Smith, Butts, and Parks were outstanding for the Bears.

Mercer 0, Marquette 30

The Mercer boys journeyed north for the second time ever to participate in an intersectional contest with Marquette University. On 27 November before a crowd of 10,000, Marquette proved too much and won by a score of 30-0.

The Mercer defense proved capable of running plays, but Marquette completed nineteen of thirty-two passes against the Bruin secondary and accounted for touchdowns in the last three quarters. The defensive line stopped the vaunted Marquette attack four times within the four-yard line. Two times the Mercer line held within the one-foot line, once with four downs to go.

Mercer went beyond midfield once to the Marquette twenty-three yard line on passes, but only four of eleven passes were completed by the Bears during the game. Members of the squad making the trip were Dick Carson, Denver Fleming, Fred Forrester, Bela Lancaster, Slew Dunn, Prentiss Neal, John Herndon, Eli McDonald, Bit Pierce, Dutch Rogers, Glen Davis, John Parks, Kay Tipton, Wallace Butts, Jimmie Glover, Gerald Teasley, Phoney

Smith, Ralph Skelton, Marion Roberts, Jack Bate, B. F. Cliatt, and Beddingfield.

By 1925 most of the large schools had dropped out of the SIAA as the Southern Conference was formed. There were twenty-one schools in the SIAA in 1925. These were: Furman, Oglethorpe, Mercer, Centenary, Loyola, Birmingham Southern, Millsaps, Citadel, Howard, Presbyterian, Georgetown, Erskine, Wofford, Charleston, Chattanooga, Centre, Southwestern, Louisiana College, Newberry, Rollins, and Mississippi College.

Although Mercer did not have a winning record during the 1925 season, there were a number of outstanding players on the team. Those receiving all-SIAA honors for the season were Bit Pierce, Slew Dunn, John Parks, and Phoney Smith, who was chosen captain of the team.

Following the 1925 season, the Mercer coaching staff changed once again. Robinson returned to Mississippi College, and Bernie Moore was hired as head coach.

Chapter 5
SECOND DOWN

The 1926 team, after a valuable but difficult year of experience in 1925, was composed of four seniors, eight juniors, and fourteen men up from the freshmen team. Under new head coach Bernie Moore, sixty men, including freshmen, reported for preseason practice at St. Simons Island on September 1. E. Parker Mosley moved up to athletic director and Sid Johnson coached the line, while J. D. Blair, former Lanier coach, worked with the freshmen.

After a twenty-day practice period in the sun and surf, the Bears returned for the opening battle with Georgia in Athens. The new starters on the team that faced Georgia were Barney Davis, Guinard Wilder, Buchanan Loser, and Walter "Big Six" Salter. All-SIAA players returning were Charlton Pierce, Joseph F. Smith, and John Parks. Butts, Fleming, Skelton, and Tipton rounded out the starting eleven.

1926

Mercer 0, Georgia 20

Mercer won the toss, elected to receive, and Salter returned the kickoff up the middle for twenty yards. Phoney Smith dashed for seven yards, then punted fifty-five yards on third down, after a second-down fumble. Georgia drove to the Mercer four-yard line, but the defense held four downs. On the first down, Smith punted the ball fifty yards and got the Bears temporarily out of trouble.

The Red and Black came storming back toward the Mercer goal, but a McCreary fumble on the Mercer eight-yard line was recovered by Barney Davis. Following three unsuccessful attempts to move the ball, Smith punted to the Bulldogs again. Moments later, when a Georgia runner broke loose, he caught him to prevent a touchdown. With Georgia on the Mercer twenty-three, Morton ran for one yard, then Sherlock made ten yards before being knocked down by Smith. Mercer took over again on the six-yard line after Smith had stopped Morton for no gain.

Hoping to improve their field position, Smith punted for Mercer. On the first down Morton lofted a pass to Sherlock for fifteen yards. Georgia then drove slowly but relentlessly to the Mercer three-yard line where Boland broke over for the touchdown. Wally Butts, the 5'6" 143-pound Mercer defensive end, broke through the defense and blocked the conversion attempt. Georgia led 6-0.

Marion Roberts returned the kickoff twenty yards to start a new Mercer drive. Skelton had two successive incomplete passes, and Mercer was penalized five yards. Buck Loser lost the ball, allowing Morton to scamper seventeen yards for a Georgia touchdown with the recovered fumble. Georgia led 13-0 on the successful extra point.

Once again Georgia kicked off, and Ralph Skelton carried the ball back fifteen yards to midfield. Dick Barnes rambled for five yards on two plays, but Skelton was held for no gain. Roberts could get only one yard, and the ball went over to Georgia. Just as the half was ending, Georgia picked up five yards on a run by Bobby Hooks, who would become the last Mercer football coach.

The second half started with Mercer's back to the wall. A determined defense held Georgia on the eleven-yard line and later on the five, but the third drive ended in a touchdown and a 20-0 score. Once again Mercer received, and Bill Bruner returned the kickoff twenty yards. Phoney Smith was able to get two yards, but Joe Powers could not gain, and Smith was forced to punt.

Although Mercer did not score in the game, the twenty-five men who went to Athens played well. The Bears were defeated by superior strength and depth. Smith and Skelton were outstanding offensively for the Bears.

Mercer 7, Citadel 12

The Citadel came to Macon for the first time and edged the Bears 12-7 after Mercer had led 7-6 with less than three minutes to play. Doyle was the hero of the day for the Citadel as he picked up a fumble on the Mercer fifteen-yard line and raced eighty-five yards for the game's winning score. The crowd watched in despair as the long-striding runner dramatically sealed the victory.

Ginny Wilder started the game by kicking off, but the ball was quickly punted back to Smith, who fumbled. The Citadel drove to the Mercer fifteen-yard line, where Meeks dropkicked a field goal. Following the interception of a Skelton pass, Blanding ran twelve yards before being stopped by Smith. Two plays later Weeks booted another fifteen-yard field goal for a 6-0 advantage.

The half ended after each team punted several times with neither getting a real advantage. Phoney Smith hit one seventy yards during the exchanges.

The second half opened with Wilder booming the ball fifty-five yards downfield. Two series later Smith punted his second seventy-yarder. Citadel returned the punt to Mercer on their ten-yard line. From here John Parks, an outstanding Mercer baseball catcher, threw a strike to the speedy Phoney Smith. Smith, running like a deer, took the ball over his shoulder and sped ninety yards for a touchdown. This established a record for the longest pass-run ever. He added the extra point and Mercer led 7-6.

The Cadets took the kickoff and tried three passes, only to have the last one intercepted by Butch Hammock. A revived Mercer crew took over, and Skelton made one yard. Smith broke loose for twenty-five yards and another first down. After an incomplete pass, Smith was held for no gain, Skelton kept the drive going by hitting Butts with a fifteen-yard pass on the next play. Marion Roberts got two yards, Skelton added four more, then Smith got five for a first down on the Citadel fifteen-yard line.

But on the next play a Barnes fumble was picked up by Doyle, who ran the eighty-five yard touchdown. Wally Butts broke through to block the point attempt, but the damage was done and the Cadets led 12-7.

Barnes hustled the kickoff back forty yards, but a Skelton pass was intercepted on the next play. Mercer got the ball back as Barnes recovered when the defense made the Citadel cough up the pigskin.

Mercer tried to come from behind on passes, but the effort ended as the final pass of the game was intercepted by the alert Citadel defense. The entire Mercer team played with great determination. Parks and Butts received praise for their outstanding work. Smith, playing with an injured shoulder, had another outstanding game and also averaged fifty-four yards on five punts.

Mercer 6, Florida 3

The lineup for the Florida game had Butch Hammack at center and Red Nightengale at right tackle as new starters for Mercer. A crowd of 6,000 was on hand to cheer the Bears to victory at Centennial Stadium. Monty Salmon, of the Rialto Theatre, helped the team get ready for the Gators. He had the Mercer varsity as guests, and short speeches were made with the players and fans responding.

Florida had the ball first, but Mercer held the Gators to no gain on three attempts, so Bishop punted. Smith returned the punt fifteen yards, then quickly added ten more for a first down. Skelton hit for no gain, but Smith got loose for fifteen yards at right end for another first down. He added another five yards up the middle, then Florida drew a five-yard penalty to give Mercer another first down.

With the crowd responding wildly, Smith and Skelton put together two five-yard runs for another first down. Buck Loser got one; Salter added two; then a Skelton-to-Loser pass accounted for twelve yards and the fifth first down in a row.

The team was really moving now, and the crowd could sense that the Bears would not be stopped. "Big Six" Salter pounded out ten yards to put the ball on the Florida fifteen-yard line. Ralph Skelton tried right tackle but was stacked up at the line of scrimmage. On the second down Phoney Smith was handed the ball, and he squirmed into the end zone behind good blocking. The extra point was down the middle, but Mercer was guilty of holding and the point didn't count.

On this drive Mercer put together six consecutive first downs for the only touchdown of the game. After several exchanges of the ball through punts, Florida picked up one first down. Then Bishop booted a thirty-yard field goal for the Gator score. It was reported later that Bishop actually attempted to punt the ball but dropped it too low and the punt became a field goal.

In the second half, Florida started on the Mercer thirty-five and quickly moved to the five-yard line. The Gators gained only one yard in three tries, and Mercer took over as a fourth down pass went incomplete into the end zone.

Later in the third quarter the Bears drove to the Florida five with a twenty-yard gainer by Smith and two runs for six yards by Skelton, but Florida held. Upon getting the ball back, a Skelton-to-Smith pass for thirty yards started another drive toward the Florida goal. Skelton picked up seven yards on three tries to the Florida six-inch line, but the Gators held again. From here

Florida began to put the ball into the air in desperation. After six straight incomplete passes, Phoney Smith picked one off as the game ended.

The Mercer defense in this game was tremendous as both the linemen and backs played determined football. On offense, Smith was the leading rusher with 123 yards in seventeen attempts, while Skelton added seventy-two on nineteen tries. Salter and Loser also ran well. The hard-charging line opened the way for twelve first downs during the game.

Mercer 3, Howard 0

The Bears edged Howard 3-0 on October 23 in Macon before an estimated crowd of 7,000. Phoney Smith's twenty-five-yard field goal was the only score of the day. The fourteen men who saw action played fierce defensive ball and held Howard scoreless despite the fact that they amassed 252 total yards. Bancroft of Howard was the leading ground gainer with 103 yards while Smith had seventy-four yards for Mercer. Although the Bears were victorious, the services of Butch Hammock were lost because of a broken arm.

Mercer 13, Ft. Benning 21

A loss to Ft. Benning in Columbus, Georgia, dropped the Bears to a 2-4 record. Most of the game was played by the reserves as Mercer started Adams, Vernon Cail, Joe Estes, Holder, Bob Bond, Cheeves, Wilder, Bruner, Towers, Barnes, and Roberts.

Ft. Benning had thirteen first downs to eight for Mercer and the Bears had only three completions in twelve passes attempted. Five passes were intercepted by Benning, two of which were returned for touchdowns. Kjelstom brought the first one back for seventy yards and a touchdown with Kelly later adding another seventy-yard score. Ft. Benning drove forty yards in eleven plays for their third touchdown.

Mercer's first serious threat started on their own twenty-two-yard line. Bruner passed to Skelton for eleven yards; Ft. Benning was penalized five yards and two more Bruner passes netted twenty-eight yards. Benning drew another five-yard penalty, then Parks faked a pass and gained twelve yards to the fifteen. Skelton scored two plays later and Bruner added the extra point.

Regular starters Parks, Davis, Neal, Loser, Smith, Skelton, and Salter played part of the second half. They cut the final margin to eight points as Ft. Benning won by a score of 21-13.

Mercer 13, Furman 13

Timely pass completions enabled the Bears to earn a tie with Furman and bring their record to a 2-4-1. Furman, playing at home in Greenville, ran twice as many plays as Mercer, but they crossed the goal line only once.

The game began as Smith kicked off fifty-eight yards. Furman ran two plays and punted. Mercer's Smith returned the punt on the third down and Schneider of Furman fumbled the boot. Marion Roberts recovered and ran to the Furman twenty-yard line.

Mercer got two yards on three plays before Smith missed on a field goal from the eighteen-yard line. The remainder of the first quarter consisted of short runs and punts as Furman kicked four times and Mercer three.

The beginning of the second quarter found Furman at the Mercer twenty-five yard line. The tough Mercer defense allowed twelve yards on five plays, then Red Nightengale threw Crawford for a five-yard loss. On the next play Davis of Furman toed a twenty-yard drop kick through the uprights for a 3-0 Furman lead.

Mercer took the kickoff but couldn't make the required ten yards for a first down. Furman started at their own forty-yard line and went to the Mercer forty-five where Davis attempted another drop kick. The half ended after each team ran two more series of plays.

Early in the second half Pipkin kicked a seventeen-yard field goal to give Furman a 6-0 lead. Mercer then went to work and produced a touchdown. Skelton gained a yard, then he passed to Parks for twelve yards and a first down. Skelton got only one yard on two carries, but Parks tossed a twenty-three-yard aerial to Smith for another first down. Roberts was held for no gain, and Smith got one before Parks threw successfully to Loser for seventeen yards and the fourth first down in a row. Smith went the last yard for the score after Skelton had been held for no gain. Smith converted and Mercer led 7-6.

The lead was short-lived as Furman came roaring back from their own thirty-six-yard line. They went sixty-four yards in twelve plays to take a 13-7 lead. The Mercer men responded to the challenge by starting a drive on the forty-six-yard line. After a play was stopped cold, Parks, with a hot passing arm, threw to Smith for seven yards. Skelton then threw to Smith for fifteen yards and a first down. Phoney was rolling now as he ran for four yards and caught another pass from Skelton for twelve yards for a first down at the Furman twenty-two-yard line. From there he blasted for eight yards. Skelton was held for no gain, and Smith could get only one yard. Big Six Salter plowed for a tough yard and a first down at the Furman ten-yard line. Phoney Smith went the remaining distance on a fake pass play to knot the score at 13-13. The game-winning extra point was blocked. Furman had one other chance to go ahead, but Pipkin missed a twenty-three-yard field goal attempt.

In the dramatic second half Mercer got ten first downs and thirteen points. Phoney Smith ran for sixty-two yards in fifteen carries. He scored one touchdown and Skelton added the other in the hard-fought battle. Parks and Skelton were particularly outstanding with their clutch passing. The defensive line, with Bit Pierce returning to action, kept the Furman team out of scoring territory most of the afternoon. Butts, Tipton, Fleming, and Nightengale drew praise for their work all through the game. Joe Estes, Bond, and Salter also saw action as 150 Mercer students were on hand for the game.

Mercer 55, Rollins 0

Roberts made the first touchdown for Mercer and Smith kicked the goal five minutes after play began. Pierce was removed from the game for slugging shortly after the first marker. This first touchdown started an avalanche of touchdowns for the Bears that ended with the score 55-0.

Skelton scored on a forty-two-yard run and Smith converted to run the score to 14-0. One more touchdown was scored in the first half. In the third quarter Loser scored to make it 27-0. He then recovered a blocked punt for another touchdown and Skelton converted for a 34-0 lead.

In the fourth quarter Skelton ran ten yards around left end for a touchdown. Vernon Cail kicked the extra point. Bill Bruner recovered a blocked kick for the seventh touchdown and Powers converted. Bruner also scored the eighth and last touchdown with a fifty-one yard run. He converted to account for the final point. In all Loser scored two touchdowns, Skelton three, Bruner two, and Roberts had one. Smith converted three times while Cail, Power, Skelton, and Bruner had one each.

Mercer 31, Oglethorpe 7

The cry was, "Let's Make It Two in a Row," and the Bears responded with a mighty roar against Oglethorpe, in Atlanta on 20 November 1926. When the dust had cleared, all the feathers had been picked from the mighty Petrels and the score read Mercer 31, Oglethorpe 7. The Petrels were stunned after the first kickoff but tried desperately to recover during the remaining fifty-nine minutes of the contest.

The incomparable Phoney Smith caught the opening kickoff on the Mercer ten-yard line. Behind a wall of blockers, he picked his way to the Oglethorpe one-yard line. Before the crowd had settled, Ralph Skelton took the ball over for the touchdown. Smith converted and Mercer led 7-0.

Oglethorpe retaliated for six points and Campbell added the extra point for a 7-7 game, but some of the starch had been removed from the talented Atlanta eleven. The ball then changed hands several times before Wally Butts pounced on an Oglethorpe fumble at the fifty-yard line. Mercer drove to the goal line but could not score. Some minutes later another fumble was recovered on the Oglethorpe six-yard line. The stubborn Oglethorpe defense held, and a field goal attempt by Smith was wide.

Oglethorpe found the going equally tough, and was forced to punt from behind their goal line minutes later. The ball struck the goal post, and an energetic Bear lineman recovered on the five-yard line as the half ended.

At the start of the second half, Mercer took the kickoff and moved the ball to the Oglethorpe forty-five-yard line. Phoney Smith then broke loose off tackle and, with Pierce leading, went for the touchdown. He converted and the score was 14-7.

Some minutes later Mercer recovered another fumble, and Smith booted a twenty-yard field goal. The Oglethorpe team was rattled as the vicious Bear defense applied pressure. A fumble on the Oglethorpe thirty-five-yard line set up another touchdown on a Skelton-to-Smith pass. Roberts got into the scoring act by intercepting one of Oglethorpe's desperation aerials and going fifty yards for a touchdown.

The Bears had a great second half, scoring twenty-four points and holding a good Oglethorpe team scoreless. The defensive line of Parks and Butts at end, Pierce and Estes at tackle, Tipton and Davis at guard, and Fleming at center was too tough for the Oglethorpe eleven. Adams also assisted greatly in the second-half onslaught.

The backfield was superb, both offensively and defensively. The Mercer offense was triggered by long runs and returns of intercepted passes. Phoney Smith, in one of his greatest performances, got 157 yards from scrimmage, scored two touchdowns, four extra points, and one field goal. His efforts for the day gave him sixty points for the season. Skelton's touchdown pushed his point total to thirty-six.

Mercer 0, Parris Island 0

The final game of the season was a 0-0 battle with the undefeated Parris Island Marines. Twice the Marines turned the Bears back at the six-yard line. In the fourth quarter Mercer went to the one-foot line but couldn't push the ball across.

The 1926 season ended with four wins, three losses, and two ties. Mercer scored 128 points while the opposition got seventy-six. The all-SIAA selections included John Parks at left end, Charlton Pierce at left tackle, and Phoney Smith at left halfback. He was also selected captain of the 1926 team.

1927

Expectations for the 1927 season were high and tickets went on sale at $8.00 for the five home games. The nine lettermen returning were Phoney Smith, Doyle Barnes, Big Six Salter, Buck Loser, Bit Pierce, Red Nightengale,

Joe Estes, Butch Hammack, and Captain Wallace Butts. Bernie Moore returned as head coach with J.D. Blair coaching the line, and Kay Tipton handling the freshmen.

The coaches worked hard during the summer months getting ready for the coming season. Light shoulder pads and silk pants were part of the new equipment ordered. Coach Moore and his aides went to Knute Rockne's coaching school to learn new techniques.

Mercer 77, North Georgia Aggies 0

The season opened with a warm-up game, the fashion in that era, against the North Georgia Aggies. While Mercer was engaging the Aggies, Alabama warmed up with Millsaps 46-0, and Vandy got by Chattanooga 45-18.

The Bears not only warmed up, they got red hot and blistered the Aggies 77-0. On only fifteen first-half running plays, Mercer scored seven times to mount a 45-0 lead. Twenty-four men participated in the runaway, and several new players saw considerable action.

Phoney Smith, causing more excitement than the 1848 gold rush, scored first with a thirty-five yard canter and eventually totaled four touchdowns and twenty-eight points. Art "Yank" Wright had four touchdowns, Jimmy Matthews one, Bill Alderman two, and Wilbur Smith got one. Phoney also had four extra points, while Alderman added one.

Although scoring twenty-eight points, Smith missed the first three extra points he tried. The goal posts were placed ten yards deep in the end zone rather than on the goal line as in the past. This caused some difficulty for kickers on extra points and field goals.

According to Bit Pierce, the Bears' favorite play was an off-tackle slant by Smith. With Pierce at tackle and Butts at end, the play was very effective. "Wally had the ability, although he was small, to get up under the defensive tackle and push him out of the way. Then with a halfback blocking the end, I could move through and get the linebacker or run interference. Phoney then would come bursting through, pointing to me to get this one or that one, and he then would be on his way."

Mercer 6, Citadel 0

Before a crowd of 5,000 in Savannah, Mercer slipped by the Citadel 6-0. Phoney Smith scored from the six-inch line to end a second-quarter drive. It started as the Cadets went to the Mercer one-yard line. A strong Mercer defense caused a fumble, and the ball was recovered by Mercer. Phoney Smith then made a forty-yard run to get Mercer rolling toward the Citadel goal. New men in the lineup for this game included Dan Garrett, Hicky Godby, Luther Ray, Art Wright, and Bill Alderman.

Mercer received the kickoff to start the game. Wright was thrown for an eight-yard loss, but a pass for thirteen yards recouped the deficit. However, on fourth down the ball was punted to the Citadel. The Cadets marched to the Mercer one-yard line and stalled. Smith ran for forty yards to get Mercer out of trouble. After several small gains, big Bill Alderman broke loose to the Citadel three-yard line. Smith slashed over on the third down for the touchdown. The extra point was missed, and there were no more serious threats during the remainder of the quarter.

The Citadel began to move in the second quarter, picking up five first downs on the way to the Mercer four-yard line. From there Blanding went for two yards, but on the next play Blanding fumbled. Smith picked the ball up and ran forty yards before being caught.

The second half was a punting-and-passing exhibition with Mercer punting five times. Hammack and Alderman intercepted passes while Wright of Mercer had one stolen by the Citadel defense.

Mercer 13, Furman 27

Mercer was not quite as successful against a strong Furman eleven in Macon the following weekend, losing by a score of 27-13. In a game featuring the knockout punch and the long run, Capps returned a punt eighty-five yards for a Furman score. Whitey Rawl was the star runner for the Paladins.

On offense for Mercer, it was Phoney Smith who once again thrilled the fans with runs of eighty-seven and fifty yards for touchdowns. His ferocious running and the determination of the Furman defense to stop him resulted in his being knocked out three times during the game.

While Phoney was galloping on offense, Pierce and Butts were playing their usual aggressive game on defense. Buck Loser played a big part in the Mercer attack with his punts, as two went for seventy and sixty-five yards.

Mercer 26, Presbyterian 7

Phoney Smith and Bill Alderman carried the offensive load for the Bears in a 26-7 victory over Presbyterian College for the third win of the season. Smith led with three touchdowns and 130 yards in three quarters of play. Alderman scored one touchdown, made two conversions, and gained 117 yards in thirteen carries.

While this offensive show was going on, the defense, led by Mallard, Butts, and Pierce, really gave the Blue Hose offense a tough time. Mallard was credited with his greatest game, while Captain Butts was his usual determined self. Buck Loser directed the Bears from his quarterback post. He also put the Hose in difficulty several times with his outstanding punting. One punt went for eighty yards after he booted it from behind his goal line. Art Wright got off a forty-yard run to bolster the offensive charge.

Mercer 0, Howard 14

Howard proved too strong for the Bears and edged them 14-0 in Macon the following weekend. With Phoney Smith out with fractured ribs, the offensive efforts were drastically reduced. He came into the game in the third quarter and almost single-handedly carried the ball to the Howard five, but Mercer couldn't score.

Mercer 6, Florida 32

Old enemy Florida took the measure of the Bears 32-6 in Gainesville before a crowd of 9,000 Homecoming fans. Florida ran up twenty-two first downs and Mercer got only four as the Gator defense made the going rough. Wally Butts, although outstanding as a defensive end, played with a badly bruised kidney. Phoney Smith got the only touchdown for Mercer on a sixty-five-yard run.

Mercer 21, Oglethorpe 6

Before a Homecoming crowd of 7,000 on Armistice Day, Dad's Day, and Phoney Smith Day on 11 November 1927, Mercer played Oglethorpe in Macon. Wilton "Bill" Alderman kicked off, and one of the greatest games ever seen in Macon was under way.

Oglethorpe returned the kickoff fifteen yards, got a first down, but then Smith intercepted a pass for Mercer. With Mercer in possession on the forty-yard line, Art Wright ran for five yards, Smith got three, and then added four more for a first down. On the next play Smith darted off tackle for twenty yards and another first down. Oglethorpe got tough here and stopped three running plays. Mercer's pass went incomplete over the goal line, and Oglethorpe took over on the twenty-yard line.

Oglethorpe gained eight yards in three attempts and punted on the fourth down. Smith returned the ball fifteen yards to the Petrel forty-six-yard line. Mercer couldn't move, and Loser was forced to punt. Oglethorpe took the ball again, got one first down, and Mercer got the ball back again at the forty-one-yard line.

Wright got two yards and Smith added one before Wright found daylight and sprinted twenty yards for a first down. Smith followed with an eighteen-yard run around right end. With the ball on the eighteen-yard line, Wright was dropped for a seven-yard loss. Alderman then fumbled, and the drive was stopped as Oglethorpe took over on the twenty-five yard line.

The third time that Mercer got the ball in the second quarter resulted in a touchdown. With the ball on the Oglethorpe forty-six, Smith ran for two yards. On the next play he passed twenty-nine yards to Wright for a first down on the

Petrel sixteen-yard line. After a five-yard penalty on Oglethorpe, Alderman ran the remaining ten yards for the touchdown. Alderman converted and Mercer led 7-0.

Alderman kicked off once again, and Fox returned the ball fifteen yards. Following a play for no gain, Garlington was hit hard by Butts for a five-yard loss. Garlington punted on the fourth down, and Smith returned the ball twenty-five yards to the Oglethorpe thirty-six-yard line.

Smith ran two plays for twelve yards and a first down. Alderman hit a stone wall and got nothing, but the slippery Smith got away for five yards on the next play. A Smith-to-Loser pass accounted for fifteen more yards and another first down. Smith then threw a short two-yarder to Wright to put Mercer on the Oglethorpe six-yard line. Smith hit the line hard twice for no gain, and Alderman added only two yards as Oglethorpe stopped the Bears' threat at the four-yard line.

At halftime two autographed balls, signed by Butts, Pierce, and Smith were punted into the stands. Buck Flowers, a former Georgia Tech standout, punted one. Charlie Morgan, a former great athlete for Mercer in baseball and basketball and a record-holding professional baseball player, punted the other.

The second half started with Alderman kicking off again, with White of Oglethorpe returning it thirty yards to the Oglethorpe forty-five-yard line. Vaughn got two yards, but was then thrown for a four-yard loss by Butts. Vaughn then completed a fifty-yard pass to Clements, who was stopped by Loser on the Mercer ten-yard line. Three plays later Garlington scored, but Mercer still led 7-6 as the extra point was missed.

Mercer received and Wright returned the ball thirty-five yards; Matthews got one yard; and Loser passed to Wright for seventeen yards and a first down. Wright then lost four yards, and Alderman's pass was intercepted. Oglethorpe couldn't gain and returned the ball to Mercer at the Oglethorpe forty-four-yard line. On the first play Battering Bill Alderman broke loose for forty-four yards and a touchdown. He added the extra point, and the score was 14-6.

Two series later Oglethorpe, starting on their own seventeen, drove to the Mercer fourteen-yard line before being stopped. With White and Fox carrying the ball, two first downs were registered to the Mercer forty-four-yard line. Garlington then took off for twenty yards, only to be stopped on a saving tackle by Smith. From the Mercer twenty-five-yard line Fox ran for three yards, and White followed with two more. After Garlington was stopped cold, Fox added six yards. Vaughn was knocked back one yard by Hammack, and Garlington was dropped for a six-yard loss by Pierce. Phoney Smith deflected a third-down pass, and the fourth down pass fell incomplete.

The Bears couldn't advance and turned the ball back to Oglethorpe. From the fifty-yard line Oglethorpe launched one successful pass, but the next toss was intercepted by Smith, who weaved his way up the field for a sixty-yard touchdown. Smith booted the extra point for a 21-7 lead.

Oglethorpe added a first down, but then ran out of gas, and it was Mercer's ball on the forty-seven-yard line. Smith passed to Godby for ten yards, but then Smith fumbled. Neither team could generate a successful drive for the remainder of the game.

The Mercer Bears had once again defeated a strong Oglethorpe team. In the beginning it was Bill Alderman and his two touchdowns leading the scoring. Then the defense shut out the Petrels in the second half. Ray, Nightengale, Pierce, and Butts played outstanding defense in the line.

For the game Phoney Smith picked up 159 yards, Alderman had sixty-two, and Art Wright added thirty-six. The first downs were 12-9 for Mercer while the passing went Mercer, 6 for 14, and Oglethorpe, 6 for 13. Overall, it was an evenly matched game except for the stellar defense by Mercer and the long runs by the Mercer backs.

Mercer 7, Georgia 26

Georgia in 1927 sported one of the best college football teams in the country. The mighty Bulldogs scored a tremendous 254 points during the season while allowing their collective opponents twenty-six points. The scoring for the year against Georgia read: Auburn 3, Alabama 6, Yale 10, and Mercer 7.

The lineup for the game against this great Georgia team was Baggy Mallard and Butts at end, Pierce and Nightengale at tackle, Harvey Stipe and Luther Ray at guard, with Butch Hammack at center. The backfield consisted of Wright at quarter, Smith and Salter at half, and Alderman at fullback. W. A. Wommack, Bill "Skinny" Gear, Red Adams, J. D. Barnes, and Joe Merritt were the subs for the day.

Georgia managed four touchdowns and two extra points while earning fifteen first downs. Mercer got one touchdown, one extra point, and eight first downs. The game was not a rout, however, for Smith put the scare of the season into the mighty Dogs by taking the kickoff and racing ninety yards for a touchdown. This is considered one of his greatest runs ever. Georgia recovered, however, with Harvey Hill blasting twenty-four yards for a Georgia touchdown. Passes of twenty-three and fourteen yards led to the second Georgia touchdown.

Mercer fought hard, had many close calls and several opportunities to score additional points, but the Bulldogs rang their thirteenth consecutive victory bell over Mercer. It was as though the ghost of Herty was after the Bears again. Yank Wright was caught from behind as he streaked for the end zone. Phoney Smith dropped two touchdown passes. Also, Mercer turned the ball over to Georgia once on the six-inch line. Regardless of the outcome, this game has a special place in the hearts of those who saw the action. The hard-fighting Mercer Bears showed tremendous courage and character on that November day.

Mercer 34, Wake Forest 0

Wake Forest proved to be meat for the Bears in Asheville the next weekend. Still stinging from the defeat at the hands of Georgia, Mercer unleashed an attack that made the Deacons believe in the devil. Scoring twice in the second quarter and three times in the fourth, Mercer raced to a 34-0 win.

Bill Alderman scored twice and added four extra points, Art Wright had two touchdowns, and Phoney Smith scored one time. Alderman also punted ten times for Mercer and had a thirty-six yard average.

The 1927 season ended with a 5-4 record and was one of the most exciting in history. Crowds were larger and opponents were bigger and better. The flashy, bare-headed, fleet-footed Phoney Smith thrilled thousands as he spearheaded the Mercer offense during the season. Charlton L. "Bit" Pierce, Wallace Butts, Harry "Red" Nightengale, and Butch Hammack led a group of determined defensive players who made life miserable for many a team. These men were not only tough; they were durable. They played when they were hurt, and they played as hard as possible at all times.

Following a dinner at the Dempsey Hotel given by Buddy Black, the players were presented letters for the season. Receiving special recognition were: Lynwood Mallard, Charlton Pierce, Harvey Stipe, Luther Ray, Butch Hammack, Harry Nightengale, Wallace Butts, Joe Merritt, Amos Godby, Joe Estes, and Phoney Smith.

Much has been written and said about the football talents of Phoney Smith. Phoney came to Mercer from Tennessee. It was lucky that he happened to come at all. He first went to the University of Alabama, but after a few days there, decided that he wanted to come to Mercer. His brother, Crook Smith, was an outstanding end on the Mercer team at that time.

Phoney came and never left. In fact, he epitomized football at Mercer to many fans and alumni. He also became outstanding in baseball and basketball. He received all-SIAA honors three times, was selected captain twice, and was selected honorable mention All-America. One of the greatest tributes came from his fellow students when the 1928 *Cauldron*, the Mercer yearbook, was dedicated to him. Phoney Smith not only had football talent; he had charisma.

1928

A nine-game schedule was planned by Coach Bernie Moore for the 1928 Mercer football eleven. Helping Moore were J. D. Blair and Kay Tipton. Blair worked with the line, while Tipton coached the freshmen.

Captain Butch Hammack, a two-year letterman, along with alternate captain Buck Loser led the 1928 edition of the Mercer Bears which returned eleven lettermen. Practice began on September 3 for a battle with Presbyterian College three weeks later in Clinton, South Carolina. Starting in the first game would be Baggy Mallard, Amos Godby, Frank Branch, Skinny Gear, Red Adams, Harvey Stipe, Butch Hammack, Buck Loser, Art Wright, Jody Matt, and Bill Alderman.

Mercer 7, Presbyterian 6

Before a crowd of 3,000, Presbyterian jumped out front with a sixty-yard pass play but failed to convert the point after the touchdown and led 6-0. Mercer scored with less than a minute to play on a pass from Alderman to Wright, which covered seventy yards. Clarence Stovall threw the block which took out the last defender as Wright sailed over the line. Alderman added the extra point, and Mercer had clinched the first win of the 1928 season, 7-6.

Scoring against Presbyterian that day was tough, for Mercer had been denied touchdowns five times earlier by a stubborn Blue Hose defense. The Hose twice held within the two-yard line and twice within the ten-yard line. The defeat in Clinton was the first suffered by Presbyterian on the home field since the 1925 season.

Mercer 0, Georgia 52

Playing Georgia in Athens was another story, however. No matter how it is told, it still comes out 52-0 and is reminiscent of the '92 game. McCrary got four touchdowns during the afternoon, one being a forty-eight sprint. Bobby Hooks also added one on a twenty-five-yard run.

Georgia, with a superior number of players, started the second team. This group saw action only during part of the first and second quarters. The remainder of the game was played by some varsity members and third teamers. Mercer was limited to eight first downs while Georgia earned sixteen.

One rule change for the new season helped the Bears on this day. When a player fumbled the punt within his own thirty-yard line, the ball was returned to him. Mercer got two balls back as Matt fumbled twice. One bright spot of the afternoon was a sixty-eight yard quick-kick by Brewer Corbin.

Mercer 7, Howard 15

The Howard Bulldogs, not quite so big and not so numerous, arrived in Macon on October 13. The visitors were just as determined to win, though, and eked out a 15-7 victory after trailing 7-6 in the third quarter.

Alderman kicked off before an estimated crowd of 6,000. Howard, starting on the thirty, lost one yard, but then Burns was blasted by Mallard and Godby for a ten-yard loss. Mercer lost a chance to score early when a Wright pass was intercepted on the Howard thirty-one. He lost another pass on the Mercer forty-five-yard line some plays later, but Howard could not advance.

With Howard on the Mercer thirty, Van Buskirk was hit for a three-yard loss by Luther Ray, who had just been declared eligible to play. Following that play, Harvey Stipe put Mercer on the thirty-six-yard line by intercepting a pass.

Minutes later, after the ball was returned to Howard, Mallard blocked a Howard punt and returned it to the Bulldog thirty-eight-yard line. Alderman rambled for two yards, and Wright caught a pass for twelve yards, but Mercer was penalized fifteen yards.

A Wright pass then went incomplete, but the next one from Wright to Mallard to Alderman made all connections for twenty-seven yards. This triple pass, as it was called, started when Wright, receiving the hike from center, passed to Mallard. Mallard, from his end position, then passed to Alderman downfield. This triple pass was used throughout the season with good success.

Although the pass was caught and Mercer was on the Howard seventeen-yard line, Mercer could not score. Two series later with Howard on the seventeen-yard line, Van Buskirk was hit by Mallard for a five-yard loss. Then Mallard and Ray blocked Van Buskirk's punt, and Godby recovered on the Howard two-yard line. Art Wright scored, and Alderman added the point for a 7-0 lead.

The plot thickened as Alderman kicked off to the Howard ten-yard line. Bullard received the kick and ran it back ninety yards for a touchdown. The score read 7-6 as Mercer cranked up again.

Mercer had some exciting moments before the half, but could not put enough together for a touchdown. Corbin passed to Godby for twenty yards, but then he had one intercepted. Several plays later Wright intercepted on the Mercer twenty as the half ended.

After several minutes of play in the second half, a fifteen-yard slugging penalty on Mercer started Howard off from the Mercer thirty-five toward the goal. Van Buskirk put Howard out front shortly thereafter with a six-yard field goal, and the Bulldogs led 9-7. Mercer couldn't move the ball, and Howard started again from the thirty-one-yard line. From there a final touchdown was scored to make it 15-7.

Mercer 0, Florida 73

Little can be said about the game of the following week in Gainesville, Florida, except that it was the last football game ever played between Mercer and Florida. The record now stood at six wins for Mercer against ten losses and one tie as the Gators walloped the Bears 73-0. There was a time when Mercer and Florida could compete evenly, but Florida, like most of the larger schools, had gone into football in a big way, recruiting outside talent, and always having superior depth. As a result, a school with a twenty-two-man traveling squad like Mercer just didn't have enough personnel. As Mercer continued to schedule major colleges, this record against Florida would prove to be the best against a major opponent.

Mercer 20, Birmingham Southern 20

Back at home against SIAA member Birmingham Southern, Mercer did much better the next Saturday. Frog Newsome started the show with a forty-yard kickoff. Two downs later the Panthers punted to the Mercer twenty-five-yard line. On the first down Wright, attempting to punt, had the ball blocked by Barnes, who picked it up and scored. Barnes added the extra point, and the Panthers had a 7-0 lead before the echo of the starting whistle had faded.

One exchange later, Alderman pulled the same stunt, getting a punt blocked, and the Panthers were on the Mercer fifteen-yard line. The Bears were spared, however, as Wright recovered a Pelgreen fumble on the Mercer two-yard line. A punt later, starting on the Mercer thirty-two, the Southerners picked up two first downs and six points to lead 13-0.

This shook the Bears up, and Wright returned the kickoff thirty yards to the Mercer thirty-five. Matt got five yards, then a Wright-to-Matt pass was complete for thirty-eight yards to the Panther twenty-two-yard line. From here, Alderman went two yards; a Wright-to-Matt pass was good for twelve; Alderman ran three yards; then Wright went the remaining five yards for a touchdown. Alderman converted and Mercer trailed 13-7.

Several plays later Mallard partially blocked a Southern punt, and Mercer got the ball on the thirty-five. On the next hike, Wright raced sixty-five yards for a touchdown. Alderman was good on the point attempt, and Mercer led 14-13.

In the fourth quarter, Alderman intercepted a Smith pass and scored from the ten-yard line for a 20-13 lead. Lott returned Alderman's kickoff forty yards, but on the next play, Joe Merritt intercepted a Smith pass.

It was not Mercer's day, though, as Alderman fumbled and Birmingham Southern had the ball on the Mercer forty-six-yard line. On the very next down, Smith broke loose for forty-three yards before being overtaken by Matt at the three-yard line. Three plays later, Smith scored to make it 20-19. A pass for the extra point was completed, and the score was tied 20-20.

The game ended with both teams tossing passes and having them intercepted. What seemed to be a come-from-behind victory ended up in a tie. The Mercer men played well except for the first few minutes and the blocked punts. Mallard was particularly tough as a defensive end and made his presence continually known. Wright and Alderman were the big offensive threats, aided by Matt with his pass-receiving.

Mercer 18, Duke 38

In Durham, North Carolina, the following weekend, the battling Baptists fought the Devils hard but lost 38-18 in the first contest ever between the two schools. Duke amassed twenty first downs while limiting Mercer to only five. Duke threw twenty-one passes for 158 yards, while Mercer passed fourteen times for ninety yards but had very few completed.

Mercer drove first on a pass from Wright to Matt for fifty-three yards. Wright then hit Alderman for eighteen to the Duke three-yard line. A third pass from Wright to Mallard carried the ball to the Duke six-inch line, but Duke held for downs. Brice of Duke fumbled on the Duke fifteen-yard line after taking over, and Loser picked up the fumble and scored. Alderman missed the conversion, but Mercer led 6-0.

The lead was short-lived, though, for the Blue Devils, from the twenty-yard line, drove to the goal in seven plays with Janoski scoring from the two-yard line. Brice added the point and Mercer's lead was over for a time.

The Bears got fifteen yards from Matt on the kickoff. He then added four more on a dash inside, but Mercer drew a penalty to the nineteen-yard line. On the next play the triple pass was unwrapped. It went from Wright to Mallard to Matt for eighty-one yards and a touchdown as the defense watched in amazement. The point was missed again, but Mercer now led 12-7.

Duke scored again from the one-yard line several plays later. Coach Moore then took out the Mercer regulars and did not send them back until the middle of the fourth quarter. Duke took advantage of this and got twenty-five points on the Mercer substitutes. One of Corbin's punts was blocked for one of the touchdowns.

Mercer scored later on the triple pass which went Wright-Mallard-Newsome for sixty-four yards. This was mentioned by the scribes as a most unusual play, having not been seen frequently in the South.

Mercer 0, Oglethorpe 15

Oglethorpe finally got revenge, copping the first win since 1924 in Macon before an estimated 7,500 fans in Centennial Stadium. Mercer got ten first downs, while Oglethorpe got only nine, but Oglethorpe had fifteen points and Mercer had none. Clements of Oglethorpe kicked off fifty-five yards, and Wright returned the ball forty yards to the Mercer forty-five yard line. On the following play Merritt snapped directly back to Matt and the ball was fumbled. Asa Wall of Oglethorpe picked up the bouncing ball and sped thirty yards for a touchdown.

Since the T formation, with the quarterback receiving the snap directly from the center, had not then been established, the center would hike the ball to the runner. This took a great deal of timing on the part of both men. It also took a great deal of concentration by the center, for he was risking being mutilated at all times.

Oglethorpe started again, after a Mercer drive, on the sixteen-yard line and drove to the Mercer twenty-seven. The big play in the series was a thirty-eight-yard run by Cy Bell. From here Fox added five yards, but then Fox and Mallard were ejected from the game for being too aggressive. With the ball resting on the Mercer fourteen after a five-yard penalty, Oglethorpe ran two plays for two yards. Bell then sprinted around left end for a touchdown. Martin added the extra point for a 13-0 lead. The final two points of the contest came when Matt touched a punt as it was going into the end zone and then fell on it for a safety for Oglethorpe. The final score was 15-0.

Mercer 7, Citadel 0

With a fourth quarter touchdown on a wet field, Mercer slipped by the Citadel in Savannah before a crowd of 5,000 by a 7-0 score. Mercer's scoring drive began as the ball was received on the Citadel twenty-eight-yard line. Two plays later, while still on the same yard stripe, pass interference was called against the Citadel as Matt threw to Wright. With the ball on the Citadel three-yard line, Loser went in for the touchdown, and Alderman added the extra point.

For the Bears the punting of Alderman kept the Citadel's guns silenced all afternoon. While Wright, Matt, and Loser were outstanding on offense, Mallard was storming the Citadel from his defensive end slot.

In the third quarter Alderman went fifty-five yards for a touchdown, but the officials ruled no score. The ruling was that Wright was not the required five yards behind the line of scrimmage when he passed to Mallard, who passed to Alderman.

Mercer 14, Wake Forest 12

Mercer took the measure once again of the Wake Forest Deacons in Asheville, North Carolina, in the final game of the 1928 season. Wake Forest scored first as an Alderman punt was blocked, and Mills scored from the three-yard line. An attempted drop kick for the extra point was unsuccessful.

Mercer scored on two pass plays. After working down to the Deacon twenty-five-yard line, Matt threw to Wright for a touchdown. Alderman was true on the conversion attempt. Wake Forest came back and scored from the eight-yard line, but once again missed the point after.

Starting on the twenty-yard line, Wright passed to Matt for a thirty-five-yard gainer to the Deacon forty-five. Wake Forest got caught with a fifteen-yard penalty, and Mercer advanced to the Deacon thirty. Art Wright then reached back and flipped a pass to Baggy Mallard which covered the required thirty yards for a touchdown. Alderman converted again, and Mercer won 14-12.

By 1928 the SIAA had grown to thirty teams, and Mercer was fourteenth in standing that season. The teams in the association were: Southern College of Lakeland, Florida, Chattanooga, Mississippi College, Western Kentucky, Wofford, Transylvania, Furman, Howard, Millsaps, Louisiana College, Centenary, Citadel, Georgetown, Mercer, Birmingham Southern, Southwestern, Kentucky Wesleyan, Stetson, Newberry, Spring Hill, Oglethorpe, Louisiana Normal, Southwestern Louisiana, Presbyterian, Centre, Union, Erskine, Louisiana Tech, Rollins, and Louisville.

Chapter 6 THIRD AND LONG YARDAGE

Following the 1928 season Bernie Moore moved to Louisiana State University as an assistant, and Lake Russell came to Mercer from Carson-Newman. Moore later became head coach at LSU and established a record of eighty-two wins, thirty-six losses, and five ties from 1935 through 1947. Following this tenure he became commissioner of the Southeastern Conference, a position he retained until his retirement.

Harold McNabb and J. D. Blair were assistant coaches. McNabb also served as baseball coach while Blair coached the freshmen and served as professor of history. Blair was also president of the Macon Baseball Corporation.

1929

Mercer 6, Duke 19

After three weeks of practice with a new coach, the Bears met Duke University in Macon on 29 September 1929. Starters for Mercer in the opener were Mallard, Plunkett, Adams, Lane, Branch, Gear, Godby, Corbin, Matt, Wright, and Alderman.

The first quarter score was 6-6, but Duke scored two minutes before the half to go ahead. Mercer scored when Brewer Corbin passed to Jody Matt from the Duke thirty-five-yard line for a touchdown. Matt caught the ball on the fifteen and went over for the touchdown. Alderman missed the conversion attempt.

Duke scored after starting at the Mercer forty-nine-yard line. Robeson then caught a pass and carried the ball to the Mercer five where he was stopped by Matt. Godfrey got two yards at center but was hit for a two-yard loss by Lane and Branch on the second down. Buie scored on the fourth down.

Duke went ahead with a first down on Mercer's eleven and scored after completing two passes. Buie dropkicked the extra point for a 13-6 lead. Duke scored again in the third quarter on a fifteen-yard run up the middle for a touchdown. The Bears played well defensively and held a far superior team to just three touchdowns. Once the Bears held at the four-yard line. Baggy Mallard was outstanding on defense, along with a host of other players. For the game Duke got nineteen first downs while Mercer got four.

Mercer 7, Howard 2

The first win at Mercer for Lake Russell came over Howard College on 19 October 1929 in Macon, In a tremendously hard-fought battle, Howard got a safety on Alderman's blocked punt early in the game. Mercer scored within the last few minutes on a pass from Wright to Hollingsworth which covered thirty-one yards. Alderman converted for the 7-2 victory.

Although Mercer scored late, the game could have broken open at any time. Defensively, the action was shared by many. Mallard blocked a punt, recovered a fumble, and dropped two runners for losses. Lane shared a fumble recovery on the Howard nineteen and intercepted a pass in the third quarter. Nightengale blocked a punt and caught one runner for a nine-yard loss. Despite all this outstanding defensive work, the Bears just couldn't take advantage of the numerous opportunities to score with the ball.

The leading ground gainer for Mercer was Alderman, with thirty-six yards. He also punted ten times for the Bears. The Howard defense made ground-gaining tough as Wright carried the ball eighteen times with a long gain of twenty yards around left end. He was stopped five times for no gain, and he lost yardage on five occasions. He finished with a net of twelve yards. Matt did little better with fifteen yards in thirteen attempts. For the afternoon Mercer got seventy-two yards rushing and connected on three of fourteen passes. Mallard with a catch for twenty-eight yards and Hollingsworth with the thirty-one-yard touchdown catch led the receivers.

Starters for the game were Mallard, Godby, Emmett Waller, Branch, Lane, Gear, and Nightengale in the line. The backs were Brad Lamson, Matt, Wright, and Alderman. Subs that day were J. D. Sewell, Elder Hollingsworth, Luther Ray, Red Adams, and Lamar Plunkett. Brewer Corbin missed the game after being hurt in an auto accident.

Mercer 0, Citadel 21

The second loss of the season was to the Citadel in Charleston, South Carolina. Mercer played good ball the first half and held the Cadets scoreless. In the second half the Cadets rushed for three touchdowns and won 21-0.

Godby and Roy Johnson were outstanding at end while Wright played well on defense. Mercer had four passes intercepted and managed only five first downs. The Citadel ran up nineteen first downs during the game.

Mercer 0, Oglethorpe 26

The Petrels of Oglethorpe took the victory again by a 26-0 score in Atlanta as Cy Bell took the opening kickoff and raced ninety-two yards for a touchdown. Fox scored later on a sixty-yard punt return.

Mercer got only three first downs, while Oglethorpe had fifteen. Luke Appling, later of Chicago White Sox baseball fame, was the most consistent ground gainer for Oglethorpe.

Mercer 0, Wake Forest 13

The Wake Forest Deacons pinned the third shutout in a row on the Bears in Asheville and won 13-0. Eustace Mills clipped off runs of eighty and fifty yards for two touchdowns. Mercer, with an anemic offense, got only forty-eight yards and two first downs, lost three fumbles, and did not complete a pass.

Other losses in the 1929 season were to Presbyterian 6-0, Chattanooga 7-0, and 39-7 to Birmingham Southern. Mercer did put together a good offense with a good defense one more time during the season.

Mercer 59, Rollins 0

Rollins became the second victim of the 1929 Bears who, like the stock market, had fallen on bad times. The thrashing of Rollins by a 59-0 count helped somewhat. Mercer started a drive with Matt recovering the ball and returning it fifteen yards to Mercer's thirty-five-yard line. From here, Alderman and Matt picked up six straight first downs. Wright helped with one five-yard run. Each gained thirty-four yards, with Matt getting six points and Alderman adding the conversion.

After Nightengale recovered a fumble on the Rollins twenty-four, Matt ran for nine yards in two plays. Wright also got nine in two plays, before Alderman gained four yards up the middle for another touchdown. He added the extra point to make the score 14-0. Two punting exchanges later, Red Adams nailed Spencer for a six-yard loss. Matt returned the punt to the Rollins thirty-four, and on the next play scored to make the score 20-0.

Corbin returned the second half kickoff thirty-eight yards, but Mercer ran out of gas. Alderman punted, and on the first play Spencer ran into Nightengale for a minus two yards. Jody Matt then got seventeen yards to start another scoring drive. He then gained six yards, caught one pass for ten yards, and then caught another for a fourteen-yard touchdown. Alderman was successful on the conversion and Mercer led 27-0.

Moments later Matt returned a punt twenty-nine yards to the Rollins five-yard line. Alderman scored on the second of two runs and added the extra point to raise the score to 34-0. Johnson recovered Alderman's forty-five-yard kickoff to put Mercer in scoring position again. A drive from here, with Alderman gaining twenty-four yards, ended in an eleven-yard touchdown by Corbin.

After another punt, Rollins missed a fourth down pass from the thirty-six-yard line, and Mercer scored three plays later. Alderman ran for twelve yards in two attempts, and Matt went twenty-four yards for the touchdown. Alderman place-kicked again to raise the score to 47-0.

Rollins could not make any progress against the tough Bear defense. The "Tars" would receive, run one or two plays, and punt; this was the pattern during the game. The last touchdown came after Hollingsworth had clipped Fisher for a five-yard loss. Rollins then punted out of bounds on the forty-yard line. On the first play Alderman went in again to make it 53-0.

Rollins then put together two first downs and ended up on the fifty-yard line. Brad Lamson ran for four yards, and Hollingsworth added nine for a first down. Alderman added two yards, Matt got seven yards, and then Adams recovered a Mercer fumble on the twenty-five-yard line for a three-yard gain. Matthews lost one yard, then got it back with a seventeen-yard run. Lamson scored his first touchdown for Mercer from the five-yard line to make the final score 59-0.

For the afternoon, Mercer picked up 403 yards rushing while Rollins got only nine. The defense for Mercer was outstanding as Rollins was thrown for losses on six occasions and failed to gain on seven other running plays.

Branch, Sewell, Hollingsworth, Nightengale, Adams, and in fact the entire line were defensive standouts that day. On offense, Jody Matt scored four touchdowns and gained 138 yards in seventeen carries. Alderman had three touchdowns and five extra points for a twenty-three-point total. He gained 167 yards in 27 attempts to lead the Bears. Art Wright got into the offensive show by throwing two touchdown passes.

Mercer had finally found the team they had been looking for, in Rollins, after a number of frustrating games. The season ended with two wins and seven losses for Lake Russell in his first year at Mercer. Russell, however, had plans for better things as he recruited twenty-four freshmen who won five games, scored 101 points and allowed the opposition only fifteen points.

The freshmen accomplished what the varsity couldn't in beating the Georgia Bullpups 13-0. Johnny Cimperman intercepted a pass and went ninety-five yards for a score, and Pinky Walden scored on a fifty-yard pass play. The Mercer Cubs, under Coach Kay Tipton, had registered the first win over the Bullpups some years before.

1930

The 1930 eleven, utilizing some of the talented freshmen from the successful 1929 freshman team, played much better football and had a more successful record. Members of the 1930 squad were: Ben Murphy, Bob Smith, Joe Seryak, Dick McNabb, Bob Sperry, Red Bailey, Art Venable, Frank Branch, Captain Lamar Plunkett, Wilsie Wilder, Fate Atchley, Tom Veazey, Ralph Ricketson, Red Marshall, Roy Johnson, Pinky Walden, Jody Matt, Bradford Lamson, Bill Cooper, Bill Barton, Johnny Cimperman, Charles Lobetti, Bill Poe, Emmett Waller, and Elder Hollingsworth.

Mercer 7, Presbyterian 9

Mercer opened a new season on 27 September 1930 as Walden went fifty yards with a punt for a touchdown in the first quarter against Presbyterian. Bob Sperry converted, and Mercer led 7-0. Presbyterian got a safety some minutes later when Lobetti stepped out of the end zone while attempting to punt. Presbyterian scored a touchdown later as Walden fumbled a punt on the Mercer thirteen-yard line, and Presbyterian recovered.

Mercer got off to a strong start as Walden picked up thirty-six yards on the first play of the game but after another first down two passes went incomplete and Presbyterian took over. The remainder of the quarter saw neither team making much progress.

Early in the second quarter the Blue Hose were driven to their own twelve-yard line by a fifty-yard Lobetti punt. After two plays Green punted back to Walden, who scooted fifty yards for a touchdown. Sperry added the extra point to make the score 7-0. As the second half started, Cimperman had a pass intercepted.

Presbyterian took over on the thirty-seven-yard line and drove fifty-two yards to the Mercer one-yard line, where the Bears held. On the first play Lobetti punted, but in doing so stepped out of the end zone for a safety and a 7-2 score.

Six series later, Walden fumbled a Green punt on the Mercer thirteen-yard line. With four running plays Presbyterian scored a touchdown and led 9-7. Mercer tried desperately to get back on the scoreboard. Poe threw six incomplete passes, while Lamson missed on two attempts and had the last one intercepted to end the game.

Missing from the lineup because he had signed a professional baseball contract was former standout end Baggy Mallard. Mercer played well enough to win, but the lack of experienced varsity performers was evident.

Mercer 0, Georgia 51

Georgia fell one point short of the 1928 score while earning a 51-0 victory. Once again it was all Georgia as Jack Roberts led with four touchdowns.

Bob Smith and Roy Walden were outstanding for Mercer in a losing cause. Mercer got nine first downs but had six passes intercepted, and completed only four of twenty for seventy-four yards against the tough Georgia defense.

Mercer 33, Florida Southern 0

In Tampa, Florida, for the first time, before a crowd of 2,500, Mercer defeated Florida Southern 33-0. Mercer actually picked up eight first downs before the first counter came. During this time Southern was backed up twice to the nineteen and fourteen-yard lines.

Finally, after starting on the thirty-three-yard line, Mercer scored as Johnny Cimperman sped the final thirteen yards for a touchdown. Smith's kick hit a Southern player and bounced over the crossbar for a 7-0 lead. Mercer got two more points on a safety just before the half as Kell of Southern attempted to punt and fell on the ball in the end zone.

Early after the kickoff, Walden ran fifteen yards for a touchdown. Smith recovered a fumble several series later for Mercer. On the first play Poe passed to Walden for twenty yards to the Southern fourteen-yard line.

Walden then raced the fourteen yards for a touchdown. Smith converted for a 21-0 lead.

On the next Southern series Walden intercepted a pass and returned it sixty yards for a touchdown. The final touchdown came after Jody Matt recovered a fumble on the Southern twenty-three yard line. Poe picked up fifteen yards before Walden scored again. In all, five touchdowns were scored, and Smith converted three times for a 33-0 total.

Walden was the big man for the Bears as he ran for 140 yards on twelve plays and caught one pass for twenty yards. He also ran back an interception for a sixty-yard touchdown. The defense was outstanding, holding Southern to four first downs. One of the bright spots for Southern was Murrell's punting. He was one of the reasons Mercer didn't get more points as he had three punts that traveled over seventy yards each.

Mercer 6, Chattanooga 9

Chattanooga edged Mercer 9-6 as a Lobetti punt was blocked to give Chattanooga a safety. Chattanooga made a long drive in the first quarter on a ninety-eight-yard march to score and took a 9-0 lead.

The Mercer touchdown came on a series of pass plays as Poe passed to Walden for thirty-three yards. Walden then passed to Lobetti for ten more yards. The final pass was from Lamson to Matt for twenty-five yards and a touchdown.

In all, Mercer connected on six passes for eighty yards while rushing for 149 yards. Mercer had twelve first downs while limiting Chattanooga to only six. Smith was outstanding for Mercer by intercepting two passes and playing superb defense.

Mercer 0, Wake Forest 21

Mercer lost to Wake Forest in Wilmington, North Carolina, 21-0 as Tom Veazey, Dick McNabb, Bob Smith, and Johnny Cimperman played outstanding ball for the Bears. It was a very windy day. One ball, punted from the twenty-yard line, rolled back to the twenty-two after hitting downfield.

Walden, in one offensive threat, got off a seventy-yard run, but the play was called back because of a penalty. He later returned a pass interception fifty yards to midfield. Veazey caught four passes to lead in receiving. The Bears were not at full strength for this game as Poe, Waller, and Lobetti had been dropped from the squad for breaking training rules.

Mercer 13, Birmingham Southern 6

Back in Macon, Mercer edged Birmingham Southern 13-6 before 2,000 fans on a cold day. Birmingham Southern scored first, after starting on their own twenty-yard line. Vaughn was the big gainer with a sixty-yard sprint, before being stopped by Walden. The Panthers scored from the fifteen-yard line in five plays to lead 6-0.

Mercer scored when Walden returned a punt ninety-five yards for a touchdown with Bob Smith clearing the last man out. Bob Sperry added the conversion for a 7-6 lead.

The defense went to work in the second half with Smith intercepting a pass and Veazey recovering a fumble to stop the Southerners. Cimperman intercepted a pass several plays later and returned it forty-six yards to the Panther four-yard line. Cimperman then scored in two plays for a 13-6 count. Walden stopped Vaughn after a thirty-three-yard return on the kickoff, and then he intercepted a pass on the Mercer twenty-four-yard line to end the last Birmingham Southern threat.

It was really an outstanding day for the Mercer defense as Smith intercepted two passes to halt two final Panther drives. For the day, Southern earned twelve first downs while limiting Mercer to only three. The visitors picked up 228 yards on the ground and thirty-nine in the air. Captain Lamar Plunkett and Buckshot Veazey were described as outstanding for Mercer.

Mercer 33, Stetson 0

Mercer took another victory over the Stetson Hatters in Deland, Florida, in the second night game of the year. Jody Matt, held in check for most of the season, erupted for three touchdowns, while Cimperman took a sixteen-yard pass for another score. Frank Branch recovered a fumble for the final touchdown. Bob Sperry added three extra points in the 33-0 victory. The defense for Mercer was outstanding once again and limited Stetson to a long run of eighteen yards.

Mercer 6, Carson-Newman 13

In a poorly played game with Carson-Newman, Mercer allowed scores on a thirty-eight-yard pass and a seventy- four-yard run in a 13-6 defeat. The Bears earned ten first downs while limiting the Eagles to only five, but the offense just couldn't put together sustained drives. Jody Matt ran the ball twenty-one times for ninety-three yards. He also caught two passes as Walden completed five of twelve for fifty yards.

Mercer 2, Oglethorpe 0

The Homecoming game for the 1930 season pitted Mercer against Oglethorpe in Macon. Before a crowd of 4,500 Mercer drove to the Oglethorpe six-yard line. Along the way the Bears earned four first downs, but a tough Petrel defense stopped the drive and kept Mercer scoreless. The remainder of the first half was a defensive battle by both teams.

The second half opened, and Oglethorpe kicked off twice out of bounds, and the ball was awarded to Mercer at the forty-yard line. Mercer couldn't advance and Cimperman punted thirty-five yards to the Oglethorpe ten-yard line. Two plays later Lamar Plunkett blocked a punt for a safety and a 2-0 lead. Following this important score, Mercer earned four more first downs on a drive to the Petrel one-half-yard line but were stopped by the tough Oglethorpe defense.

In all, Mercer got twelve first downs on 197 yards rushing and thirty-four yards passing. Jody Matt got eighty-five yards and Pinky Walden added seventy-five more. Plunkett's blocked punt was the key to victory as the sophomore line of Veazy, McNabb, Branch, and Johnson proved too tough for the Oglethorpe offense.

The season ended with a record of 4-5, but the Bears were building. The 1930 freshman team went undefeated and scored ninety-one points while allowing five opponents only five points total. The Mercer Cubs had good wins over Georgia, 6-0, and Florida, 25-0. Following the Florida game, the newspapers in Gainesville suggested that the Crimson Tide, who beat Florida, play the Mercer Cubs for the southern championship.

1931

The 1931 season was the year it was finally all put together. Two years of good recruiting and learning a new system finally paid dividends. Lake Russell, Harold McNabb, and Amos "Skeet" Horner, a former Tennessee fullback, made up the coaching staff. The season proved particularly outstanding as only three games were scheduled at home. Yet the Bears established a 6-3 record. The road schedule was obtained because it was more profitable to play on the road. It was reported that every home game since Russell had become coach had lost money because of poor paying attendance.

Mercer 20, Erskine 6

Erskine became the first recipient of a Bear mauling, as sub quarterback Jake Trommerhauser scored two touchdowns on runs of fourteen and twenty-four yards in his first varsity game. Others seeing action in the opener were: Nat Reasor, Red Camp, Joe Pope, Bob Smith, Dick McNabb, Swede Olsson, Cotton Harrison, Brad Lamson, Pinky Walden, Elder Hollingsworth, Johnny Cimperman, Ernie Zinkowski, Hal Bell, Bob Sperry, Alf Bunch, Gordon Reddick, Tom Veazey, and McDaniel.

The first big play for Mercer came on a Cimperman-to-Walden pass for thirty yards. Later Harrison recovered a fumble on the Erskine seven-yard line. Following a five-yard penalty, Trommerhauser ran over from the twelve for a 6-0 lead. In the second half Walden picked up a big twenty-nine yards on one play to help move the ball to the Erskine seventeen-yard line. But the Erskine defense stiffened, and in eleven plays the Flying Fleet had scored for a 6-6 tie.

In the fourth quarter Trommerhauser got twenty-four yards on a spinning reverse play for a touchdown. Hollingsworth converted for a 13-6 lead. Erskine took over, but Walden intercepted a pass and returned it twenty-five yards to the Erskine twenty-five-yard line. Walden added twelve yards on a reverse, but the drive was stopped at the four-yard line.

Erskine couldn't advance, and after receiving the punt Mercer drove forty-eight yards for a touchdown. Trommerhauser, Cimperman, and Walden, who drove for twenty-eight yards, pushed to the one-yard line. Cimperman scored from the one-yard line and converted for a 20-6 lead. In all, Mercer accounted for 249 yards to only seventy-three for Erskine.

Mercer 26, Citadel 0

The second victim of the season was the Citadel on the home field in Charleston, South Carolina. Pinky Walden and Jake Trommerhauser ambushed the Cadets with two touchdowns each. Hollingsworth added two extra points for a 26-0 victory.

Following the Citadel's first punt, Walden sped fifty-one yards around right end for a touchdown behind good interference. Hollingsworth converted for a 7-0 score. Mercer got the ball back later and ran two plays for no gain at the Citadel forty-yard line. Then a Citadel substitute came into the game and began talking to the other players, and the Citadel was penalized fifteen yards. It was illegal for subs to bring messages into the game. From the Cadet twenty-four-yard line, Cimperman got nineteen yards on two plays. Walden scored three plays later, and Hollingsworth converted again.

Two exchanges of punts later, the Citadel fumbled and Reddick recovered on the Citadel thirty-one. Zinkowski got fifteen at left end, and Trommerhauser raced sixteen yards for the touchdown. In the third quarter Mercer had a first down on the Citadel forty-eight. After two yards on two plays, Cimperman caught a twenty-nine-yard pass to the Cadet seventeen-yard line. Following a loss of two yards, Trommerhauser sped nineteen yards off tackle for a touchdown. The second kick in a row was blocked.

The Bears were content to punt every time they got the ball for the remainder of the game. One punt was grounded on the Citadel two-yard line as once again the defense excelled. Smith intercepted two passes, returning one forty yards, and Seryak also intercepted one. The Citadel attempted eighteen passes, but the alert Mercer defenders intercepted four of them.

The Citadel was limited to only three first downs with one coming on a run and two by penalties.

Mercer 28, Stetson 7

The Hatters fell to the Bears in Macon before 2,000 fans by a 28-7 score. The first time Mercer got the ball, on the forty-nine-yard line, Walden ran thirteen yards. Jake Trommerhauser then sped eight yards, followed by a two-yard rush by Cimperman. Stetson stopped the drive, however, and took over on the twenty-yard line.

Mercer took off again from the thirty-seven, picked up three first downs, but Trommerhauser fumbled the ball to Stetson on the fourteen-yard line. In the second quarter a Trommerhauser pass was intercepted and returned forty-two yards to the Mercer eighteen-yard line. Petrie then raced the eighteen yards, and Stetson took a 7-0 lead.

Mercer recovered composure, gained five first downs and scored on the third down. Walden got the counter, and Hollingsworth gave Mercer a 7-7 tie. From the Stetson thirty the Hatters gained ten yards, but then Cimperman intercepted and went sixty yards behind good interference by Camp for a touchdown. Hollingsworth converted for a 14-7 lead.

Several minutes later, Walden returned a punt twenty-five yards to the Stetson thirteen-yard line. Cimperman got three yards, and Walden added nine for a first down. With one yard to go, Cimperman hurdled over on the fourth down, and Mercer led 21-7 as Hollingsworth booted the point again.

In the fourth quarter Walden sped fifty-four yards for a touchdown, and Hollingsworth converted for his fourth time. Reddick then blocked a punt on the Stetson twenty-yard line, and Cimperman recovered on the Stetson eighteen.

The defense had done it again as Harrison and McNabb were described as outstanding. Thus far in the season the defense had allowed only thirteen points in three games, while the offense rolled up sixty-seven points.

Mercer 21, Presbyterian 7

Mercer had now played two home games, and won them both, but lost $1200 at the gate as too many passes were issued. It was road time again, and the Blue Hose of Presbyterian College were the hosts.

With 100 Mercer fans on hand, including Athletic Committee member Dr. W. G. Lee, the Bears made another successful trip as Mercer won 21-7. It was a rough game as Mercer was penalized 135 yards for over-aggressive play. The first score came when Mercer got a first down at the Presbyterian ten, following a seventeen-yard run by Walden. Walden then rushed for one yard, Cimperman got eight through the middle, but Walden was held for no gain on the third down. Walden then blasted his 136 pounds through the line for the touchdown. Hollingsworth converted. The touchdown marked the first time that Presbyterian had been scored on in nine games. The Blue Hose were the SIAA champs during the 1930 season.

Later during the game, Mercer was penalized twenty-five yards for clipping, to put the ball on the fourteen-yard line. A punt attempt by Cimperman was blocked and recovered by the Blue Hose on the four-yard line. The defense held for no gain for three downs, but on the fourth down a penalty put the ball at the one-foot line. Presbyterian scored from here and tied the game 7-7.

Mercer was not finished, though, for Tony Long saved the day. Nat Reasor, an end, had been injured in the first quarter, and he had been replaced by Long, who weighed 156 pounds. In Long's first varsity action, he caught two passes from Trommerhauser for ninety-four yards and two touchdowns. This put the game out of reach for the Bears. The three touchdowns and conversions by Hollingsworth made the score 21-7.

Mercer 0, John Carrol 0

For the fifth contest of the year, John Carrol was the foe in Cleveland, Ohio. The Bears went into the battle without the injured Pinky Walden, who had gained 638 yards during the season. Nat Reasor was also still out with injuries.

Mercer got 183 yards, while John Carrol ran up 154 yards on the field, but neither team could cross the goal line. The game ended in a 0-0 tie, as 2,000 fans got the play-by-play action from the *Macon Telegraph* building.

Mercer 25, Wofford 7

In Spartanburg the following week a star named John Jasonis was born. He was put in to replace the injured Walden, and he almost singlehandedly wrecked the Terriers. Although he had played only about two minutes in the first five games, he carried the ball twenty times in this game for 152 yards. He played just over three quarters. Cimperman also added 116 yards on thirteen carries for the Bears. Harry Lichter was starting center for this game.

There were several punting exchanges before Zinkowski raced seventy yards for a touchdown. Mercer scored again as Jasonis had runs of thirty-two and thirty-five yards before he plunged one yard for the touchdown.

Minutes later it started over as Cimperman ran for forty yards and Jasonis got ten yards on two runs and scored another touchdown. The final touchdown came as Cimperman intercepted on the Mercer twenty-five and went seventy-five yards for a score. He was tackled on the five, but slid over for the touchdown.

Wofford scored when Hollingsworth intercepted on the Wofford twenty-yard line and lost the ball in the air on the forty-five-yard line. Willis of Wofford grabbed it and sped fifty-five yards for the touchdown. The defensive lineup of Veazey, Camp, Pope, Lichter, McNabb, Olsson, Harrison, Bell, Reddick, Bunch, and Long were just too strong for the Terriers as Mercer was now undefeated in six games, a new record.

Mercer 0, Centre 3

The string ended, though, in Danville, Kentucky with the Praying Colonels on 31 October 1931. Against a very strong Centre team, the Bears managed only twenty yards rushing while giving up 223; yet the score was only 3-0. Olsson played the best game of his career in this game. The Centre offense was difficult to contain. Reddick intercepted a Centre pass to stop one drive, but the big 215-pound Centre fullback led the Colonels to victory, eating up big chunks of yardage.

Olsson and Sperry also had a big eating day, but it was not yardage. It was reported that they ate everything they could find at the pregame meal. The two consumed two platters of steak, ten pieces of toast, four huge baked potatoes, two saucers of butter beans, four dishes of ice cream, four cups of coffee and they emptied all butter dishes.

This was the first trip to Danville by the Mercer team. Herbert Smart, a generous supporter and long-time fan of Mercer football, who was later mayor of Macon, made the trip along with Joe McClain, dean of the Mercer Law School.

Mercer 12, Birmingham Southern 0

The Bears returned to their den the next weekend for a Homecoming game with Birmingham Southern. A gala celebration with a parade of 200 automobiles, with Governor Russell and golf great Bobby Jones as celebrities, thrilled the excited crowd. Forty merchants placed advertisements in the *Telegraph* on 6 November 1931 with pictures of Mercer players. This was one of the best displays of local spirit ever.

Mercer was rough and ready for the game as Walden, Zinkowski, and Cimperman accounted for sixty-two, seventy-one, and sixty yards rushing. The tough Bruin defense limited the Panthers to only thirty-eight yards. Each team punted the ball thirteen times, and the ball was actually in the air a total of fourteen times before Mercer scored. The touchdown was scored from the sixteen-yard line as the half ended. Zinkowski got two yards, followed by a one-yard run by Trommerhauser. Zinkowski then went thirteen yards around end for the score and a 6-0 lead.

In the last few minutes Mercer started again on the Panther thirty-eight yard line. Cimperman ran for four yards up the middle, and Walden drove quickly around end for ten more and a first down. Zinkowski, Cimperman, and Walden pushed the ball eleven yards to the fourteen-yard line. After another first down was made, Zinkowski scored from one yard out for a 12-0 final score.

Mercer 19, Chattanooga 27

In the annual battle with the Moccasins, Chattanooga got on the board first with an eleven-yard run following a punt return to the Mercer thirty-four-yard line. Two minutes later Gordon Reddick blocked a Chattanooga punt, and Swede Olsson recovered for a Mercer touchdown. Hollingsworth added the point and the score read 7-7.

Chattanooga stormed back and scored on a spinner play over left tackle from the eighteen to make the score 13-7. A few plays later Zinkowski fumbled on the Mercer eighteen-yard line. Mercer held one play but then gave up a seven-yard touchdown to Harwell to make the score 20-7.

The Bears scored again after marching down the field on Walden's eighteen-yard run. Trommerhauser passed to Long, who had just come into the game, for seventeen yards and a touchdown. Hollingsworth missed the conversion attempt.

Mercer played hard in the third quarter and threatened to score twice. In the fourth quarter Mercer marched to the goal from the Chattanooga forty-seven-yard line. The final yards and the touchdown came on a pass from Walden to Zinkowski for twenty-four yards. Hollingsworth missed again, and the Moccasins led 20-19.

Chattanooga scored once again after Trommerhauser's pass was intercepted at the forty by Forialetto. Smith scored from the one-foot line, after Mercer had been penalized for roughing. The final score stood 27-19 as a bleeding Pinky Walden received a tremendous ovation from his native Tennesseans.

Mercer 20, Oglethorpe 0

In the first quarter of the annual battle with Oglethorpe, Mercer ran fourteen plays and got three first downs, but didn't score. Cimperman had a run of thirty-four yards, and Walden sped thirty yards around end from the Mercer thirty-eight as the quarter ended.

After being held for no gain, Walden passed to Harrison for thirteen yards to the Oglethorpe eighteen-yard line. Walden then ran three times for eighteen yards and a touchdown. Hollingsworth added the extra point, and Mercer led 7-0.

Later, after Walden lost seven yards, Herrin fumbled a Mercer punt and Camp recovered on the Mercer forty-eight. Zinkowski got fifteen yards on the second down, then fumbled the ball to the Petrels on the Oglethorpe thirty-seven-yard line. Zinkowski intercepted a pass on the next play and raced fifty-eight yards for a touchdown. Hollingsworth converted again for a 14-0 lead.

In the fourth quarter Cimperman punted seventy-three yards, and Cotton Harrison downed the ball on the Oglethorpe one-yard line. The Bears, trying to force the Petrels into fumbling, got the ball back on a Trommerhauser interception at the Oglethorpe forty-nine. Walden led the offense from here with thirty-five yards gained and a touchdown from the eleven-yard line. Seven substitutes came into the game, and Walden intercepted the ball as the game ended.

The Bears had a great day, making sixteen first downs and 270 yards from scrimmage. The entire team played well and kept the Oglethorpe offense caged all afternoon. Following the game, the team was treated to a banquet with the Atlanta alumni at the Winecoff Hotel.

The season ended, and Hollingsworth received praise as the greatest blocking halfback in Mercer's history. Cimperman was marked as the best all-around back. He was an excellent blocker, great punter, fine line plunger for his weight, and a great defensive player. Coach Russell and his aides had finally put it together and developed the most successful team in Mercer history. The team scored 171 points while limiting the opponents to just 58 all season.

1932

On 5 September 1932 practice began for a new season under head coach Lake Russell. J. C. "Tiger" Bennett, former Georgia star, and Skeet Horner served as assistants. Harold McNabb, who had been an assistant for a number of years, went to Albany High School following the 1931 season.

Captain Johnny Cimperman led a twenty-six-man squad that undertook one of the most difficult schedules in Mercer history. Missing on opening day were Gerald McQuaig and Harry Lichter, who were out with injuries.

Mercer 7, Vanderbilt 20

The season opened in Nashville against the Vanderbilt Commodores before 5,000 loyal fans. Bob Sperry kicked off, and Roberts set sail to the thirty-three-yard line. Roberts was a busy man during the first series as he carried the ball seven times while picking up thirty-nine yards and a touchdown. Big Swede Olsson blocked the extra point attempt.

During the remainder of the quarter Mercer ran three plays, punted three times and earned one yard. Vanderbilt picked up only forty-seven yards as Reddick, Harrison, and Zinkowski made key stops. In the second quarter Mercer couldn't advance, but Harrison got the ball back by intercepting a Vandy pass on the Mercer seventeen-yard line. Zinkowski ran for three yards, then Cimperman boomed a punt a record eighty yards to the Vandy goal line where the ball was downed by Harrison. After a four-yard gain, Vanderbilt quick-kicked. The ball was touched by Zinkowski and recovered by Vandy on the Mercer six-yard line. On the second down Roberts ran the ball over and Vandy led 13-0.

Vanderbilt kicked off, and then recovered a Walden fumble on the Mercer thirty-five-yard line. On the second play, after a two-yard gain, Walden got the ball back with an interception. As the third quarter started, Mercer picked up two first downs on passes covering thirty-seven yards. Mercer's offense didn't click, and Vandy eventually took over on the thirty-one.

In the fourth quarter, with the ball on the Mercer twenty, Reasor passed fifty yards to Walden on the Vandy thirty-two-yard line. Mercer's threat ended as Vanderbilt took over on the twenty-seven-yard line. However, three series later Mercer had the ball on the Vanderbilt thirty-six-yard line.

Two passes then accounted for thirty-three yards. Cimperman caught one for eighteen yards. Three plays later, Walden ran three plays and lost one yard, but on the fourth down Trommerhauser passed to Reasor for a four-yard touchdown. Sperry converted and the score stood 13-7. The last touchdown was scored by Roberts on a sixty-one-yard run. Beasly added the point in the 20-7 game. Mercer had played well against superior strength but was just not able to contain the strong Commodore team. Harrison, Olsson, and Reasor were the defensive leaders for the Bears.

Mercer 21, Howard 6

With the Bears starting some of their biggest men ever, Howard College became victim number one in the second game of the season. With Reddick, Smith, and Olsson weighing in at 200 pounds, along with Harrison and Camp at above 180 pounds, the biggest starting line in history was on the field. Other starters were Sperry, Trommerhauser, Pope, Zinkowski, and Cimperman. Substitutes that day were Bob Lee, Walden, Bell, Bowie Gray, Al Davino, and Bunch.

Mercer had an outstanding day, gaining 205 yards from scrimmage while limiting Howard to eight yards. Cimperman was the leading ground gainer for Mercer with eighty yards. Mercer scored first as Zinkowski ran across the goal from the eighteen-yard line. Sperry converted. In the second quarter Trommerhauser passed to Sperry for a thirty-seven-yard touchdown. Sperry converted again, and Mercer led 14-0. Cimperman was the big ground gainer in the second quarter with fifty yards in four carries.

The next score came in the third quarter as Howard was driving toward the goal following Cimperman's blocked punt. After Howard picked up two first downs, Walden intercepted a fourth down pass on the Mercer thirteen-yard line. He raced eighty-seven yards for a touchdown with Sperry blocking the last man. Sperry hit his third extra point in a row, and Mercer led 21-0.

Mercer was rolling now as Smith, Harrison, and McNabb were running wild on defense. Howard attempted to punt from the thirty-one, but McNabb broke through and blocked the ball. Sperry recovered on the Howard twenty-nine-yard line. After Walden had bucked for one yard, Trommerhauser lofted a pass toward the end zone. Ewing intercepted the ball for Howard and sped ninety-four yards to the one-yard line before being tackled by Cimperman. Moore scored for Howard on the next play and the game ended 21-6.

Mercer 52, Presbyterian 0

The following weekend Mercer received the kickoff against Presbyterian and ran eight plays before turning the ball over. Presbyterian punted on the first down, and Mercer ran four more plays before the Blue Hose got the ball back. Minutes later Trommerhauser ran for one yard from the thirty-nine-yard line. On the next play he passed to Zinkowski for a sixty-yard touchdown. Sperry converted, and Mercer was ahead 7-0 in a game that would become the biggest rout in history between the two institutions.

Several plays later Harrison recovered a fumble on the Presbyterian twenty-seven-yard line. After Zinkowski got twelve and eight yards on two carries, Cimperman got the touchdown with a one-yard plunge to raise the score to 13-0. The Blue Hose got hot and picked up three first downs, but then Trommerhauser intercepted a pass on the Mercer forty-one-yard line. Zinkowski had a long gain of twenty-one yards, but the drive stalled at the thirty-yard line. Starting again, after receiving a punt, Walden got twelve yards on two carries. He then caught a Trommerhauser pass for twenty-three yards to the twenty-one-yard line. Walden hit the middle for three followed by a slant for three by Pope. Then Walden sped around end for fifteen yards and a touchdown. Sperry converted and Mercer led 20-0.

Pope lofted a beautiful sixty-two-yard punt which was grounded by Harrison. On the first play Presbyterian lost six yards on a tackle by Sperry. Sims got off a short punt for five yards, and Mercer was in business at the Blue Hose eight-yard line. On the first play Zinkowski raced in for the touchdown. After the kickoff Smith intercepted on the first play to give Mercer the ball on the Presbyterian thirty-six-yard line. On the first down Zinkowski scored his third touchdown to raise the score to 32-0.

Mercer then got five first downs before Jasonis scored from the one-yard line. Bell converted to make it 38-0. Jasonis and Walden were the big guns in this drive. Presbyterian started again but ran into trouble.

Walden intercepted and returned the ball twenty-five yards. Jasonis then raced twenty-two yards around left end for a first down on the opening play. Bob Lee carried the ball around right end for twenty-three yards and another first down. Walden ran for three yards before Jasonis burst off tackle for two yards and a touchdown. Sperry kicked the extra point for a 45-0 count. The final score of the contest came as Walden ran forty yards for the touchdown after Presbyterian failed to gain again. Sperry converted for the final point of the game.

Presbyterian was not able to combat the aggressive defensive play of Harrison, Reddick, Sperry, and McNabb. The Mercer secondary allowed only two completions in ten attempts. In all, Mercer got 349 yards from scrimmage while Presbyterian ran for thirty yards. Walden led Mercer with 127 yards while Zinkowski had ninety-three yards.

Mercer 0, Furman 2

The Homecoming game for the Bears matched Furman with Mercer in Macon on 22 October 1932 before a crowd of 8,000. This was probably the greatest defensive battle the Macon fans ever saw, and the statistics indicate that it was quite a show.

Mercer earned two first downs while Furman had none. There was a total of thirty-eight punts during the game with Mercer punting eighteen times and Furman kicking twenty. Mercer connected on three of twenty-one passes for thirty-seven yards but had three intercepted. In all, Mercer had minus seven yards rushing while Furman picked up forty yards.

Starters that day were Bowie Gray and Cotton Harrison at end, Red Camp and Swede Olsson at tackle, Gordon Reddick and Dick McNabb at guard, Captain Bob Smith at center, Jake Trommerhauser at quarterback, Joe Pope at left halfback, Ernie Zinkowski at right halfback, and Johnny Cimperman at fullback. The substitutes were Nat Reasor, Hal Bell, Pinky Walden, and Bob Lee.

Early in the second half with the ball at the nineteen-yard line, a Cimperman punt was blocked for a Furman safety. That was all the scoring for the game. The Mercer defense was led by Camp, Olsson, and Harrison in this great defensive battle.

Mercer 57, Parris Island Marines 0

The Bears got back in the win column with a 57-0 thrashing of the Parris Island Marines in Savannah. Mercer gained 503 yards from scrimmage as six Bears scored touchdowns. Zinkowski led with three, Walden scored two, and Cimperman, Lee, Jasonis, and Pope scored one each. Cimperman converted once and Sperry twice. Scores resulted from a forty-one-yard run by Zinkowski, a seventy-yard dash by Lee, and a sixty-yard return by Walden as the Bears unleashed long range weapons.

Mercer 8, Centre 0

Returning to Danville for a battle with Centre, Mercer wrecked the Homecoming festivities by edging the Colonels 8-0. After a scoreless first quarter, Mercer threatened in the second quarter by driving to the Centre one-foot line. Centre held, then attempted to punt on the first down. Pope smashed through to block the kick, and Mercer led 2-0.

In the second half Centre tried the flying wedge but had no success as Camp and Sperry broke it up. Centre finally advanced to the Mercer thirteen-yard line by passing. On the fourth down a field goal was attempted, but Pope broke through again to block the ball and recovered on the Centre twenty-two-yard line. Once again the Bears couldn't advance consistently. Several plays later Pope knocked down a pass and then blocked another punt to get Mercer the ball at the Centre seventeen-yard line. After three running plays, Trommerhauser passed to Cimperman for an eleven-yard touchdown. The extra point was blocked, but Mercer led 8-0.

Centre came flying back and earned four first downs, but the game ended with the ball at the Mercer one-yard line. Cotton Harrison, Nat Reasor, and Joe Pope were outstanding in this dramatic battle with a gallant Centre team.

Mercer 25, Chattanooga 0

Four hundred fans accompanied the team to Chattanooga the following weekend. Mercer got on the scoreboard one minute before the half with a forty-five-yard pass from Trommerhauser to Zinkowski as Ernie got behind three defenders to take the throw. Chattanooga threatened first and actually scored, but the touchdown was called back when the Moccasins were penalized. Then, starting from the Mercer twenty-one-yard line, after a Zinkowski fumble, Chattanooga drove to the Mercer one-yard line where the Bears held.

In the second half Zinkowski intercepted, and Mercer drove to the Chattanooga four-yard line but couldn't score. Smith intercepted a pass moments later, but Mercer again failed to score. Then Cimperman intercepted a pass and returned it twenty-four yards to the Chattanooga twenty-yard line. Walden took the ball and gained a first down and then followed with a touchdown from the five-yard line. Sperry converted.

A few minutes later another interception by Smith led to a three-yard touchdown by Cimperman. The final score resulted when a Cimperman interception put Mercer on the thirty-five-yard line. After a one-yard gain by

Pope, Walden ran thirty-four yards around end for the final touchdown.

The Mercer defense, particularly the secondary, completely outclassed the Chattanooga team. Mercer got 249 yards rushing and fifty-two yards passing, returned punts for forty-six yards, and got fifty-four yards through interceptions in a great offensive show. Chattanooga had a total of only eighty-six yards.

This win also enabled Mercer to finish high in the Dixie Conference championship. This conference was composed of Mercer, Birmingham Southern, Millsaps, Chattanooga, Centre, Mississippi College, Howard, Southwestern, and Spring Hill.

Mercer 7, Oglethorpe 6

In a rugged game in Atlanta on Thanksgiving Day, Mercer edged Oglethorpe 7-6 on a five-yard run by Pinky Walden and Bob Sperry's conversion. Zinkowski was sidelined with injuries for the contest. Walden and Pope were the offensive leaders as Mercer gained 116 yards and six first downs.

Reasor started things by recovering an Oglethorpe fumble on the Petrel thirty-five in the first quarter. Pope went off tackle for eleven to the twenty-four-yard line; then Walden, Pope, and Cimperman pushed to the thirteen-yard line. Here the defense became stubborn and four plays later Oglethorpe took over on the seven-yard line.

A few plays later, Harrison threw to Wren for a six-yard loss to the Oglethorpe one-yard line. Then an Oglethorpe punt was good for only thirteen yards to the fourteen-yard line. On the first play Cimperman fumbled and lost one yard. On the second down Walden lost another ten yards, but Oglethorpe was penalized fifteen yards to the twelve-yard line. After Walden got six yards in two attempts and Cimperman had added one, Walden bulled in from the five-yard line for the touchdown. Bob Sperry kicked the extra point.

Oglethorpe got the ball in the second quarter and drove eighty yards, getting five first downs, and scored on a fourteen-yard run. The extra point was partially blocked and Mercer led 7-6. The defense held off Oglethorpe five more times in the second half to clinch the victory.

The 1932 team was regarded as one of the best in Mercer history. The Bears scored 177 points while the opponents got thirty-four as the season ended with a 6-2 record. Centenary College was originally scheduled, but the game was canceled and the Parris Island Marines team was a replacement.

The composite All-Dixie team in 1932 had Harrison, Olsson, Smith, Zinkowski, and Cimperman on the first team. Sperry and Walden were selected to the second eleven. First team all-SIAA berths went to Olsson,

Smith, and Zinkowski, while Sperry, Walden, and Cimperman made the second team.

Fifteen men were awarded letters at the end of the season. A number of visiting dignitaries were present at the awards ceremony. Ralph McGill, sports editor of the *Atlanta Constitution*, observed, "It is difficult for me to understand how Mercer's team could be as strong as it was during the season considering the fact that material was scanty and that equipment was not on par with other schools." The men receiving letters were: Nat Reasor, Kingsport, Tennessee; Cotton Harrison, Temple, Texas; Bowie Gray, Perry, Georgia; Lester Olsson, Akron, Ohio; Red Camp, Thorndale, Texas; Gordon Reddick, Cairo, Georgia; Dick McNabb, Erwin, Tennessee; Bob Smith, Akron, Ohio; Jake Trommerhauser, Augusta, Georgia; Ernie Zinkowski, Norwood, Massachusetts; Roy Walden, Knoxville, Tennessee; Al Davino, New York, New York; John Jasonis, Maine; Joe Pope, Akron, Ohio; and Johnny Cimperman, Akron, Ohio. Harry Lichter missed the 1932 season because of an appendectomy.

1933

The coaching staff for the new season remained Lake Russell, head coach, with Horner and Bennett as assistants. J. D. Blair was athletic director.

Mercer 44, Spring Hill 3

A new season opened with Spring Hill College of Mobile, Alabama, playing the Bears in Macon before a crowd of 3,000 on 23 September 1933. Mercer ran roughshod over the visitors, amassing eighteen first downs and 428 yards. Spring Hill was limited to only fifty-eight yards rushing and three first downs.

On the first exchange Pope intercepted a pass at the Spring Hill thirty-five-yard line. Trommerhauser ran for one yard, then Bob Lee raced thirty-four yards for a 6-0 lead. Spring Hill then drove to the Mercer thirteen-yard line, where Traynor dropkicked a field goal.

In the second quarter Oran Curry blocked a Spring Hill punt at the thirty-three-yard line. Mercer took over with Zinkowski and Tom Porter rushing for a first down. The drive stalled, however, at the seventeen-yard line. On the first play for Spring Hill, Gene NeSmith intercepted on the eleven-yard line.

Zinkowski on the first down lost five yards, but on the second down he ran for fourteen yards around end. Pope pushed forward one yard, and then

Tom Porter scored his first Mercer touchdown to make the score 12-3. Porter later served as assistant football coach, track coach, basketball coach, and principal of Lanier High School.

Early in the second half, with Trommerhauser, Pope, and Zinkowski running, Mercer made four first downs before Zinkowski raced twenty-one yards for a touchdown. Bob Lee then recovered a fumble on the kickoff at the Spring Hill thirty-three-yard line. Lee ran for eighteen, then Pope sped for seventeen more and a touchdown. The score became 26-3 as Bell converted.

When Mercer got the ball again, Lee and Porter carried it from the forty-seven to the five-yard line and Porter scored from there. Lee gained twenty yards and Porter thirty-five in the drive. Opie Gilbert put Mercer back in action by intercepting a pass at the thirty-three-yard line. On the second down Bob Lee scored on a thirty-two-yard burst up the middle.

Henry Allen then came into the game for Mercer and returned the kickoff thirty-six yards. Allen got five yards on an off-tackle play on the first down. On the second down he broke free at right end and went fifty yards for a touchdown. Bowie Gray converted and Mercer led 44-3.

In all, twenty-five men saw action, with Bob Lee running for 117 yards, Allen adding eighty-seven, and Zinkowski getting eighty-eight more. The defense was superb in this opening game and never allowed Spring Hill to become a serious threat.

Mercer 6, Army 19

One of the most memorable games in history occurred on 30 September when the Mercer Bears tangled with the West Point Cadets. This is one of the games that the alumni always talk about, but few remember the real story. Mercer was not up to full strength for this contest as McQuaig, Zinkowski, and Pope were injured while Bell and Reasor were suffering from boils.

Army scored first as Buckner sped forty yards, knocking off three tacklers on the way. Minutes later a blocked Pope punt resulted in two first downs and another six points for the Army. In the second quarter Trommerhauser passed to Lee for fifty-three yards to the Army four-yard line. Lee ran three plays and got three yards and Porter blasted into the end zone for the touchdown. Army led 13-6.

In the second half Army scored again after a march from the Mercer thirty to make the count 19-6. Then Lichter intercepted a pass to start Mercer on a drive again. Trommerhauser ran for seventeen yards to the Mercer forty-six-yard line. Pope got three, Lee added fifteen more, and Porter gained three yards to the Army forty-four-yard line. From here Trommerhauser passed to Lee for nineteen yards and a first down. Three plays later Trommerhauser hit Lee again for nineteen yards and a first down at the Army nine-yard line. Porter got one yard, but three plays later Army had the ball back after ambushing the Mercer drive.

Mercer launched the last drive from the twenty-three-yard line, mainly using passes. After four straight completions for thirty-nine yards, Tom Porter ran for one yard and a first down. Time ran out as a triple pass from Trommerhauser to Gray to Pope went eight yards. This pass was completed twice for fifteen yards during the passing series.

Playing a determined game, Mercer got fourteen first downs while the Army got only seven. Army had a great day passing, however, with 178 yards. Members of the squad seeing action that day were: Nat Reasor, Red Camp, Gordon Reddick, Harry Lichter, Swede Olsson, Cotton Harrison, Jake Trommerhauser, Ernie Zinkowski, Joe Pope, Gerald McQuaig, Tom Porter, Oran Curry, Bob Lee, Al Davino, Bowie Gray, Gene NeSmith, Paul Ward, and H. P. Bell, Jr.

Mercer 6, Navy 25

Taking on the Naval Academy the following weekend was an unprecedented occasion for a Mercer team. Never before had a Mercer squad played two such notable opponents back to back. Gerald McQuaig put Mercer on the scoreboard just before the first period ended. Navy scored three minutes later. Zinkowski then returned the kickoff twenty-nine yards to the Mercer forty-yard line, where he was stopped by the safety man.

In the second half Mercer received the football but could not advance. Navy then sailed for three straight first downs and a touchdown to lead 12-6. Trommerhauser carried Mercer forward with two first downs on passes, but Navy held. For the remainder of the game, it was Navy which generated the offense. Two more scores were added by the Middies, one on a sixty-yard pass play. In all, Navy gained 339 yards while limiting Mercer to 144 yards.

Mercer 0, Birmingham Southern 0

Mercer returned south only to battle Birmingham Southern to a 0-0 draw in Birmingham. It was not Mercer's day once again as the Bears did everything but score. Mercer got twelve first downs while holding the Panthers to only three. The Bears hit on nine of twenty-five passes for 125 yards, while the Panthers went zero for six, but the Bears couldn't score and the game ended 0-0.

Mercer got inside the seventeen-yard line four times, but lost the ball on a fumble and an interception, and as time ran out to end the half. In the second quarter Olsson and Lichter blocked a punt, and Joe Pope fell on the ball for a touchdown; but the play was called back and Mercer was penalized for being offside.

Curry and Pope were outstanding on defense, and Gray recovered a fumble. Henry Allen intercepted a pass in the closing minutes to set up Trommerhauser's pass completions for thirty-three and twenty-eight yards in the closing minutes. Tom Porter helped push the Panthers back with eleven punts for a thirty-five-yard average.

Mercer 12, Georgia 13

One of the finest and closest games ever between Mercer and Georgia was staged in Macon before 8,340 fans. Ticket prices for the game were $2.25, $1.65, and $1.10 for the Homecoming Day game.

Georgia got the ball first and promptly lost two yards on two plays as Cam and Lichter were hitting hard. Mercer took over on the twenty and Zinkowski raced twenty yards for a first down. He then picked up nine yards in three plays, and Porter was forced to punt.

After several exchanges of the ball, Pope blocked a Georgia punt, and Bell recovered at the Georgia five-yard line. McQuaig ran for one yard, but Zinkowski lost five yards in two plays as Georgia was hitting hard. On the fourth down Trommerhauser shot a pass into the end zone, but it fell incomplete.

Georgia punted, and Mercer started again on the Georgia thirty-yard line after Zinkowski returned the punt sixteen yards. McQuaig ran the ball four straight times and picked up a first down at the nineteen-yard line. Georgia was then penalized to the two-yard line. McQuaig ran three plays and scored to give Mercer a 6-0 lead. Zinkowski's drop kick attempt was blocked.

In the second half, following a Porter punt to the Georgia thirty-five, Grant ran forty-four yards for a touchdown, then booted the extra point for a 7-6 lead. As Mercer got the ball back, Zinkowski fumbled and Georgia recovered. Zinkowski was hurt on the play.

Moments later Lichter recovered a fumble to return the ball to Mercer. Once again the mighty Bulldogs held the Bears off, and Georgia took over once more. The Red and Black took the ball at the seventeen-yard line and drove eighty-three yards for the touchdown. Chapman went the final eight yards, but the big play was a forty-three-yard run by Brown.

Henry Allen entered the game and returned the kickoff twenty-six yards to the Mercer thirty-five. Davino was held for no gain, but Allen ripped off runs of six and twenty yards for a first down. McQuaig got seven and Davino added four yards before Allen slashed the remaining ten yards for a touchdown. A pass for the extra point went incomplete.

The game was a rough affair as Lichter was injured, Zinkowski required five stitches in a torn right ear, and Pope cracked his knee. Olsson, Reddick, Lichter, Camp, Harrison, among others, were outstanding defensively for Mercer in this close game with Georgia.

Mercer 6, Furman 6

Mercer and Furman fought to a 6-6 tie in Greenville before a Homecoming crowd on 28 October. The Mercer score came as Allen scored on a forty-eight-yard pass from McQuaig. Mitchell of Furman, who had blocked a punt for a safety in the 1932 game, batted the ball into Allen's arms for the touchdown. Bell missed the extra point attempt. Furman scored on a pass after Allen's punt was blocked in the quarter. Henry Allen, Swede Olsson, Red Camp, and Nat Reasor were outstanding for the Bears.

Mercer 7, Chattanooga 0

The Bears got back into the win column with a 7-0 triumph over Chattanooga. Action started as Allen picked up eleven yards on two runs, then carried the ball twenty-three yards to the Chattanooga ten-yard line. The drive ended here, but Chattanooga could make no progress as Olsson and Camp were crashing through.

Lee returned the punt fifty-two yards behind outstanding blocking, but four plays later the ball went back to the Moccasins. In the middle of the second quarter Allen ran for seventeen yards and then added five more. Chattanooga was penalized to the sixteen-yard line on the next play. McQuaig got four yards, but Allen lost three. Lee ran off tackle for eight yards, but the gain was not enough and the ball went over.

Mercer tried once again later as Lichter recovered a fumble on the Chattanooga eleven, but the half ended with Mercer on the four-yard line. In the second half Lee threw to McQuaig for twenty-four yards on two passes to the Chattanooga seven-yard line. Lee then fumbled and Chattanooga recovered on the one-inch line.

Finally Allen returned a punt to the Chattanooga eighteen-yard line. McQuaig ran for eleven yards, and Trommerhauser got to the one-inch line on three plays. On the fourth down McQuaig scored and Gray converted for the 7-0 score.

Mercer 13, Clemson 0

Clemson became victory number three for the Bears in Savannah on 18 November as 600 fans from Macon attended the game. Joe Pope scored both touchdowns on one-yard runs, and Bowie Gray converted once for a 13-0 win.

Mercer started from the Clemson nineteen with Lee running for two yards. Zinkowski, playing with a bandaged ear, added seven yards on two runs. Pope slashed forward for three yards, Zinkowski got five more, and Pope bulled over from the one-yard line. Gray's conversion made the score

7-0. The second touchdown drive started as Allen picked up fifteen yards from the Clemson thirty-four-yard line. Pope, Trommerhauser, and Lee carried the ball with Pope going over again from the one-yard line. Mercer drove to the Clemson six-yard line in the last minute of play on a forty-three-yard run by Allen but couldn't score.

Olsson and Reddick were outstanding in the line that day. Allen and Trommerhauser aided on defense by intercepting passes. Allen was the leading ground gainer for Mercer with eleven yards.

Mercer 31, Oglethorpe 0

The final game of the season matched Mercer and Oglethorpe in Macon. Nine seniors were playing their last game for Mercer. In the first quarter Reddick recovered a fumble on the Oglethorpe thirty-one, and Zinkowski scored from the thirteen after McQuaig went sixteen yards on a fake kick.

In the second quarter Mercer was held for downs, but the Bears were stopped only temporarily. Eddie Anderson, the Oglethorpe punter, attempted a punt from behind the goal and had the kick blocked. Oglethorpe recovered. As Anderson attempted to punt again, Pope blocked it; and Camp recovered for a touchdown.

For the first ten minutes of the second half, Oglethorpe fought hard before turning the ball over at the Oglethorpe thirty-three-yard line. McQuaig ran sixteen yards followed by a two-yard jaunt by Lee. Four plays and fourteen yards later McQuaig broke into the end zone. Bell, playing with a broken nose and no protective guard, added the extra point.

Corbett Williamson recovered an Oglethorpe fumble on the Oglethorpe twenty-one on the kickoff. Trommerhauser lost three yards, and McQuaig gained one on the next play. Trommerhauser then passed to Reasor, who lateraled to Pope. He lateraled to Lee for a twelve-yard touchdown in a razzle-dazzle display. Pope scored the last touchdown on a five-yard run.

After this score Oglethorpe made a first down on the Mercer twelve-yard line, but the tough Bear defense allowed nothing in four attempts. After an exchange of punts, Pope went over from the five-yard line following a march down the field, which accounted for five first downs.

Reasor played the greatest game of his career, while Cotton Harrison, Camp, Olsson, and Reddick were described as outstanding. Reddick blocked two punts during the game. Following the season Olsson made the all-SIAA team. He also made the all-Dixie team, along with Lichter and Trommerhauser.

Olsson ended his career in 1933 as one of Mercer's greatest linemen ever. He made honorable mention All-America, along with Camp and Lichter. He was also selected to the all-Georgia team, and played in the North-

South game in New York. He was later a standout with the Washington Redskins for a number of years. Olsson was the only Mercer player ever to make it in the National Football League. Following his career in professional football, he was a very successful football coach in his native Toledo, Ohio.

1934

The 1934 Mercer football team, consisting of twenty-six men, was coached once again by Lake Russell. Assisting him were Jimmy Slocumb, a former Georgia Tech end, and Carter Townsend.

A number of sophomores came up from the Cub team to aid the experienced regulars in this rebuilding year. Some of these were Carl Altonen, Eugene Warlick, J. C. Thomas, Manuel Mamalakis, George Tyson, David Hazlehust, John Hemple, Allen Bloodworth, John Ellis, Billy Smith, Edwin Varner, and Jack Morris. Gerald McQuaig was missing from the squad because he had signed a professional baseball contract.

Mercer 6, Presbyterian 7

The first game of the season was played in Macon before 1,700 fans, with Presbyterian edging the inexperienced Bears 7-6. In a rough affair, Mercer drew 105 yards in penalties while Presbyterian was not guilty of a single infraction.

Mercer got a touchdown first as 140-pound Allen Bloodworth, with Varner blocking, returned a punt seventy-five yards for a touchdown. The extra point was missed, but Mercer led 6-0. Mercer got eighty-seven yards rushing during the game while Presbyterian earned 120 yards.

The Mercer sophomores went into the game in the second quarter for needed experience and held the Blue Hose scoreless. In the third quarter Presbyterian got four straight first downs, but the drive ended at the Mercer twenty-yard line. Following a Mercer punt, Presbyterian came back for a first down at the Mercer ten-yard line, but the Bears held once more.

Presbyterian finally mustered a drive of four first downs, one on a penalty, to the Mercer two-yard line. On the third down Higbee went one yard for a touchdown on a reverse. The extra point was good for a 7-6 victory.

Twenty-three men saw action for Mercer in this opening game of the new season. Altonen and Allen intercepted passes, while Thomas and Altonen recovered fumbles to help hold the visitors. Allen, Lee, and Bloodworth were the principal ball carriers for Mercer.

Mercer 0, Loyola 21

Loyola of New Orleans made it two losses in a row for the 1934 Bears with a crowd of 5,000 fans on hand. Before Mercer really got warmed up, Loyola was off and running. Picking up sixteen first downs in the first half alone, Loyola scored three touchdowns and three extra points to earn a 21-0 victory.

Billy Ray scored from the thirteen for the first counter. Then after Mercer couldn't move, Loyola picked up five first downs to the Mercer five-yard line, but the Bears denied a touchdown. After an exchange of punts, Bloodworth got eleven yards but then fumbled. Loyola recovered and got four more first downs and a touchdown.

The final score for Loyola came as two runs of twenty-five yards, plus a penalty, put the ball on the Mercer six-yard line. Daigle scored, and Ray added his third extra point. It was just too much Loyola as Mercer managed seventy-eight yards passing and sixty-eight rushing to Loyola's total of 355 yards. In addition to all other handicaps, Mercer lost three fumbles.

Mercer 0, Birmingham Southern 14

The starting line-up for the Birmingham Southern game listed Warlick and NeSmith at end, Williamson and Porter at tackle, Mamalakis and Tyson at guard, Lichter at center, Bloodworth at quarterback, Smith and Varner at halfback, and Allen at fullback. The only thoroughly experienced men on the squad were Lichter, Porter, Williamson, NeSmith, and Allen. Porter had played in the backfield, but he was now a tackle and was inexperienced in that position.

In addition to inexperience, injuries had taken a toll as Carl Altonen and Charley Brown were out with preseason injuries. Al Davino, Roger Dodd, Johnny Hemple, Red Tyson, and Bob Lee were also hurt in some fashion.

Allen Bloodworth, in a great offensive show, played the entire sixty minutes against the Panthers, carrying one punt to the Panther ten-yard line. Just before the half, Bloodworth completed three straight passes to Billy Smith and Jack Morris to get a first down on the Southern fifteen-yard line. Mercer got nine yards on two tries but lost the ball on the fourth down at the six-yard line.

In the third quarter Bloodworth tacked McKay on the Mercer twenty-six-yard line after a long run. Teel then scooted twenty-two yards to the Mercer three-yard line. The Bears held here for four downs in one of the great defensive efforts of the day.

Southern scored two touchdowns during the game and converted after each for a 14-0 victory. Outstanding that day for Mercer was Lichter, with two pass interceptions, along with NeSmith and Porter, who were defensive stalwarts.

Mercer 3, Furman 9

In an evenly matched game, Furman edged Mercer 9-3 in Greenville, South Carolina, to hand Mercer the fourth straight loss of the season. In rushing Mercer had a net of fifty-five yards while Furman got twenty-one yards. Mercer made seventy yards passing, and Furman got ninety-one yards on six of ten throws. The Bears were successful on only four of fourteen passes that day. Each team punted twelve times. Mercer fumbled five times, while Furman fumbled four. Everything was about even during the game except the score.

Henry Allen was ill from the flu, and Eugene Warlick missed the game with dengue fever. Johnny Hemple, Buster NeSmith, Oran Curry, and Harry Lichter were outstanding. The Mercer line repelled the Furman backs on one occasion from the Mercer thirty-yard line for a twenty-six-yard loss.

The game was a punting duel. Just before the half, Furman received one on the fifty-yard line. Furman then got three first downs to the eight-yard line. Furman attempted a field goal, but NeSmith blocked it. Lichter recovered.

After an exchange of punts in the second half, Mercer got the ball on the fifty-yard line. Bloodworth passed to Lee for nine yards, and then Smith went up the middle for a first down. Bloodworth took to the air again and hit NeSmith for thirteen yards. Bloodworth ran for four yards and Ed Varner slashed for six yards to the Furman twenty-yard line. Smith ran straight ahead for three yards, and Bloodworth skirted end for 10 yards for the fourth first down. On the third down Bloodworth kicked a perfect goal from seventeen yards out, just inside the side line.

Furman scored as a Lichter pass deflection was caught by Roper, who went to the Mercer twenty-seven-yard line. Three plays later Blair passed nineteen yards to Stevens for a touchdown and a 6-3 lead. The final points for Furman came as Bloodworth attempted a pass from the Mercer one-yard line. The ball was intercepted at the Mercer seventeen-yard line, and King of Furman booted a field goal on the fourth down.

Mercer 6, Stetson 0

The Bears finally found a victim, but it was not a willing one. The Hatters of Stetson fought gallantly in Jacksonville, Florida. In an evenly matched game Mercer got ninety-nine yards rushing and sixty-three passing. In addition, Stetson had twelve first downs and Mercer eight, but the Bears were penalized eighty-six yards.

Stetson ran first from the thirty-eight and picked up twenty-seven yards on two plays. On the third down NeSmith tackled Slade for an eleven-yard loss. Mercer, starting from the thirty-two, moved eleven yards on Varner's sprint around right end. Allen went around left end for thirty-eight yards on the second down. After that run, Bob Lee passed eight yards to NeSmith on the Stetson eight-yard line. Here the Hatters became tough, and four downs later Mercer had gained only five yards.

Stetson took over on the three-yard line. The Hatters earned four first downs to the Mercer eleven, but then Slade lost eight yards on a tackle by Smith, and the ball was turned over.

On the first down Lee passed to Allen for thirty-four yards after faking an end run. After two running plays had been held in check, Lee passed to Allen for fifteen yards and a touchdown. Lee missed the conversion attempt.

In the second half Stetson drove from the Mercer thirty-six to the one-yard line but couldn't score. Varner dropped the ballcarrier for a loss on the fourth down.

In the fourth quarter Lee passed to NeSmith for thirteen yards to the Stetson fifteen-yard line. From here Lee attempted a pass, but Lawton of Stetson intercepted. Lee, the lone remaining defender, avoided blockers and slowed Lawton down enough for Ward and Porter to make the stop on the Mercer thirty-five yard line. The Bears had won their first game of the season by defeating a good Stetson team 6-0.

Al Davino was outstanding on defense after he replaced Varner, who was injured early in the game. In all, eighteen men saw action in the contest.

Mercer 30, Washington and Jefferson 7

Returning to Macon to host Washington and Jefferson before a sparse crowd of 920 paid, Mercer enjoyed a 30-7 win as the entire team played well. Bob Lee put Mercer on the scoreboard first by recovering a fumble and running twenty-five yards for a touchdown. Bloodworth, with touchdowns of forty-four and ninety yards, along with a field goal from the eighteen-yard line and two extra points, was the offensive leader for the day. Ed Varner got the other touchdown on a one-yard run.

Lichter, Tyson, Porter, and Warlick were outstanding in the line. Billy Smith was a 60-minute man and had a forty-three yard run to his credit. John Hemple caught a forty-two-yard pass. The young Mercer team had at last put together a good offense.

Mercer 13, Chattanooga 13

It rained in Chattanooga the next weekend as the Bears and the Moccasins went at it again. Mercer scored first as Bloodworth skipped in for a score and added the extra point. A fifteen-yard penalty on a Bloodworth punt helped Chattanooga get a touchdown. Hinds passed to Perry to the Mercer twenty-eight-yard line. After two running plays and no gain, Chattanooga passed for twenty yards and a touchdown. Mercer led 7-6 as the conversion was missed.

Mercer then got a first down at the Chattanooga twenty-five-yard line with Smith leading the way. Smith ran for nine yards, but the play was called back, and Mercer was penalized fifteen yards. Allen then passed to Varner for eight yards, but Mercer was penalized again.

In the third quarter Opie Gilbert intercepted a pass on the Chattanooga eighteen-yard line. Jack Morris ran for six yards on the first down, but Mercer was offside again. In the fourth quarter Bloodworth intercepted and returned the ball sixty yards, but the play was called back and another five-yard penalty was administered. Chattanooga scored on a twenty-five-yard run after getting the ball.

The Bears became angry now, and Bloodworth took to the air. He hit Warlick on a thirty-eight-yarder. Then Smith made runs of seven and ten yards as the offensive line was pushing the Moccasins back. Lee followed by driving to the one-foot line. Smith was stopped on the next two plays, but Bloodworth then scored with Lee, Smith, and Allen leading the interference. Bloodworth missed the extra point, and the score remained tied.

Mercer was the victim of tough breaks on offense as several crippling penalties were assessed. The Bear defense did well, though, by holding Chattanooga within the fifteen-yard line at least six times during the game. Tom Porter was particularly effective on defense as he stayed in the Moccasin backfield all afternoon knocking down ball carriers.

Mercer 0, Clemson 32

Clemson got revenge for several defeats as the Jess Neely-coached team blasted Mercer 32-0 before 4,000 fans in Savannah. The Tigers proved far superior after a scoreless first quarter by scoring one touchdown in each of the second and third quarters and three times in the fourth quarter.

Mercer's offense couldn't get started because of the aggressive Clemson defense, which limited the Bears to sixteen yards rushing and nine yards passing. Smith gained seventeen yards, Bloodworth had eleven, but Varner lost twelve to account for all the Mercer yardage. The Bears got into scoring position only twice and were forced to kick from behind the goal line several times. The Clemson offense accounted for 166 yards and five touchdowns.

Mercer 13, Centre 16

Playing in the annual Centre Homecoming game in Danville, Kentucky, Mercer fell 16-13. Centre scored ten points in the last three minutes on a sixty-eight-yard run for a touchdown by Hendren and on a twenty-five-yard field goal by Marks. After a listless first half which saw Mercer earn only one first down, the Bears scored thirteen points in the second half. Centre scored first, however, after starting from the Mercer thirty-eight-yard line. Later Centre threatened again after a fumble was recovered on the Mercer eighteen-yard line. Centre drove to the four-yard line, but the defense held and Mercer got the ball back.

In the second half NeSmith recovered a fumble on the Centre forty-five for Mercer's first trip into Centre territory. Later Bloodworth and Davino put together runs of four and seven yards for a first down. Jack Morris was hit for a three-yard loss, but Davino got one yard up the middle. On the fourth down and sixteen yards to go, Bloodworth passed to NeSmith for a touchdown, and Mercer led 7-6 with Bloodworth's conversion.

In the fourth quarter Mercer got the ball on the Centre forty-two-yard line. On the first play Bloodworth tore around right end and cut back to go across standing up for the touchdown. The extra point was missed, but Mercer led 13-6.

Mercer tried to kill time since the end of the game was near but was finally forced to punt. Hendren returned the punt sixty-eight yards for a touchdown, and the conversion made it 13-13. Mercer took the ball, but an aroused Centre team charged hard, and the Bears couldn't advance. Bloodworth punted and the ball was blocked with Centre recovering on the Mercer twenty-seven. Two plays later Centre advanced to the Mercer eleven-yard line. Mark then booted a twenty-five-yard field goal for the 16-13 victory.

In the second half Mercer really came to life and deserved to win but unfortunate breaks gave Centre the victory. NeSmith was described as magnificent, while Altonen was regarded as the finest guard that Centre had faced all year.

Mercer 7, Oglethorpe 6

In Atlanta in the rain, Oglethorpe and Mercer tangled once more with Mercer slipping by with a 7-6 victory. Oglethorpe scored in the opening minutes with Park Puryear going seventy-five yards for a touchdown. A pass attempt for the extra point was incomplete.

Allen Bloodworth made three touchdown-saving tackles after the runners had eluded every would-be tackler except him. Lichter was also outstanding as he intercepted two passes while Varner stopped one drive with an interception. Tom Porter and Carl Altonen were the big thrust in the offensive line. Al Davino ran wild on offense the second half after being a blocking back for three years.

In the second half Oglethorpe punted out of bounds on the thirty-yard line. Allen got nineteen in two attempts and the Oglethorpe team was penalized to the one-foot line for roughing. Davino and Allen each ran once and only inched the ball forward. On the third down Davino blasted in for the touchdown. Bob Lee, who was playing with a taped shoulder, booted the extra point for the victory.

(text continues after photograph section)

This 1896 team won over Georgia Tech

The 1906 team dressed in the football uniform of that year

The 1908 Mercer team practicing in Tattnall Square Park

Coach Stroud and the 1911 team on the steps of the Administration Building

The 1922 Starting Backfield—Dave Rice, George Harmon, Shorty Poore, Kid Cecil

The 1934 Starting Eleven in Centennial Stadium

Members of the 1935 squad, which posted a record season

Touchdown for the Bears in a 1936 battle at Centennial Stadium

The Mercer Bears in action, circa mid-1930s

Alumni Athletic Breakfast, May 1970, Macon, Ga.—Many years of athletics at Mercer University are represented in these men who came together for a reunion of former athletes. *From left*—Wallace Butts, head coach at the University of Georgia for 22 years and a 1928 graduate of Mercer; Lake Russell, who coached football at Mercer for 12 years beginning in 1929; and Robert Wilder, Chairman of the Department of Physical Education, who served as basketball coach at Mercer for 14 years (1957-1970)

Charter Members of Mercer University Athletic Hall of Fame, 1971

Front—J. F. "Phoney" Smith, Malcolm Green, E. B. "Crook" Smith, J. B. "Stick" Roddenberry, J. A. "Red" Simmons, J. W. "Wally" Butts

Back—Les "Swede" Olsson, Zeb Vance, Jim Cowan, Lake Russell, Wright Bazemore, Bob Wilder (nonmember)

Members of the Mercer University Athletic Hall of Fame, 1971-1978

1971

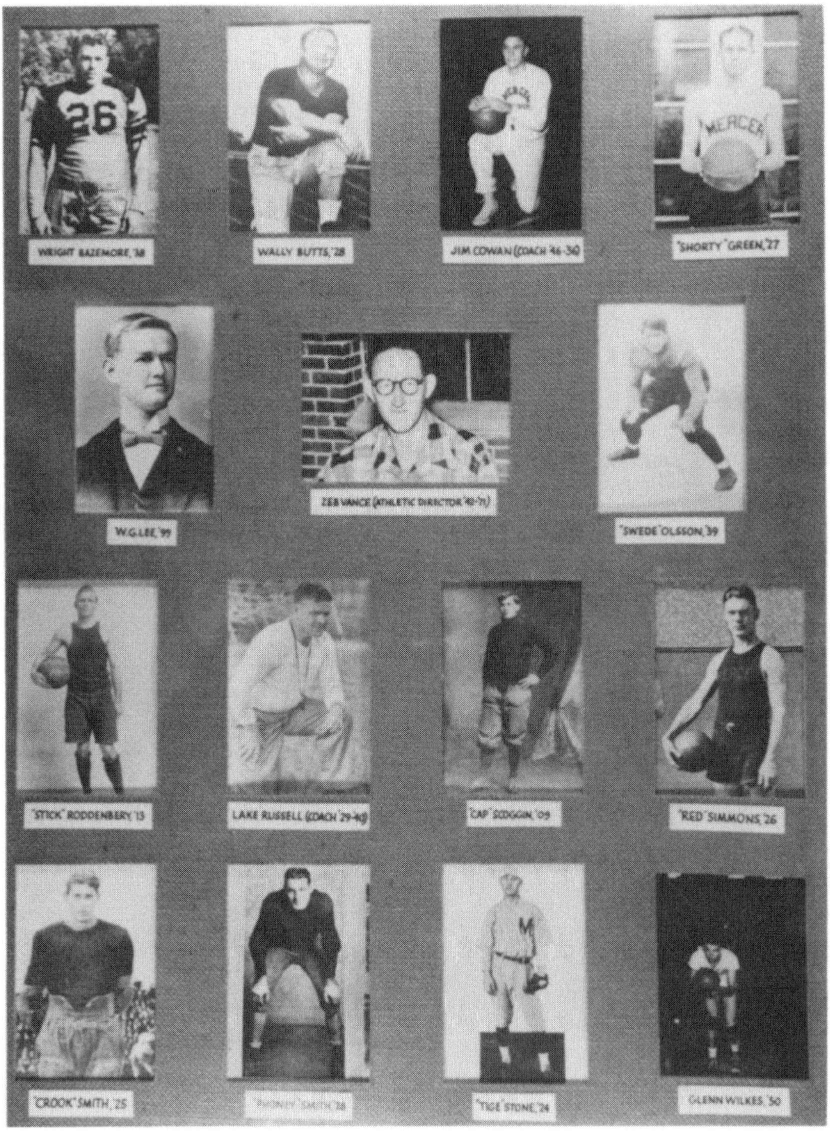

1972

BILL ALDERMAN, '30
ALLAN BLOODWORTH, '37
LUTHER BLOODWORTH, '18
LAMAR CLEMENTS, '51
CHARLIE MORGAN, '17
"SKIPPER" COCHRAN, '14
JOHN PARKS, '14
BOB REEDER, '51
CLAUDE SMITH (COACH '43-'77)
"DUCK" SWANN, '16
JOHN WESTMORELAND, '14

1973

NORMAN CARTER, '60
J.C. CLEMENTS, '17
HERSCHEL FORESTER, '15
GEORGE HARMON, '25
BOB SMITH, '33
WALTER GRACE, '15
TOM PORTER, '36
"BAGGY" MALLARD, '30
BOBBY PINKSTON, '26
RICHARD REID, '54

1974

GLENN CASSELL '52
JOSH CODY (COACH '21-22)
BOB GAMBLE '22
FRANK HUNT '15
CARL LANCASTER '23
BOB LEE '35
HARRY LICHTER '36
TOMMY MIXON '55
BOB WILDER '52

1975

"SCOOPER" DEWBERRY, '15
BRADLEY HOGG, '11
"SPEC" LANDRUM, '40
BERT SCHWARTZ, '34
MANLY McWILLIAMS, '24
AL OWEN, '39
"SLAP" RENTZ, '22
ERNIE ZINKOWSKI, '34
NAT REASOR, '34
JOE POPE, '34
BOB SPERRY, '35

1976

NEAL ALLEN '41
JIMMY CARNES '56
"COTTON" DORSEY '17
SID ELLISON '25
GEORGE GIBSON '14
DAN HAMMACK '23
OSCAR LONG '26
"SHORTY" POORE '25

1977

MAYES DOBBINS,'50
BILLY SMITH,'38
FERROL SAMS,'14
KING DUNN,'25
ERNIE SINCLAIR'20
"BUNCIE" SKINNER '27

1978

Steve Moody, '67 Emmett H. (Bubber) Pope, '25 Tommy Day Wilcox, '65 I. Giddens Wilkes, '23

1935

The 1935 season started with ten seniors back for their final year as Russell, Slocumb, and Harry Lichter got the men into shape. Lichter worked with the freshmen. J. D. Blair returned as athletic director. Freddie Sington, a former Alabama All-American signed as an assistant coach.

Tickets for the games were $1.50, $1.00, and $.25. The attendance at home games had been poor a number of years, and a poll was taken to see if the Macon fans would support night football. The Bears created a new image with new uniforms consisting of silk pants, which were blazing red in the front with black stripes on the legs. The jerseys were orange wool with black stripes on the arms. Helmets were orange with black stripes. Orange and black shoes completed the uniform and probably served to scare the opponents.

Mercer 0, Georgia 31

Mercer went into the Georgia game without Carl Altonen, who was ill with malaria. In the early part of the game NeSmith, Curry, and Tyson were injured.

Once again the Bulldogs were a tough team, running for 446 yards and passing for eighty-two more while accumulating twenty-five first downs. Georgia scored first. Midway in the opening period Johnny Bond burst through the middle for a sixty-two-yard touchdown. Mercer had actually driven to the thirty-seven on a twenty-seven-yard pass from Bloodworth to Allen for a first down. Georgia held, and then Bond ran for the touchdown.

Mercer recovered a fumble on the Georgia thirty-seven, but Allen's fourth down pass was intercepted to end the drive. Georgia then got four straight first downs and scored on a pass to begin the quarter. Mercer punted on the first play after the kickoff in the second quarter, and Bill Hartman sped forty yards to the Mercer fourteen-yard line. Al Anderson scored from the fourteen to make the score 18-0.

Mercer kicked off in the second half, and Georgia scored in three plays after being stopped on the first down. It began as Mindt raced twenty-five yards on a pass before being stopped by Thomas. Green then passed to Charlie Harold for thirty-one yards and a touchdown. Georgia got the last touchdown after gaining five first downs, starting from the twenty-five-yard line to cap the 31-0 game.

Allen was the major ground gainer for Mercer with seventy-two yards in nine attempts, but Mercer finished with a net sixty-five in twenty-six runs as several ball carriers lost yardage. Wright Bazemore was outstanding on defense.

Bazemore, a sophomore, had come to Mercer from Fitzgerald High School, where he had been coached by former Mercer great Bill Alderman. In 1933 at Fitzgerald, Bazemore scored 128 points in six games and gained 882 yards for a team that won four games and lost two. Bazemore later became one of the most successful high school coaches ever in Georgia, winning thirteen state championships through 1969.

Mercer 0, Navy 27

Mercer took on tough Navy for the second time in Annapolis on 5 October with Navy winning 27-0. The starting lineup for Mercer was John Hemple and Wally Byrom at end, George Tyson and John Fitzpatrick at tackle, Paul Ward and Roger Dodd at guard, Opie Gilbert at center, Don Lockert at quarterback, J. C. Thomas and Allan Bloodworth at halfback, and Tom Porter at fullback.

Navy scored first after Bloodworth punted to the Navy forty-five. Navy was penalized fifteen yards, but on the first play Navy recovered with a seventy-yard pass play for a touchdown. The receiver was hit by three Mercer players but broke away for a touchdown. In the second quarter Navy had the ball on the Mercer forty-five-yard line. Two plays netted ten yards, but then Pratt passed to Fellows for thirty yards and a touchdown.

Mercer couldn't advance, and Navy began once again on the Mercer forty-two-yard line. With straight running plays, the Cadets pushed the ball to the Mercer three-yard line. Two plays netted no gain, but then Pratt passed for a touchdown.

Roger Dodd recovered a fumble on the Navy twenty-three, but Owen of Mercer fumbled, and Navy recovered. Schmidt of Navy fumbled, and J. C. Thomas recovered on the Navy fifteen-yard line. Owen got five yards in two plays against the tough Middie line, but the half ended and so did Mercer's threat.

In the third quarter Navy's third team played even with Mercer for most of the period; then Corbett Williamson recovered a fumble on the Mercer 49. Bloodworth ran for seven yards around end, and Porter hit the middle for Mercer's first first down of the game. Bloodworth had an incomplete pass, but Allen raced fourteen yards around end for another first down at the Navy twenty-six-yard line. The Bears did not score, however. As the fourth quarter began, two passes fell incomplete and a third was intercepted to stop Mercer's biggest threat.

Navy couldn't move the ball, and Bloodworth returned a punt to the Mercer forty-seven, but a penalty gave Mercer the ball on the Navy forty-eight-yard line. Henry Allen then broke loose around end for twenty yards to the Navy twenty-eight for another first down. Bloodworth lost seventeen yards while attempting to pass on the first down. The Navy first unit came back into the game and stopped the drive. The Middies then drove from the eighteen to the Mercer eight-yard line for a seventy-four-yard advance. Mercer held, and Billy Smith batted down a fourth down pass.

Bloodworth punted and Navy drove back, but Fitzpatrick recovered a fumble at the Mercer five to stop a score. Bloodworth ran to the thirteen, and Smith got a first down at the fifteen-yard line as the game ended.

Navy, with a tremendous show of power, got fourteen first downs on 456 yards rushing and 165 yards passing. Mercer got five first downs and one hundred yards rushing. The defense for Mercer in the second half was outstanding as the Navy team was held scoreless.

Mercer 14, Birmingham Southern 0

In a Friday night game before 3,500 in Macon, Mercer entertained Birmingham Southern and earned the first win of the season. Mercer amassed 351 yards to only eighty for Southern in the biggest offensive show of strength for the 1935 season.

New men in the starting unit were Ewing Edge at right tackle and George Rosich at right end for this game. The scoring for Mercer was by Tom Porter and Henry Allen, with Bloodworth adding the two extra points in the 14-0 victory.

In the first half Mercer was stopped twice on the six-inch line. Later Birmingham Southern punted, and Allen Bloodworth returned the ball thirty yards to the Panther twenty-eight-yard line. Bloodworth then passed nine yards to Allen, and Porter went off tackle for five yards for a first down at the fifteen-yard line. Bloodworth got nine and Porter added three for another first down at the three-yard line. Porter hit the middle twice and got to the six-inch line. After Porter failed to gain on the third down, Al Owen was pushed back on a reverse, and Southern took over.

The Panthers punted, but the play was called back and they were penalized three inches for offside. The remainder of the first half was a defensive battle with neither team mounting much of a threat.

In the second half a penalty put Mercer back on the five-yard line. Bloodworth broke loose on the first play for eighty-two yards, only to be hauled down at the Southern thirteen-yard line. Porter scored from the five after Bloodworth had skirted end for eight yards.

Henry Allen scored the second touchdown when he went off left tackle and cut back to score from seventy-six yards out as Opie Gilbert cleared the last defender. In the final quarter Wally Byrom attempted a nineteen-yard field goal but was unsuccessful. For Mercer Bloodworth had 108 yards, Porter 105, and Allen ninety-one as the principal ground gainers.

Mercer 14, Presbyterian 7

The Bears made it two in a row with a win over Presbyterian on October 19 as Allen Bloodworth scored all the points in a 14-7 win. Porter led a drive in the first quarter to the Presbyterian five-yard line, but the Blue Hose held for downs as Bazemore's fourth down pass was incomplete.

Presbyterian intercepted a pass in the second quarter and drove to the Mercer five-yard line. The Bears held for three downs, but Holliday scored a touchdown on the fourth down. Thomason added the extra point, and Mercer was behind 7-0. In the second half, Mercer came back to score as J. C. Thomas returned the kickoff to the Mercer forty-two. Porter carried the ball from here five times for twenty-three yards, Allen got thirteen on one dive, and Bloodworth added twenty-two on four runs. His last run was for twelve yards off tackle for a touchdown.

The final score came after an exchange of punts. Bloodworth started at the Presbyterian forty-six and went off tackle. After being nearly caught at the Blue Hose twenty-six-yard line, he slipped into the end zone for a touchdown. Mercer earned sixteen first downs and 266 yards rushing as Bloodworth led with ninety-two yards. J. C. Thomas was outstanding during the game as a blocker, earning back his starting halfback spot.

Mercer 0, Furman 32

Mercer ran up against a strong Furman team in Greenville and lost by a score of 32-0 as Furman had one of the greatest lines ever. The Paladins scored two touchdowns before Mercer made a serious threat. Mercer's longest effort was a twenty-six-yard pass from Allen to Owen to the Furman thirty-six as the half ended.

In the third quarter Furman started at the forty-six and drove to the Mercer eleven-yard line. In three plays, only eight yards were gained. On the fourth down a Blair pass was batted down by Gilbert, but Bob King grabbed it for a Furman touchdown. Mercer was never able to get into the game and managed only ninety-five yards total, compared to 287 for Furman.

Mercer 0, Clemson 13

Mercer played the best game of the 1935 season against a good Clemson team, and the Tigers won 13-0. Bloodworth was out of action, and Russell started his second unit backfield.

Owen and Smith carried Mercer to the Clemson thirty-eight, but Owen fumbled and Clemson recovered. After an exchange of punts with neither team advancing, Clemson drove to the Mercer twenty-six yard line. Ward, Rosich, and Lockert stopped the Tigers for two downs, but Clemson scored on the third down to take a 6-0 lead.

Clemson sent in a new team, and Owen got a first down at the Mercer twenty-five yard line following the kickoff return. Smith raced around right end for sixteen yards, Varner added seven, and Bazemore got one yard. On the third down Allen punted to the Clemson nine-yard line. Clemson got six first downs and went to the Mercer one-yard line but couldn't score.

Later Owen passed to Byrom for twelve and twenty-one-yard gains to the Clemson fourteen-yard line. Varner's pass to Byrom just missed and was intercepted. Clemson drove to the Mercer twenty-five yard line but couldn't score.

Allen, who was outstanding all day, ran for four yards; then Varner gained one yard. Allen then reversed his field three times and gained twenty-seven yards to midfield but fumbled while being tackled and lost the ball. A Berry-to-Lee pass for Clemson resulted in a fifty-yard touchdown.

Mercer tried to score as Owen hit Byrom for twenty-one yards and then connected for three yards with Rosich. Paul Ward ran for three yards, but the game ended with Clemson winning 13-0.

Actually the game was nearly even statistically, but Mercer was under constant pressure and couldn't put together a sustained drive. Al Owen was outstanding for Mercer and particularly effective as a passer that day.

Mercer 7, Chattanooga 12

Chattanooga took the measure of Mercer before the 3,500 fans in Chattanooga on Homecoming Day, although Mercer came from behind to lead in the second quarter 7-6. Chattanooga scored first as Watland sped thirty-five yards, sidestepping Allen, Bloodworth, and Thomas for the touchdown.

Tom Porter picked up twenty yards, earning two first downs in the first quarter. A new Mercer team, led by Own, came in during the second quarter. Minutes later Mercer got the ball on the Chattanooga thirty-one. Varner picked up four yards at end, then an Owen-to-Byrom-to-Smith-to-Varner pass accounted for seven yards and a first down at the Chattanooga twenty. Owen ran for five yards on the first down. On the second down Ed Varner sped through right tackle for fifteen yards and a touchdown. Byrom added the extra point, and Mercer led 7-6.

In the second half Bazemore, Smith, Varner, and Owen worked in the backfield. Mercer got only short yardage before Chattanooga, from the twenty-two, got forty-eight yards on a pass to the Mercer twenty-seven-yard line. A second pass was complete for twenty-seven yards and a touchdown. Chattanooga led 12-7.

Mercer's first unit came back into the game, and Porter and Altonen recovered a Chattanooga fumble at the Mercer ten to stop a drive. Minutes later, after the ball had been returned to Chattanooga, Altonen recovered another fumble on the Chattanooga thirty-nine yard line. Bloodworth ran for one yard, and Porter got twenty-two yards on a fake pass. Porter then bulled for eleven yards on two plays to the Chattanooga three-yard line. Chattanooga held for two plays, then Porter fumbled, and the Moccasins recovered behind the goal line.

Altonen, Ward, Curry, Tyson, and Bazemore were the defensive leaders for Mercer. Porter was the major ground gainer with fifty-five yards, although he sat out much of the game.

Mercer 21, Alabama Teachers 7

In a double header on 15 November 1935, Lanier High School lost to Miami High School 13-7, and Mercer defeated Alabama Teachers 21-7. (Teachers later became Troy State.) There were 7,000 fans in attendance for the games. This was the largest crowd since the 1932 Georgia game.

Russell started his second team, and the first quarter was mainly a punting duel. Bazemore fumbled a punt to give the Teachers the ball on the Mercer thirty-six yard line. He then deflected a pass on the fourth down to get Mercer the ball at the five-yard line. Owen punted and followed with an interception at the Mercer five to stop a threat. Billy Smith punted to the Teachers thirty-seven where "Turk" Rosich recovered a fumble on the first play.

Mercer's first team entered the game at the beginning of the second quarter. Allen passed to Hemple for fourteen yards, but other gains were small, and Teachers took over again. Mercer, starting from the thirty-seven, then went to the one-yard line. Bloodworth fumbled, and Teachers recovered on the five-yard line.

The Bears were having a difficult time. It seemed that they would never score, even after getting very close to the goal. On the last drive Mercer picked up five first downs. Bloodworth ran once for thirty-seven yards in the drive.

Cook of Teachers punted and then intercepted a Bloodworth pass. He returned it forty-eight yards and was stopped by Bloodworth, who eluded four blockers to make the tackle. The remainder of the first half was played with neither team making progress.

Bazemore returned the kickoff forty yards to the forty-eight yard line. Billy Smith hit center for seven, followed by a blast off tackle by Owen for five yards and a first down. Smith got seven on two runs, but Owen threw an incomplete pass. Smith punted to the Teachers three-yard line.

Starting again from the thirty-eight after Teachers had run one play and punted, Smith hit the middle for two yards. Varner ran for thirteen at left end for a first down at the Teachers twenty-yard line. Owen ran for three, then added thirteen more for a touchdown. Byrom booted the extra point.

Later in the game Bazemore intercepted a pass and returned it fifty-three yards to the Teachers forty-two-yard line. Owen got ten yards on two runs, Smith added six, but Owen then lost two yards. After Smith dashed off tackle for three yards, Owen passed to Byrom for ten yards and another first down at the fifteen-yard line. Smith went up the middle for five yards, and the first team returned to action.

Bloodworth skirted end for eight yards. Porter followed with seven yards in two plays for the touchdown. Bloodworth converted for a 14-0 lead.

After an exchange of the ball, Bloodworth fumbled, and Teachers recovered on the Mercer twenty-six-yard line. Three plays later Elmore passed to Meredith for an eighteen-yard touchdown. Cook hit the extra point for a 14-7 score. Mercer scored last as Bloodworth took the kickoff on the twenty and sped eighty yards for a touchdown as Rosich cleared the last defender. Bloodworth converted for a 21-7 win.

Mercer 19, Oglethorpe 0

The final game of the 1935 season brought Oglethorpe to Macon as eight seniors played their last game. J.C. Thomas, Corbett Williamson, Henry Allen, Tom Porter, Paul Ward, Opie Gilbert, Oran Curry, and Carl Altonen finished careers with a 19-0 victory over the Petrels.

Corbett Williamson was one of the most durable players ever to play for the Bears. He had played every minute of every game in the 1934 season. Gene NeSmith, who had been a standout, had been hurt in the first game of the 1935 season and had still not recovered as the final game of the year was played.

For the year Mercer won four and lost five, closing the season on a victory note. Al Owen started things off two minutes after the opening kickoff by going forty-four yards through left tackle for a touchdown. Later in the quarter Owen, Smith, and Varner drove to the six-yard line but were halted by a fifteen-yard penalty.

In the second quarter a backfield consisting of Allen, Thomas, and Porter went into action. Allen recovered a fumble on the Petrel sixteen-yard line. Porter went up the middle for six yards, then Allen raced around left end for the touchdown. Oglethorpe came back with successful passes to the Mercer ten-yard line as the half ended.

In the third quarter Jimmy Sullivan of Oglethorpe drove to the Mercer twenty-five on runs of twenty-one and twenty-six yards, but Ed Varner intercepted a pass to end the threat. Owen then had great runs of thirteen, nineteen, and seventeen yards, but Mercer lost the ball on an interception while attempting a pass.

The seniors returned to the game, and Bazemore and Porter carried the ball to the Oglethorpe two-yard line. Porter scored off left tackle, and Don

Lockert converted. One final drive for the Bears, with seven players carrying the ball, went to the two-yard line of Oglethorpe as the game ended. Varner had thirteen and Owen sixteen yards as the big gainers in this drive.

Starters for the Bears that day were Wally Byrom, Red Tyson, Corbett Williamson, Candler Hicks, Roger Dodd, Oran Curry, George Rosich, Al Owen, Ed Varner, Don Lockert, and Billy Smith. Substitutes were Manny Mamalakis, Paul Ward, Tom Porter, J. C. Thomas, Opie Gilbert, Henry Allen, Carl Altonen, Allan Bloodworth, Peter Demetros, John Hemple, Ewing Edge, Wright Bazemore, and John Fitzpatrick.

Mercer picked up 341 yards rushing. Al Owen accounted for 146 yards in sixteen attempts for a 9.1 average. In all, eight men were ball carriers that day. J. C. Thomas and Carl Altonen had a great day blocking and tackling.

1936

There were some changes in the coaching staff prior to the 1936 season. Lake Russell returned as head coach and had John "Cotton" Harrison and Gene NeSmith as his assistants. Carter Townsend left following the 1935 season to coach at Lanier High School.

Roger Dodd captained the 1936 team, and he was the first permanent captain in several years. Fifteen lettermen were back, including Dodd, Manuel Mamalakis, Wright Bazemore, Allan Bloodworth, Edwin Varner, Ewing Edge, Bubber Lawrence, Billy Smith, Phil Chastain, Al Owen, Jack Morris, Johnny Fitzpatrick, Candler Hicks, George Rosich, and Red Tyson. Sophomores included Vernon Robinson, Grady Rainey, Jess Corona, Johnny Mattox, Jack Mehrens, John Sutherland, Marion Hagler, and Hunter Hurst. Junior college transfers were Martin Kumse, Felix Johnson, Art Barrow, and Bill Bryant.

Mercer 40, South Georgia Teachers 0

South Georgia Teachers College from Statesboro, Georgia, was first on the 1936 schedule for the Bears. The Teachers were coached by former Mercer great Crook Smith. Mercer got within scoring position in the early minutes of the game but fumbled on the five-yard line.

This, however, was only a slight delay as Mercer started over at the thirty-five yard line a short time later. Bloodworth ran for eight around end and then passed to Varner for eighteen yards and a first down at the nine-yard line on the next play. Al Owen then went over in two plays for a touchdown.

Near the end of the first quarter, Owen ran for nineteen yards off tackle to put the ball in scoring position. Billy Smith followed with a thirteen-yard sprint for a touchdown. Minutes before the half Jack Morris raced for twelve yards after Bazemore got twelve around left end. Bazemore then carried the ball seven yards off tackle. Morris followed with a sixteen-yard jaunt around end for a touchdown. Bazemore converted, and Mercer led 19-0 at the half.

Russell, substituting freely, used a different team in each of the first and second quarters. The first unit started the third quarter, and Varner got a touchdown on a sixty-four-yard run. Later an eighty-yard drive resulted in a touchdown in five plays. Owen ran for twenty, Smith got thirteen, and Bloodworth broke free for thirty-eight yards around end. Bloodworth lost three yards on the next play but recovered on the second down for ten yards and a touchdown.

In the fourth quarter Morris ran for sixteen yards for a first down. Smith got five up the middle, but Art Barrow was held for no gain. Smith then got twenty-seven through center, and Bazemore broke through tackle for thirteen more yards. Morris climaxed the drive with a spurt around end for fourteen yards and the touchdown. In all, six touchdowns and four extra points were scored against the Teachers. Bloodworth and Bazemore had two conversions each.

Mercer 6, Georgia 15

Mercer took on Georgia in 1936 in Athens before 7,000 fans and played the Bulldogs a close game. Georgia scored first after starting at the twenty-four-yard line as Hartman passed to Anderson for a touchdown. The big runs in the drive were twenty-seven yards around right end by Anderson and a twenty-six-yard run around left end by Jones.

After four exchanges of the ball, Mercer sent in a new team, with the exception of Marion Hagler. Georgia then drove to the Mercer eighteen-yard line. After Georgia was penalized fifteen yards, Green ran for fourteen yards. Tensley added fifteen more for a touchdown and a 13-0 lead.

Hagler of Mercer kicked off, and Robinson recovered a fumble on the Georgia forty-one for Mercer. Bloodworth ran twenty-seven yards around left end to the Georgia twenty-yard line. The Bulldogs were then penalized five yards. Bloodworth lost two yards but gained the yards back on the next play. Georgia was penalized five yards again, and Bloodworth ran for a first down on the Georgia fourteen-yard line. The drive halted on Bloodworth's fumble on the next play, and Troutman recovered for Georgia on the eighteen-yard line.

Green, for Georgia, got three yards on the first down. Green then started around left end but lost the ball in the air and Bloodworth caught it and ran to the Georgia thirty-six yard line. After that great play, Bloodworth, Owen, and

Morris drove for a first down at the Georgia fifteen-yard line. Owen ran for five yards, and Bloodworth added five more to give Mercer a first down at the Georgia five-yard line. Allan Bloodworth passed to Owen, and he scored the seventh touchdown in history for Mercer against Georgia. Georgia took the kickoff, and Jim Cavan ran twenty-three yards for Georgia as the half ended.

In the second half Hartman punted to the Mercer five-yard line, and Bloodworth returned the ball fifteen yards to the twenty. Bloodworth then cut through center for ten yards, and Morris added three yards off tackle. After one incomplete pass, Bloodworth hit Rosich with a twenty-six yard aerial. Morris was held for no gain, and then Owen fumbled and Georgia got the ball back on the fifty-yard line.

Mercer got it right back as Kumse intercepted at the Mercer forty-four. Two plays later Hartman intercepted on the Georgia forty-eight. Eight plays later Hartman punted to the one-foot line. Bloodworth attempted to punt back, but the punt was blocked by Hall. Haywood made the tackle to give Georgia a safety for the 15-6 score.

Hunter Hurst, who had seen little action up to this game, played more than anyone else after replacing Mamalakis on the opening kickoff. Hurst later had a career in the U. S. Marine Corps and retired recently after reaching the rank of general.

Georgia had twelve first downs and 305 yards total, while Mercer got nine first downs and 166 yards. The defense for Mercer played well and forced Georgia to punt nine times.

Mercer 20, Oglethorpe 6

Mercer played a game in Albany, Georgia, before 6,000 fans and defeated Oglethorpe for the seventh consecutive time by a 20-6 score. Al Owen missed the game with malaria, Varner had a sprained ankle, and Mamalakis was out with a bruised chest.

The remaining twenty-two men made it rough for the Petrels after a slow start as Jack Morris fumbled at midfield shortly after the kickoff, and Oglethorpe recovered. Jack Puryear ran for thirty-five yards. A pass then put the ball on the Mercer three-yard line. A second pass resulted in a touchdown, and Oglethorpe led 6-0.

Mercer got into the action as Roger Dodd recovered a fumble. Bazemore, Smith, and Bloodworth alternated carrying the ball, and Bloodworth scored from the eight-yard line. Later Bloodworth tried a twenty-two-yard field goal but missed.

In the fourth quarter Mercer got the second touchdown when Billy Smith scored before the home folks on a one-yard plunge. Bloodworth went forty-five yards for the last touchdown with Corona leading the way. Bloodworth also added two extra points.

Mercer 0, Birmingham Southern 6

A rapidly improving Birmingham Southern team fought Mercer for a 6-0 win in Birmingham on 10 October 1936. The hard-charging Panther line allowed Mercer only one first down, and this came in the closing minutes of the game.

Mercer got into Southern territory only twice. Bloodworth returned a punt twenty-five yards to the Southern thirty-two, and Al Owen intercepted a pass and went to the Birmingham Southern forty-two, but both drives failed.

Southern scored on a flat pass for eleven yards, but the Bears threw the Panthers back from the goal on three other occasions. Outstanding defensively for Mercer were Marion Hagler, Grady Rainey, and Billy Smith. Smith tore a ligament in his right knee and was treated by trainer Max Knolls. Birmingham Southern ran up eleven first downs and 206 yards, while Mercer was able to get only twenty-seven yards total.

Mercer 0, Howard 0

Mercer and Howard battled to a 0-0 tie before 3,500 fans in Macon on a Friday night. Bloodworth went fifty-six yards on a punt, but the play was called back when Mercer was penalized for clipping. Mercer got to the Howard twenty on a pass but couldn't get any closer during the game.

John Wilcox of Howard intercepted four Mercer passes and carried the ball to the Mercer five-yard line one time, but Howard could not put the ball over against the strong Bear defense. Wright Bazemore was described as a savage tackler for Mercer.

Mercer 9, Furman 20

Furman ran over the Bears 20-9 in Macon before a Homecoming crowd, picking up twenty-two first downs while allowing Mercer only three. Furman scored in the first two minutes as June Scott returned the kickoff to the Mercer twelve, a run of forty-eight yards. Joe Foster from Griffin, Georgia, carried the ball four times for a first down at the Mercer two-yard line. Joe Watson then scored on a double reverse.

The Bears fought uphill all day, throwing Furman back from the goal three times. Bloodworth scored to tie the game as Jack Morris batted a Furman ball into his arms, and he raced ninety-six yards for a touchdown, and then Bloodworth converted.

In the third quarter Furman drove eighty-one yards for a touchdown, scoring on a twenty-five yard pass. Captain Bob King of Furman was outstanding during the game as he made two extra points, caught several passes, and made numerous tackles. Candler Hicks intercepted a pass on the Mercer five-yard line and ran twelve yards before he lateraled to Bloodworth. Bloodworth took the lateral and went forty-four yards to the Furman thirty-nine.

It just wasn't Mercer's day as Furman scored twice in the third quarter. Mercer's safety was the result of a fumble in the end zone by a Furman back.

Mercer 0, Chattanooga 6

On a wet and soggy field in Chattanooga for Homecoming, Mercer dropped a 6-0 game to the Moccasins. It was a scoreless game through midway in the fourth quarter as Mercer fought off Chattanooga's attempts to score.

Dodd, Rosich, Hicks, Rainey, and Hagler were tough in the line, while Bazemore and Morris were outstanding in the secondary. Every player fought hard and contributed to the defense for the Bears. Jack Morris knocked down two passes that would have gone for touchdowns. Rosich recovered a fumble on the Mercer nine-yard line, and Bazemore intercepted a pass on the Mercer five-yard line.

Chattanooga scored as Scott returned a punt thirty yards to the Mercer thirty-eight. A successful pass put the ball on the Mercer twenty-seven. Another pass carried down to the Mercer thirteen-yard line and Bazemore made both stops. Morris and Rosich knocked down a third down pass at the Mercer two-yard line. Scott lost two yards after being hit by Bazemore and Rod Tuach, but on the next play Scott scored from the two-yard line.

Mercer 20, Presbyterian 6

Mercer came up with a good game against Presbyterian and rolled up 454 yards rushing to win 20-6. Bloodworth got 160 yards in twenty-one carries, although he didn't play in the third period. Owen matched this distance on twenty carries for a tremendous double effort.

Mercer didn't score until the third quarter when Owen sped sixty-five yards to tie the score 6-6. This touchdown came after two touchdowns were called back. Billy Smith broke loose for a touchdown later to put Mercer ahead 13-6 as Bloodworth converted.

In the final few minutes Wright Bazemore raced sixty-seven yards from scrimmage for the last touchdown. Bloodworth kicked true again for the 20-6 victory. Owen and Bloodworth had great days rushing and ripped off long yardage. Owen had runs of sixty-five, thirty, and sixteen yards while Bloodworth had six runs of ten yards or better in this well-played game. Early in the action Roger Dodd suffered a knee injury. Red Tyson and Candler Hicks played outstanding defense for the Bears.

Mercer 0, Miami 13

Mercer played in the Orange Bowl against the University of Miami before a crowd of 8,000 on 30 November 1936. Miami was unbeaten, and the Bears made it tough for the Hurricanes before bowing 13-0 in a game played in severe heat. Miami got a sixty-eight-yard punt return for a touchdown. The score came just before the half when the runner broke free after being surrounded by a group of tacklers. Until this touchdown, Miami had gotten beyond midfield just once against this rugged Mercer defense.

Bloodworth on one occasion had a fifty-two-yard punt to the Miami one-yard line. In the third quarter Mercer pushed Miami back three times in a great defensive battle. In the fourth quarter Eddie Deen had two runs of thirty-five yards to put the ball in scoring territory. He scored for Miami from the two-yard line.

Mercer charged the Hurricane goal late in the game with Bazemore getting ten yards. Bloodworth added another first down, and Owen picked up twenty-two yards for a third first down, but the attack was stopped. Mercer made three serious attempts to score in the last half but couldn't push the ball across. This game was one of the best of the season.

Mercer 0, Mississippi State 32

The final game of the season pitted Mercer against Mississippi State in Starkville, Mississippi. Mercer had played the Maroons in 1907 and 1914 and lost both games by shutouts. The 1936 battle was no exception. The win for State was not easy as the Bears put up a rugged battle. Bloodworth aided greatly by averaging forty-eight yards on seven punts, with one going for seventy-six yards. He also kept the Maroons uneasy with his punt returns. In the third quarter he raced forty-one yards on a punt return to start Mercer toward the State goal.

Mercer held State during the first period, but superior strength and depth took a toll. Russell could make only ten substitutions while Frank Cariedo of State used three teams. State scored two touchdowns in the second quarter, two in the third, and one in the fourth. In the second half the Tigers scored after driving to the Mercer sixteen-yard line and losing the ball. Walters blocked a Bloodworth punt and caught it for the touchdown.

Bloodworth's punting and tackling were outstanding for Mercer. Phil Chastain, sophomore center, intercepted a pass with one hand and returned it thirty-eight yards to the Mississippi thirty-one in a big defensive play. The Maroons took advantage of the Bears by running for twenty first downs and 369 yards. Mercer was held to five first downs and seventy yards rushing.

The Bears ended the season with a record of three wins, six losses and one tie as Lake Russell completed his eighth season at the helm of Mercer football. Allan Bloodworth, a standout performer for the Bears for three years, made the All-Dixie team at quarterback and George "Red" Tyson made the All-Dixie second team. It was during the 1936 season that Allan Bloodworth punted a football from the top of the Capitol theatre to a crowd of fans below. The ball had been autographed by the members of the very successful 1932 team, and George May caught it. The twelve men graduating from the 1936 team were George Rosich, W. H. Bryant, Jack Mehrens, George Tyson, Roger Dodd, Manuel Mamalakis, Marion Hagler, Candler Hicks, Jack Morris, Billy Smith, Jessie Corona, and Felix Johnson.

1937

The 1937 team had ten sophomores on the squad of thirty-one players as the season opened. Seventeen boys were from Georgia, while the remainder were from out of the state. Perry Hill, an Indian halfback from Kansas, left the squad and went home because he was homesick. Lake Russell was assisted by Cotton Harrison, who worked with the line, and Joe Dougherty, who coached the backs. Rufus Sams was the manager. The freshman team was coached by Billy Smith and Red Tyson.

Mercer 77, South Georgia Teachers 0

The first game of the season brought South Georgia Teachers College from Statesboro, Georgia, up for a night game on 24 September 1937. It was more like a track meet than a football game. The Bears scored twelve touchdowns while amassing a record 580 yards rushing and fifty-four yards passing. The Mercer backs scored almost at will as five different men crossed the goal line.

All twenty-four men saw action, and the starters were listed as Neal Allen, Henry Lawrence, James Fitzpatrick, Ewing Edge, Grady Rainey, Martin Kumse, Phil Chastain, Wright Bazemore, Al Owen, De Vernon Robinson, and Rod Tuach. Others seeing action on opening day were Tom Steadman, Pete Demetros, Max Fair, Wimpy Jones, Al Gerhardt, Hunter Hurst, Gordon Lashbrook, Grady Gillon, A. F. Harrison, Roscoe Cline, Johnny Mattox, Pepper Martin, and James Landrum.

The game started as Bazemore capped a drive of fifty-five yards in five plays with a thirty-yard touchdown run. Owen followed with a forty-one yard score, then added another from thirteen yards out. Bazemore sped seventy yards for a touchdown, and Cline came back with a seventy-seven-yarder for six points. Bazemore followed with the sixth touchdown on a fifty-nine-yard run. Owen reentered the race for the goal and scored on a fifteen-yarder and a fifty-three-yarder. John Mattox scored on short runs of five and three yards for scores number nine and ten. James Landrum came in and scored from the thirteen-yard line after Steadman had recovered a fumble. Wright Bazemore capped the scoring with a thirty-four-yard run.

The Teachers were not strong enough to fight the Bears and gained only one yard rushing while getting forty-five yards through the air. Bazemore ran ten times for 205 yards, followed by Owen with 163 yards in 12 trips. Cline averaged twenty yards on four carries.

Mercer 0, Georgia Tech 28

The Yellow Jackets of Georgia Tech stung the Bears by a score of 28-0 in Atlanta before a crowd of 10,000 in the second game of the season. Tech, with a powerful attack, had 237 yards rushing and 151 passing. The Jackets put the game out of reach with four quick first-half touchdowns. One score came as an Owen quick-kick was blocked for a touchdown.

For Mercer Johnny Mattox, Neal Allen, Captain Jim Fitzpatrick, and Phil Chastain were the heroes on defense, while Al Owen and Gordon Lashbrook intercepted passes to halt the Jackets. The Mercer offense just couldn't move against the strong forward wall of Georgia Tech. Although Mercer often seemed ready to break into the scoring column, the closest threat went to the Tech twenty-six-yard line. Bazemore tried the usually successful reverse play nine times but never got away. Coach Alexander of Tech used three teams, while Russell called upon twenty-three of his twenty-five-man squad.

Mercer 0, Howard 7

In his long tenure as coach of the Bears, Lake Russell and his teams always had a difficult time with the Bulldogs of Howard in Alabama. The rain and slippery turf, particularly in the first half, kept both teams from scoring. Mercer's vicious tackling caused Johnson, a starting halfback, to be replaced by Clyde White, a 155-pound back. White carried for 104 yards in the second half in fifteen runs to lead a charge for Howard.

Mercer threatened several times, and in the first quarter went ninety yards to the Howard five-yard line, only to fumble the ball away. In the third quarter Howard drove to the Mercer one-yard line, but Mercer recovered a fumble to stop the threat.

Finally, Arthur Harrison took a high pass from center while attempting to punt. He missed the ball completely as he attempted to kick it, and Boyce Smith recovered for a Howard touchdown. Dougherty made the extra point, and Howard led 7-0. Mercer pushed back but could not score. Cline and

Gillon came into the game and took the ball into scoring territory. Cline passed beautifully in the closing minutes, but the ball was batted out of the hands of Mercer receivers four times to save touchdowns.

Mercer 0, Birmingham Southern 7

The third loss of the 1937 season came after Mercer outplayed Birmingham Southern for fifty-seven minutes before a crowd of 6,000 in Columbus, Georgia. Tuach hit a four-yard punt to the Mercer thirty-three yard line following a twelve yard pass play. McMichael of Southern lofted a pass to his receiver, who caught the ball and then fumbled it out of the end zone for a touchdown. Mercer drove to the Southern three in the last minute but lost the ball. Spec Landrum was outstanding in the drive.

Mercer had fifty-nine running plays, while Birmingham Southern had only twenty-five. In all, Mercer got 200 yards on fourteen first downs, while the Panthers had eighty-three yards on eight first downs. Owen led Mercer ballcarriers with seventy-six yards in seventeen attempts. Bazemore ran the ball twenty-six times for sixty-four yards.

Mercer 0, Georgia 19

The Bulldogs of Georgia expected an easy game against the struggling Mercer Bears, but Coach Harry Mehre had to use his regulars until the last minutes of the fourth quarter to win 19-0. Mercer threatened seriously in the first few minutes, and the Dogs knew it would be a full day's work.

In the third quarter Mercer ran up six first downs to one for Georgia and went seventy-two yards, only to be halted at the three-yard line. This was one of the most inspired games in years for the Bears.

In the second half Georgia got on the board as Vassa Cate raced eighty-five yards on the kickoff. In the fourth quarter Oliver Hunnicutt scored from the two-yard line after a fifty-seven yard march which had begun with an interception by Troutman.

There were many outstanding players for Mercer, and the starters played most of the game. Mercer used only seven subs. Five of these came into the game in the last two minutes. Chastain played sixty minutes, got a broken tooth and a cut on his lip, and was outstanding on defense. Mattox, Bazemore, Kumse, and Rainey were also tough for the Bears that day. Allen, Fitzpatrick, and Bazemore were sixty-minute men.

Al Owen, with eighty-seven yards in twenty-two attempts, was the leading rusher for Mercer. Bazemore followed with fifty-seven yards in eight runs. In all, Mercer had 162 yards compared to 306 yards for Georgia. Mercer hit on five out of nine passes for forty-two yards, while Georgia failed to complete a pass. Rainey, Chastain, and Bazemore led in tackles for the Bears.

Mercer 13, Oglethorpe 6

Mercer got back on the winning track by defeating the Oglethorpe Petrels in Macon 13-6 as Johnny Mattox and Phil Chastain led a determined defense. Chastain intercepted a pass early in the first quarter and returned it thirteen yards to the Oglethorpe fifteen-yard line. Owen ran for two yards, followed by a seven-yard dash by Bazemore. On the third down Owen blasted off tackle for six yards and a touchdown. Bazemore converted, and Mercer led 7-0.

Later, Rod Tuach recovered a fumble at the Oglethorpe thirty, but a third-down Landrum pass was intercepted by Oglethorpe to stop the drive. Starting at the twenty-one, the Petrels then drove seventy-nine yards to score in nine plays. Rainey blocked the extra point to preserve the lead for Mercer.

Just before the half ended, Owen fumbled at the Oglethorpe forty-nine yard line. Schwabe got off a forty-seven yard run to the Mercer two-yard line, where he was hauled down by Bazemore in a dramatic chase. King got one yard, but the half ended before the Petrels could score.

Mercer went on offense again as Cline returned the kickoff fourteen yards. Cline and Mattox, the principal ball carriers, took the ball into Oglethorpe territory. During the drive Owen passed to Steadman for nine yards and later hit Allen for seventeen. Bazemore scored a touchdown from the six-yard line on a reverse as Mercer ran thirteen plays and earned five first downs.

The Petrels started from the twenty-one and ran three plays before the ball was intercepted for Mercer by Chastain. Mercer began at the Oglethorpe forty-six and picked up thirty-six yards on ten plays, but finally lost the ball on downs. It was Mercer all the way as the Bears ran fifty-five plays and gained 200 yards rushing and forty passing. Bazemore continued his assault on ball carriers as he led the Bears in individual tackles.

Mercer 25, Presbyterian 13

The Bears traveled to Clinton, South Carolina, to play winless Presbyterian, which had scored only once during the season. Mercer got a touchdown on the second series of plays as Owen passed to Lawrence for twenty-six yards to the Presbyterian thirty-yard line. Owen then ran for sixteen yards, followed by a fourteen-yard touchdown sprint by Tuach. Mercer led 6-0.

After another exchange, Mercer started again at the Blue Hose forty-four yard line. Owen got twenty-two on two plays, but Mercer was penalized fifteen yards. Bazemore and Owen then carried the ball to the goal, and Owen scored on a four-yard run. In the series Bazemore gained twenty yards on two carries while Owen got nineteen on three runs. Bazemore missed his second conversion attempt, and Mercer led 12-0.

Several plays later Mercer was at the twenty and was penalized fifteen yards to the five-yard line. Tuach hit a short punt, and Presbyterian recovered at the Mercer seventeen-yard line. After three incomplete passes, the fourth was caught at the five-yard line. On the next down Dennard scored to make the count 12-7. Mercer began again at the twenty. Two plays later Tuach's punt was blocked, and Presbyterian had the ball at the Mercer seven-yard line. Dennard went the seven yards on the first play. The winless Blue Hose now led 13-12, and Mercer couldn't put together a sustained drive for the remainder of the half.

Presbyterian returned after the half with new spirit but had a punt partially blocked on the thirty-one, and Mercer recovered. On the first play Owen got thirteen yards at end, and Tuach added five yards at center. Owen then went back to pass, got trapped, but then ran thirteen yards for a touchdown. Bazemore missed his third extra point attempt, but Mercer led 18-13.

After a pass interception by each team, Mercer had the ball at the Presbyterian forty-three. Owen passed to Allen for twenty-eight yards. On the fourth down Owen passed to Allen again for thirteen yards and a touchdown. Bazemore hit the extra point for a 25-13 score.

Pete Demetros intercepted a pass and returned it twelve yards, but Mercer fumbled. Phil Chastain intercepted and returned the ball to the Presbyterian forty-yard line. Owen then passed to Allen for twenty-nine yards, but Dennard intercepted the next pass. On the second down Bazemore intercepted again. Owen then ran the ball three times for thirty-eight, eleven, and fifteen yards; and the game ended.

Starters that day for the Bears were Neal Allen, Bubba Lawrence, John Fitzpatrick, Al Gerhardt, Rainey, Kumse, Chastain, Owen, Bazemore, Robinson, and Tuach. Al Owen had a great day for the Bears as he passed twenty-six yards to Lawrence and ran sixteen yards to put the ball in position for the first touchdown. He ran forty-one yards in five plays for the second touchdown. He then went thirteen yards for the third while attempting to pass. He passed twice to Allen for a final touchdown. In all, he had 186 yards on twenty-seven carries for a seven-yard average. He also returned three punts for fifty-two yards, and ended the day completing three of eight passes for sixty-two yards.

Mercer 20, Tampa 0

The Bears fought the Spartans of Tampa in the Sunshine State and came back with a 20-0 victory as Al Owen continued his assault on the opposition. Owen carried the ball a record forty-eight times and earned 219 yards. Tampa ran sixteen plays during the game and had one yard rushing and twenty-three yards passing.

Red Robinson, Martin Kumse, Grady Rainey, and Neal Allen blocked and tackled well and were outstanding defensively. The team blocking was exceptional, and Owen's play was superb as he scored two touchdowns. He scored a third running fifty-five yards, but it was called back because of an offside penalty. Bazemore scored the other touchdown and added two extra points.

Phil Chastain played all but two minutes in spite of a collarbone injury from the Presbyterian game. Rod Tuach had also been hurt in that game. In a rare quote about the play of an individual, Russell said, "Al Owen has reached a great peak. Nobody has stopped him this season. The way he was running against Tampa, he could have made Macon by sunup."

Mercer 7, Chattanooga 19

The final game of the season found Mercer suffering from injuries as Chattanooga served as host. The Bears arrived in Chattanooga and rested before the game at the Key Hotel, which was once a hideout for the John Dillinger gang.

The Moccasins were the bad guys that day and quickly found that Chastain was playing with injuries. Chastain was not able to tackle due to a dislocated shoulder, but he had to stay in the lineup because he was the only center on the squad. Chattanooga took advantage of his injury and drove at him repeatedly and with determination.

Mercer got one touchdown on a pass from Owen to Bazemore and Bazemore converted. Chattanooga scored one touchdown on a pass. The defenders on this play were Lawrence and Robinson. During the play, Lawrence stumbled and fell on the bank, and Robinson fell into a ditch. Leading the Moccasin runners were Scott on four runs for ninety-eight yards and Nardon with ninety yards in five plays, all going through the middle.

Mercer played well, but injuries hurt the Bears' chances of having a winning season, as Chattanooga won 19-7. Rod Tuach played outstanding defense and booted one punt for seventy-five yards from his own ten-yard line.

Lake Russell felt that the 1937 team had one of the strongest offensive punches of all times. Owen led the team with 890 yards in eight games on 169 carries. He also accounted for 331 yards on twenty-seven passes for a total of 1221 yards for the season. Russell had now been the Bear mentor longer than any other coach. His teams had established a record of thirty-three wins, thirty-six losses and five ties. His teams had scored 900 points while allowing the opposition 747.

1938

In the 1938 season Grady Rainey was elected captain of a team that consisted of four seniors, six juniors, and twenty sophomores. Rod Tuach was lost for the season due to injuries, and Vernon Robinson left Mercer to enter medical school. Lake Russell had Joe Dougherty coaching the backs, and Gordon Reddick returned to Mercer to coach the line.

Mercer 14, Wofford 0

Although fifteen men suffered with ptomaine poisoning before the Wofford game, the Bears triumphed 14-0. Earl Lewis, Mercer's sophomore punter, missed the opener because of a knee injury. The Bears opened the season with a starting line-up that consisted of Allen, Lawrence, Jones, Gerhardt, Rainey, Alex Tannas, Horace Richter, Spec Landrum, Art Pledger, C. W. Howland, and John Mattox. Of these men, Tannas, Richter, Pledger, and Howland were sophomores. In all, thirty men, one of the biggest squads in recent times, saw action.

Art Pledger played outstanding ball and intercepted a pass. Mattox also made an interception. Neal Allen recovered a fumble on the second play after the kickoff, and Landrum passed to Allen for fifteen yards on the first down. Allen then went ten yards on an end-around for a touchdown. Pledger converted for a 7-0 lead. The second score came as Landrum returned a punt fifty-one yards for a touchdown in the second quarter. Grady Gillon converted for the 14-0 score.

Mercer earned eight first downs, with five coming in the first quarter and three in the third. In the second quarter there were thirteen punts between the teams as Wofford ran only thirteen plays. Mercer got 121 yards with Howland earning forty-three, Mattox thirty-four, and Landrum adding twenty-seven.

Mercer 0, Georgia Tech 19

Georgia Tech eased by the Bears 19-0 in Atlanta as Tech scored on a four-yard run by Gibson just minutes before the half. Tech scored in the second half when Landrum's pass was intercepted by Howard Ector at the Mercer thirty-nine and was returned for a touchdown. The final touchdown came on a short run by Bartlett with Buck Shaw dropkicking the extra point.

Mercer had a difficult time on the ground, gaining a net two yards while Tech got 163 yards rushing and 106 passing. It was not easy for Tech, though, as the Jackets were forced to punt nine times. The Bears held the Jacket backs for no gain on eight occasions and dropped them for losses twice.

Neal Allen, playing although his father had died the night before, was outstanding on defense, and he made twenty tackles. Jones, Pride, Gerhardt, Hendricks, Lawrence, Cline, and Paulk played outstanding defense.

Mercer 19, Georgia 28

Mercer scored more points on Georgia in the 1938 game than ever before. In fact, only forty points had been scored on the Bulldogs in the nineteen previous games and the Bears got nineteen in a close 28-19 defeat. Joel Hunt was head coach of Georgia, and Wally Butts coached the line. Georgia had fifty-nine running plays for 251 net yards as they lost twenty-two on five runs.

The game started with the ball on the twenty-yard line, where the Bulldogs picked up a first down in two plays. Three plays later, Hise punted to Mercer on the forty-seven. The Mercer backs got nothing on two attempts, and Pledger punted to the Georgia nineteen, where the tackle was made by Allen. Hise punted on the first down, and Spec Landrum took the punt and sped sixty yards for a touchdown. Pledger converted to make the score 7-0.

Pledger kicked off and Fordham ran for eight yards, but Hise was hit for a one-yard loss by Tannas. Hise then fumbled, and Howland recovered at the Mercer forty-five. Mattox sprinted for ten yards for Mercer, but fumbled and Georgia got the ball back.

Later Georgia started at the Mercer forty, and Fordham and Hise took the ball to the Mercer twelve-yard line. The Georgia runners were then stopped in their tracks three straight times by Rainey. Tannas blasted Fordham at the Mercer one-yard line, and Mercer held. Rainey, for his continually aggressive defense during the game, was regarded by sports writer Morgan Black as one of the greatest guards he had ever seen.

Georgia scored after starting from the Mercer twenty-seven as Mims, a substitute back, set up the touchdown with a twenty-three-yard run. Fordham scored the touchdown and Badgett converted for a 7-7 tie. Following this score, a new team came in for Mercer, and Georgia started from the twenty-nine-yard line. Cate got thirty-five to help move the ball to Mercer's twenty-six-yard line. On the first down Hunnicutt was stopped. A Mims pass then went incomplete, but Cate ran for twelve yards to the Mercer fourteen on the third down. Seven plays later Hise scored, and the extra point put Georgia ahead 14-7. Pledger passed to Paulk for a twelve-yard gain, but the Mercer drive was stopped by an interception by Georgia just before the half.

Mercer returned after the half with new determination and stopped Georgia on two series. Pledger punted after Mercer couldn't move, and Matthews returned the punt twelve yards. On the next play Mims passed to Eldredge, who sped fifty-five yards for a touchdown. Badgett toed the extra point for a 21-7 lead.

In the fourth quarter Cate was hit for a ten-yard loss, but he recovered and got fourteen yards with the Statue of Liberty play on the next down. Four plays later Hunnicutt went one yard for a touchdown. Georgia led 28-7 with the conversion.

Pledger started passing after the first play lost nine yards. He hit Davis for a twenty-one yard gain on the second down. Howland lost five yards, but Veo Yon got eleven on the second down. Pledger then had a pass intercepted by Mims at the Georgia twelve-yard line. After two plays and minus two yards, Georgia attempted to punt on the third down. Davis and Gerhardt partially blocked Mims's punt, and Mercer recovered. Pledger passed to Bob Hendry for fifteen yards on a fake reverse. Gillon lost four, but on the fourth down Pledger passed to Davis for a touchdown. The score was 28-13 with four minutes to play.

Georgia started from the twenty-five, but after stops by Richter, Lawrence, and Slappey, Mims punted, and Mercer got the ball at the fifty-yard line. Pledger ran for fifteen yards after going back to pass. With one minute left, Yon got three yards, then Pledger raced twenty-two yards with twenty seconds left on the clock. Landrum then lofted a twenty-five yard pass to Davis for the final touchdown to make the score 28-19. Martin Kumse recovered the ball on the kickoff as time ran out.

The entire Mercer team played well. Rainey, Paulk, Landrum, Davis, and Allen were particularly outstanding. The Bears had a good day passing as six of ten were completed for ninety yards against the strong Georgia team.

Mercer 0, Tulane 51

Tulane proved much too tough for the Bears the next weekend as the Green Wave ran up 489 yards rushing and sixty-one yards passing for a staggering twenty-seven first downs. Mercer had only twenty-eight yards rushing and made five first downs in the 51-0 romp. Tulane scored in every quarter to crush the Bears.

Mercer 33, Oglethorpe 7

Oglethorpe fell for the ninth and last time to the Bears by a score of 33-7 in a game that was statistically close. After Pledger had returned the kickoff thirty yards, Landrum got nine yards on the first down. Mattox then sprinted off tackle for fifteen, and Oglethorpe was penalized five yards. On the next play Landrum sprinted thirty-four yards for a touchdown to give Mercer a 6-0 lead.

Three series later from the thirty-four, Mercer got two runs for four yards from Landrum, and Howland followed with fifteen yards on the third down. After the first two downs netted no gain, Landrum raced thirty yards around end to put the ball on the Oglethorpe sixteen-yard line. Mattox failed to gain, and Mercer was pushed back to the thirty on a penalty. Landrum tried a pass on the first down, but it went incomplete. On the second down Pledger passed to Howland for thirty yards and a touchdown. Pledger converted, and Mercer led 13-0.

A new team then came into the game, and Oglethorpe started again. Forkner got thirty-nine yards before being stopped by Bob Smith. Three plays later Oglethorpe had a first down at the Mercer fourteen, but Kelly lost one yard on a tackle by Plunkett. George lost two yards, and Presley was hit for a three-yard loss by Bud Love. The Mercer defense came to life and took over the ball on the twenty-one-yard line. Two exchanges later Kelly ran sixty yards for Oglethorpe on a trick reverse and was stopped by Paulk at the Mercer ten-yard line. Tannas and Howland led the defense, and Mercer took over once again at the Mercer three-yard line.

Later Landrum went thirteen yards from the Oglethorpe thirty-eight, followed by Mattox with a two-yard gain. Howland lost six yards. Landrum ran for two yards, then passed to Howland for twenty-four yards to the Oglethorpe three-yard line. It took three plays, but Yon ran over for a touchdown, and Pledger converted for a 20-0 score.

Oglethorpe took the ball on the thirty-five following the kickoff. Kelly lost six yards on two plays before George ran for eleven. On the fourth down a Kelly punt was blocked, and Gerhardt picked it up and sped twenty-five yards for a touchdown. Later an Oglethorpe punt was partially blocked, and Mercer had the ball at the forty-four yard line. Hendry got two yards, then Oglethorpe was penalized fifteen yards. Hendry passed to Cline for five yards. Cline then completed two consecutive passes to Davis for thirteen and fifteen yards with the last pass going for a touchdown. The extra point was blocked, but Cline picked it up at the twenty-eight-yard line and ran it across.

With Oglethorpe at the forty-three yard line, a pass was good for five yards. George then ran for thirteen yards on a triple reverse. Kelly tossed a lateral to Forkner who went thirty-six yards for a touchdown. The final score read 33-7.

Although Mercer got thirty-three points, the rushing yardage gained was 154 for Mercer and 159 for Oglethorpe. Allen was outstanding on defense and on punt coverage. Earl Lewis got into action for the first time and carried the ball for four yards on the last play of the game.

Mercer 28, Presbyterian 0

Mercer continued on the offensive ways with a 28-0 victory over Presbyterian College in a Homecoming game in Macon. Coach Russell used thirty-three players in the contest. This was the largest number of men to see action in recent years.

Mercer scored on the ninth play of the game as Dennard fumbled when he was hit by Allen and Lawrence. Rainey recovered on the Blue Hose fourteen-yard line. Cline ran for two yards, then passed twelve yards on the second down to Howland for a touchdown. Pledger converted.

Presbyterian threatened later as Thompson completed a pass to Sutton for twenty-four yards to the Mercer sixteen-yard line. Malcolm Thomas and Paul Davis took over and stopped the visitors on two downs and two passes fell incomplete.

In the second quarter Presbyterian ran one play and Mercer got the ball at the twenty-nine following a punt. Landrum ran three times for thirty yards, and Oglethorpe received two five-yard penalties. Mattox gained forty-two yards on five runs, and Landrum ran three yards to the Mercer one-yard line. Mattox broke over for the touchdown, and Pledger converted again.

Mercer was on the Presbyterian forty-three as the third quarter began. On the first play Landrum lost five yards, but Pledger then passed to Lawrence for seventeen yards and a first down. On the next play, Pledger hit Allen on a thirty-five yard strike for a touchdown. Pledger booted the extra point.

Presbyterian got the ball at the twenty, and Wenges ran for seventeen yards before falling in the open field. Three plays later Mercer had the ball at the thirty-five-yard line. Mercer ran nine plays with a Cline-to-Bob Alley pass good for five yards and a touchdown. Veo Yon booted the extra point for a 28-0 score. In the drive Pledger passed to Lawrence for thirteen yards and to Frank Pride for five yards. The big play was a twenty-three-yard run off tackle by Cline.

For the game Mercer had sixteen first downs with 163 yards rushing and eighty-eight yards passing. Pledger, with four of five completions, led the Mercer passers. Spec Landrum got to the game late because of illness in his family.

Mercer 21, Mississippi College 26

The Bears dropped another game to Mississippi College, a team they had never beaten, by a score of 26-21 in Macon before a crowd of 3,200. The Choctaws consistently befuddled the Bear defense with reverses during the game. The game was not close until the closing minutes when Mercer scored twice.

Mercer got on the scoreboard first as Frank Pride led the drive with forty yards on a reverse around left end. Pride started in place of the injured Howland. Pledger scored the touchdown and kicked the extra point for a 7-0 lead after Landrum and Pride had carried Mercer into scoring position.

Mississippi College scored from the Mercer thirty-four-yard line after Pledger had booted a short punt. Herrington then got nineteen and fifteen yards on reverses for the visitors. Majuse then scored from the one-yard line. The conversion tied the score at 7-7. In the third quarter the Choctaws scored on a reverse went seventy-five yards for a touchdown. In the fourth quarter a new Mercer team entered the game, and a Cline pass was intercepted at the fifty-yard line. On the first play Tadlock caught a twenty-five yard pass, but Mississippi was penalized fifteen yards. On the next play Hitt caught a pass for forty yards and a 26-7 lead.

Two series later Pledger passed to Love for four yards from the Mercer sixteen-yard line. After an incompletion Pledger passed to Cline for eleven yards and a first down. Yon then ran for two yards before Pledger passed to Paul Davis for a sixty-seven yard touchdown. Pledger hit the extra point, and Mississippi led 26-14. After an interception by the visitors, Richter got the ball back by recovering a fumble on the Mississippi thirty. Pledger threw two incomplete passes before connecting with Landrum for thirteen yards on the third down. After another incomplete pass, Pledger threw to Allen for a fifteen-yard touchdown. Pledger converted to make the final score 26-21.

Stanley Robinson, a former Mercer coach, was the Mississippi College mentor. Mercer outgained the Choctaws 333 yards to 294 but couldn't get enough points. The passing for the Bears was nine for twenty-three for 146 yards and two touchdowns. Through this game Mercer had gained 582 yards on passes. Thus far in the season thirty-nine of 101 passes were completed with the passers completing twenty of forty-six in the last three games.

Mercer 7, Chattanooga 9

The final game of the season was played with snow on the ground in Chattanooga with the Moccasins winning 9-7. Chattanooga had a 9-0 lead at the half. In the second half Landrum scored a touchdown, and Pledger converted. Actually the game was close, and Mercer could have won with a little luck. Mercer led in first downs 9-8. Two passes were dropped in the end zone in the final minutes of the game that would have meant victory. One pass came after Bill Jones had recovered a fumble on the Chattanooga twenty-four yard line.

Prior to this game Bobby Norris wrote in the *Macon Telegraph* on 24 November 1938 about the Chattanooga-Mercer series.

> Looking back on this Mercer-Chattanooga series now since Lake Russell succeeded Bernie Moore:
>
> In 1929 the Moccasins scored a touchdown on a fluke pass play in the third quarter to win 7-0. First downs and total yardage gained were about even. They played between the twenty-yard lines.
>
> The next year a safety in the opening period and a touchdown in the second quarter beat Brad Lamson's touch-

> down for the Bears and Chattanooga won 8 to 6. Probably the most spectacular game of the series in 1931 ended in a 27-19 triumph for the Moccasins. Ernie Zinkowski, Swede Olsson, and Tony Long scored touchdowns. Olsson fell on a punt behind the Chattanooga goal line which was blocked by Gordon Reddick, now assistant coach of the Bruins. First downs were all even.
>
> Mercer hit the high road of victory in 1932. Zinkowski scampered half the length of the field for a touchdown in the second period. Pinky Walden scored twice and Johnny Cimperman once in the fourth quarter and the Bears won 25 to 0, for the Dixie Conference title.
>
> The next year the team struggled in a mud battle. It was Mercer's greatest team. But it took a fourth quarter line plunge by Gerald McQuaig to subdue the rivals 7-0.
>
> It was a tie in 1934. Allan Bloodworth, the mighty midget, scored two touchdowns and kicked the extra point for a 13-13 draw. The Bears had an edge in the first downs 9-6. The last three years the Moccasins have dominated. Ed Varner galloped 40 yards for a touchdown and the Bruins led at the half 7-6, but lost the battle of 1935 by a score of 12-7. Mercer's luck reached rock bottom in the ball game.
>
> In 1936 the Moccasins scored in the fourth period to win, 6-0. Last year it was 19-7.

The 1938 season ended with a record of four wins and five losses as Mercer scored 122 points and the opponents got 147. Mercer gained 1537 total yards during the season and gave up 2261 yards. Landrum and Davis had four touchdowns, Allen had three, and Howland had two. Several others had one each. Captain Grady Rainey, Martin Kumse, Henry Lawrence, and Johnny Mattox graduated.

1939

The 1939 season consisted of a ten-game schedule, including Georgia, Alabama, and Tennessee. Lake Russell had Joe Dougherty as backfield coach and Bill Peters as line coach. Joe Kilgrow and Norman Whitter worked with the freshmen. The squad consisted of thirty-four men who were led by Captain William "Wimpy" Jones.

Mercer 12, Wofford 0

The opening game pitted Mercer against Wofford in Spartanburg, and the Bears triumphed 12-0 as Jack Richards and Bob Hendry scored touchdowns. In all, Mercer had eleven men carrying the ball with Yon, Pride, and Richards getting thirty-five, twenty-seven, and twenty-six of the 122 total yards rushing. Mercer connected on seven of fourteen passes for 122 yards. Wofford was held to minus-fourteen yards rushing and earned only twenty yards passing.

Sophomore Jack Richards passed and ran the ball in the third quarter for a touchdown after an eighty-five yard march. He passed twenty-three yards to Tom Heaton and then scored from the twelve-yard line on an off-tackle play.

Landrum was also effective passing as he hit Allen for twelve yards and Heaton for twenty-three. Bob Hendry scored the second touchdown. In all, Wofford ran eighteen plays against the stubborn defense and earned one first down. Wofford did slow the Bears somewhat by intercepting two passes.

Mercer 0, Presbyterian 7

Presbyterian retaliated for several defeats, by slipping by 7-0 in Macon as Mercer managed only eighty-eight yards rushing and twenty-eight yards passing. Presbyterian had six first downs and 112 yards total offense but managed to run forty-three plays while the Bears had only thirty-two.

It was not a day for the Bears as Presbyterian scored in the first quarter after Mercer had fumbled on the thirty-one yard line. Meisky hit Coleman for a forty-four yard touchdown and Coleman converted to account for all the scoring.

Mercer drove to the Blue Hose eleven in the third quarter, but a pass interception stopped the drive. Later Presbyterian fumbled on the eighteen and Pride recovered, but Landrum's pass was intercepted as the Bears tried to score. Thomas, Tannas, Jones, and Allen were outstanding in the losing battle.

In all, Richards had three passes intercepted. Yon lost a fumble to Presbyterian. Cline and Landrum had interceptions, and Landrum fumbled a punt. The luck was against Mercer that day as the alert Presbyterian defense took advantage of the mistakes to prevent the Bears from scoring.

Mercer 7, Carson-Newman 0

Carson-Newman fell 7-0 as Mercer ran up 295 yards rushing as twelve men carried the ball a total of fifty-nine times. Starting for Mercer were Neal Allen and Tom Heaton at end, Wimpy Jones and Al Gerhardt at tackle, Frank

Wary and Tom Yurasich at guard, Malcolm Thomas at center, with Art Pledger, Frank Pride, Spec Landrum, and Veo Yon in the backfield. Others getting into the game were Bob Hendry, Jack Richards, Alex Tannas, Bill Howland, Ellis Paulk, Quenton Plunkett, Tony Mazarek, Joe Dowd, Bud Love, Harry Karsznia, Horace Richter, Carl Stager, Bob Alley, Bob Smith, Tony Page, Jolly Dizadyk, Bob Dutton, and Ed Cassell.

Tony Page, Bob Dutton, and Carl Stager, three sophomores, sparked the victory in the fourth quarter. Mercer started on the twenty-four yard line and drove seventy-six yards in twelve plays to score. Page carried four times and gained nine yards. Stager picked up thirty-five yards on two runs. Dutton earned twenty-seven yards on six attempts and scored from the one-yard line. Pledger converted for the 7-0 score.

Carson-Newman used only fifteen men in the contest and drove once to the Mercer five-yard line but couldn't score. The Mercer backs had a difficult time holding the ball and fumbled nine times, losing four. Pledger lost three yards on kickoffs, and Landrum lost one. Pride, Howland, and Yon also fumbled, but the defense was tough against the visitors. Carson-Newman got only seventeen yards rushing and twenty-four passing for two first downs during the game. Bob Dutton led Mercer with forty-seven yards in nine carries. Stager had forty-four, Richards thirty-nine, Landrum thirty-eight, Pride thirty-six, and Yon thirty-four in a display of balanced running ability.

Mercer 0, Alabama 20

The Bears took on the Crimson Tide for the first time ever in a game in Tuscaloosa, Alabama. The Mercer line played outstanding against the Frank Thomas-coached team. Wary, Jones, Allen, and Thomas led the Bears. Cassell replaced Yurasich at right guard, while Cline was at halfback and Karsznia went in at fullback.

In the first quarter Alabama drove from the twenty-eight to the Mercer twenty-four, where Nelson fumbled and Malcolm Thomas recovered for Mercer. Mercer couldn't make any progress and Alabama finally got in Mercer territory at the forty-one and scored. The Tide rolled down the field with precision and ran ten straight plays for the touchdown. Spencer scored from the one-yard line, and Pig Davis booted the extra point.

Pride gained two yards just after the kickoff, and Alabama sent in a new team. After an exchange of punts, Mercer had the ball at the Alabama thirty. Landrum passed twelve yards to Pledger, then Landrum added five yards to the Alabama fifteen-yard line. Pride carried the ball four yards, and Landrum took the ball to the nine but was hurt on the play. Richards came in and lost five yards. Richards then connected with Pledger for one yard, followed by a two-yard run by Stager through center. On fourth down Richards's pass went incomplete over the end zone, and Alabama got the ball at the twenty-yard line.

The second half began as Nelson carried the kickoff back thirty-four yards for Alabama. Fifteen plays later Blackwell ran ten yards for a touchdown and a 13-0 lead. Allen returned the kickoff ten yards to the thirty-eight. Frank Pride raced eight yards, but then Mercer lost twenty-one yards on a bad snap from center. Blackwell blocked Pledger's punt, and Alabama recovered on the Mercer sixteen-yard line.

Five plays later Alabama led 20-0 after a touchdown and Davis's extra point. Mercer did not threaten again, but Alabama had one more scoring chance following a fumble at the Mercer fourteen-yard line. The Tide was able to get only seven yards, and Mercer took over for one last play. Seven Mercer backs managed only twenty-seven yards rushing against the strong Alabama line. Frank Pride gained seven yards in eight carries to lead the Bears.

Mercer 10, Birmingham Southern 0

Mercer defeated Birmingham Southern after three consecutive losses by a score of 10-0 in Macon. The Homecoming game attracted 4,500 fans and was the Panthers' last visit to Macon. Birmingham Southern dropped football following the 1939 season.

Tony Page, Frank Pride, Bob Dutton, and Spec Landrum ran the ball for Mercer during the first quarter but did not get into scoring territory. In the second quarter many subs came in, and Richards, Howland, Yon and Landrum made up the backfield.

Love blocked a punt, and Plunkett recovered on the Mercer thirty-nine-yard line. Richards got ten yards on two plays, and Yon punted on third down. Mercer got the ball back, but a third-down pass by Landrum was intercepted. Birmingham Southern put together the longest drive of the game by running ten plays before Cochran was hit for a sixteen-yard loss by O'Quinn.

Landrum passed to O'Quinn twenty yards down the field and followed with an eleven-yard pass to Pride. Landrum then sped twenty-six yards to the Panther six as the half ended.

In the second half Landrum, Karsznia, Pledger, Pride, and Page ran the ball. Pledger punted fifty-three yards to the Southern two-yard line, where O'Quinn made the tackle. Karsznia got twelve on two carries after Mercer got the ball back. Page ran for one, then Pride added three more up the middle. On fourth down Pledger booted a thirty-yard field goal with Karsznia holding for a 3-0 lead. This was the first field goal for Mercer since 1934.

In the fourth quarter Richards intercepted a pass and returned it fifteen yards to the Southern twenty-yard line. Richards then ran the ball twice for ten yards and a first down. Karsznia lost two yards, and Richards earned six on two carries. On fourth down a pass from Richards was incomplete, and Southern took over on the eight-yard line.

Two exchanges later Mercer scored after Petrite punted to the Panther thirty-nine yard line. Yon made two runs for nineteen yards, followed by a seven-yard dash around left end by Cline. Yon lost one, but then Cline passed to Pledger for a touchdown. Pledger added the extra point for a 10-0 score. Landrum, Richards, and Pledger were outstanding in the backfield, along with Karsznia, who had been performing well recently.

The Mercer line limited Birmingham Southern to eighteen yards rushing and two yards passing as they held the great McMichael in check after he had averaged fifteen yards per carry in the last game. In all, Birmingham Southern lost eighty-three yards rushing. McMichael lost thirty-seven in eight plays because of the very determined Mercer defense.

Mercer 0, Tennessee 17

Mercer took on the Tennessee Vols in Knoxville on 28 October 1939. The Volunteers had not been scored on thus far in the 1939 season and shut out the Bears 17-0. This Vol team later played in the Rose Bowl. All the scoring came in the first half of the game. Roscoe Cline missed the action, while Jones, Pledger, Pride, Allen and Landrum suffered injuries during the game.

Tennessee had the ball after Landrum kicked off sixty-five yards over the goal. Tannas put Mercer in business by recovering a fumble on the Tennessee twenty-yard line two plays later. Landrum was held for no gain, and Howland lost two yards. Landrum gained one on third down, and then Pledger missed on a fourth-down field goal attempt.

Tennessee took over, and John Butler went thirty-five yards on a reverse to the Mercer twenty-five-yard line. Four plays later Butler sped eighteen yards off tackle for a touchdown. Foxx converted for a 7-0 lead.

Landrum returned the kickoff twelve yards to the Mercer twenty-nine yard line. Landrum ran the ball on first down and lost one yard but then gained nineteen on the next two. Yon got six in three plays, and Landrum added seven more, but Yon fumbled and Tennessee recovered on the Vol twenty-two yard line. Waller ran for eight yards, then Foxx broke through for a seventy-yard touchdown. Foxx converted, and Tennessee led 14-0.

In the second quarter Tennessee drove to the Mercer fifteen-yard line before Mercer got the ball. Tennessee took over again on the Mercer thirty-nine. On the first play Warren was stopped for no gain by Plunkett. Warren then completed a pass for thirty-two yards as Paulk made the stop. Newman got six yards, but Warren was hit for a three-yard loss by Karsznia. Newman then kicked a field goal for a 17-0 score.

In the second half neither team could generate an offense as both were kept out of scoring range. Mercer, although defeated, had played an outstanding game against the strong Tennessee team, making the deepest penetration thus far in the season.

Mercer 9, Georgia 16

Georgia finally won in the 1939 season after losing four in a row. Alex McCaskill caught a fourth down pass from Billy Mims in the last twenty-five seconds of the game for a 16-9 victory. Mercer was penalized thirty-five yards in the final two minutes of the game as Georgia drove to the goal.

Cliff Kimsey for Georgia ran twenty-seven times for 142 yards, hit on two of five passes for sixty-three yards, and personally accounted for ten of Georgia's fifteen first downs. Mercer ran the ball thirty-five times for eighty-three yards, led by Landrum with thirty-four.

Mercer scored first as Cate fumbled the first punt of the game, and Gerhardt recovered on the Georgia ten-yard line. After three plays and only a two-yard gain, Pledger kicked a field goal for a 3-0 lead. Georgia took the ball and gained thirty-nine yards but was forced to punt. Mercer got the ball on the four-yard line and Pledger punted back to the forty-eight. On the first play Kimsey passed to McCaskill for twenty-eight yards, and Landrum made the stop. Kimsey ran the ball three times and scored from the ten-yard line. McCaskill converted, and Georgia led 7-3.

A new team entered for Mercer and Richards, from the thirty-yard line, led a drive to the Georgia four-yard line. From here Mercer lost seven yards in three plays, and Georgia took over on the twenty after an incomplete pass.

In the second half Georgia took the ball at the twenty-one and drove seventy-two yards to the Mercer seven-yard line. The big play was a thirty-five yard pass from Kimsey to McCaskill. Mercer took over on downs. On the first play Pledger stepped out of the end zone on a pass attempt, and Georgia got a safety to lead 9-3.

Georgia took the ball following the free kick after the safety and drove to the Mercer twenty-five yard line before losing the ball. Yon picked up one yard in the drive, then Richards fumbled while running around right end, and Georgia recovered. The Bulldogs marched to the Mercer two-yard line before they were stopped. Richards punted to the fifty-yard line, and Georgia returned the ball to the forty-five-yard line. Mercer then substituted a new team.

Mercer got the ball when Pledger intercepted Allen's pass and returned it twenty yards to the Georgia forty-yard line. On third down Landrum passed to Pledger for ten yards and a first down. After an incomplete pass, Landrum got fifteen yards on a fake spinner to the Georgia fifteen-yard line. Landrum ran for five yards on first down on a fake pass. Howland then went seven yards on the Statue of Liberty play. Karsznia sped three yards for a touchdown, and the score was tied 9-9.

Pledger kicked off to the Georgia thirteen-yard line, and Fordham returned the ball to the thirty-seven, where he was stopped by Bob Smith. On the next play Yurasich stopped the runner for a three-yard loss. Allen then lost seven as Wary and Plunkett made the stop on second down.

Later Georgia punted only twenty-three yards to the forty-seven-yard line. Mercer got the ball, and on the first play Mercer was penalized fifteen yards for holding. Karsznia got one yard, but Allen lost eight on an end-around. After an incomplete pass, Mercer was penalized another fifteen yards to the seventeen-yard line for pushing. Pledger then punted forty-seven yards to the Georgia thirty-nine-yard line.

Kimsey ran the ball from here six times for fifty-one yards. Mercer was penalized five yards. From the seven-yard line Mims tossed an incomplete pass, but on second down he hit McCaskill for a touchdown. Stegeman added the extra point, and Georgia had won 16-9. Mercer was able to run only three plays before the game ended.

This was the closest game in a number of years for the Bears against the Bulldogs. In all, Mercer ran the ball thirty-five times for eighty-three yards while Georgia had 257 on fifty-nine carries. The defense for Mercer was outstanding. It held Georgia until the final minutes of the contest.

Mercer 0, Mississippi College 15

Mississippi College clipped the Bears again by a score of 15-0 in Clinton, Mississippi. Mercer was able to get only one first down in the first half and four in the second. The Choctaws scored on a blocked punt for a safety and on a long pass on the last play in the first half for a 9-0 lead.

Mercer 3, Howard 7

Howard College pinned the sixth loss of the season on Mercer in Albany, Georgia, before a crowd of 3,500 as Neal Allen played an outstanding game in his hometown. Howard scored when Willard Huckaby blocked a Jack Richards punt from behind the Mercer goal, and Jack Moore recovered for a touchdown. The extra point put Howard ahead 7-0. Mercer had contributed to the blocked punt by losing seventeen yards on broken signals before the attempted kick.

Neither team had a big offensive day. Mercer had only seventy-six yards rushing and Howard had twenty-seven. Each team punted often, and Mercer kicked thirteen times for a thirty-five-yard average. Howard punted sixteen times for a thirty-seven-yard average.

Mercer got a field goal as Page returned a punt fifteen yards to the fifty-yard line. Page then got thirty on two plays. Karsznia ran for five, and Page added three more before Howard was penalized to the Mercer seven-yard line. Three plays later, after Page had been stopped once and Karsznia had gotten one yard, Pledger kicked the field goal.

The Bears ran the ball forty-eight times with Page as the big gainer with forty-six yards in ten carries, mostly in the second half. In all, the Mercer backs lost yardage seven times and failed to gain on six occasions. The Howard defense held the Bears even though their offense couldn't advance. Allen and co-captain Al Gerhardt had outstanding games for Mercer.

Mercer 18, Chattanooga 21

The last game of the season resulted in the seventh loss as Chattanooga bested the Bears 21-18 with Landrum scoring all three Mercer touchdowns. The three extra-point attempts were blocked, and Mercer finished the season with three wins and six losses. Three of these losses were to major institutions. Following the season Neal Allen was selected to the Little All-America Second Team.

The 1939 squad, consisting of twenty-nine players, had only four sophomores up from the freshman team. Players that graduated following the season were Bob Alley, William Jones, Bud Love, Bob Smith, Frank Wary, Ed Cassell, Alex Tannas, Art Pledger, Grady Gillon, James Landrum, and Jack Richards.

1940

Lake Russell began his last season as coach of the Mercer Bears in 1940 after a tenure of twelve years. He had guided the Bears longer than anyone ever and also had established the best record.

Tony Mason, who had changed his name from Masonek, was captain of the 1940 team. Joe Dougherty served as the only assistant coach, all others had been released to save money. The team consisted of thirty-three men, one of the largest in years. Sixteen of these were sophomores, nine were juniors, and there were ten seniors. The members of this squad were Raymond O'Quinn, Tom Heaton, Joe Dowd, Don Spice, Bill Nee, Tony Mason, Robert Holt, Robert Wagner, Frank Wary, Holly Mitchell, James Wary, Elton Wall, Thomas Slappey, Quenton Plunkett, Harry Lee Smith, Frank Mazza, Horace Richter, Malcolm Thomas, Lou Popp, Bill Howland, Carl Stager, Art Yancey, James Barfield, Ellis Paulk, Frank Pride, Harold Shepard, Veo Yon, Harry Karsney, Jolly Dizadyk, Rex McIlvaine, Tony Page, Rodney Blaylock, and Leo Lazar.

Mercer 0, Tennessee 49

Tennessee was the first foe of the 1940 season.. Mercer played well the first half, holding Tennessee to two touchdowns. The Bears stopped the Vols at the one-foot line in the second quarter. The first touchdown for the Vols came in the first five minutes after ten plays. The second was scored in the middle of the second quarter.

An unusual touchdown was made in the third quarter when a pass from Butler to Hurt was dropped, but Foxx caught it before it hit the ground for a touchdown. Later Steiner scored on a blocked kick. The Vols got three other touchdowns in the 49-0 romp. Seven extra points were kicked by six different players.

Mercer got forty-three yards rushing, while Tennessee ran up a whopping 544 yards. Tennessee also got seventy-one yards passing for a record 615 yards against the Bears.

Mercer 0, Alabama 20

Mercer continued the assault on the major schools with another battle with the Crimson Tide in Tuscaloosa, Alabama, on 5 October 1940. It was the opening game for Alabama, and the Tide rolled to a touchdown in the first five minutes on a seventy-one-yard drive.

The second score came when Harry Karsznia's punt was blocked on the Mercer thirty-seven and rolled to the Mercer fifteen-yard line. Spencer scored for Alabama four downs later. The third touchdown came in the third quarter in the 20-0 game.

Malcolm Thomas had an outstanding day for Mercer punting. Tony Page intercepted a pass on the Alabama thirty and returned it to the Alabama twelve just as the half ended for Mercer's closest threat. Richter, Thomas, Karsznia, Rowland, Page, and Paulk were outstanding for Mercer in the game.

Mercer 0, Louisiana State University 20

LSU, with former Mercer coach Bernie Moore at the helm, defeated the Bears by the same score, 20-0, in Baton Rouge. The Bears played better, but fumbles and errors in addition to the superior strength of the Tigers brought defeat. The Tigers scored first when Page fumbled on the Mercer thirty-two yard line. Dodson went over from the four-yard line after five plays. LSU went to the Mercer fourteen after an exchange of punts, but a recovered fumble by Tom Heaton stopped the drive. Later Mercer recovered another fumble at midfield.

Mercer and LSU both substituted new teams, and the Tigers went seventy-five yards to score. Bird ran forty-six yards to the Mercer eighteen-yard line, then he passed to Weaver on second down for the touchdown. After starting at the Mercer forty-five in the third quarter, LSU moved twenty-five yards to the Mercer twenty in two plays. Two plays later Dodson raced around right end for fourteen yards and a touchdown.

Mercer held on the six-yard line after a thirty-nine yard run by Weaver to the eight-yard line. Later Dizadyk intercepted a Tiger pass on the Mercer fifteen. Page fumbled and LSU recovered on the Mercer twenty-six, but Mercer held as the quarter ended and took over on the five-yard line. The Bears staged a two-first-down rally here with passes, but Blaylock was eventually forced to punt. Mercer's last chance to move the ball came when O'Quinn recovered a fumble, but the Bears couldn't move against the strong LSU team.

Mercer 45, Erskine 0

Mercer won the fourth game of the 1940 season by romping past Erskine 45-0 running forty-two plays for 350 yards. The Bears were frustrated after a three-game losing streak. Carl Stager and Rod Blaylock scored two touchdowns each, while Art Yancey, Raymond O'Quinn, and Don Spire got one each. Ellis Paulk made two conversions, and Plunkett added one. In all, thirty-three men saw action as the Bears used a three-unit backfield.

Harry Lee Smith, held out in 1939 with a leg injury, started his first game for the Bears. Other starters were Joe Dowd, Raymond O'Quinn, Frank Wary, Tony Mason, Holly Mitchell, Horace Richter, Veo Yonn, Bill Howland, Joe Page, and Harry Karsznia.

Mercer scored first when Arthur "Scooter" Yancey, a junior college transfer, returned the opening kickoff forty yards, then lateraled to Don Spice, who went for a touchdown. Yancey got the second on a seventy-two yard romp around right end.

Rod Stager, with a new team, sped fifty-seven yards in the second quarter for a touchdown as Bill Nee knocked down the last defender. Stager scored again five plays later, running over from the twenty-yard line, following a punt return for thirty-one yards by James Barfield.

In the third quarter Leo Lozar ran for twenty yards, and on the next down passed to O'Quinn for a ten-yard touchdown. In the fourth quarter Blaylock sparked a sixty-seven-yard drive with a thirty-seven yard jaunt for a touchdown. Later Blaylock returned a punt by Charlie Todd, son of the Erskine coach, for a seventy-yard touchdown. Ellis Paulk had two conversions, and Plunkett added another.

Mercer 2, Presbyterian 3

On a rainy afternoon in Albany Georgia, Presbyterian defeated the Bears 3-2 as Dick Miesky and Frank Sutton went fifty-five yards in the last three minutes to kick a fourth-down field goal from the Mercer fifteen-yard line. Miesky held and.Sutton kicked.

Mercer got a safety in the second quarter when Leo Lozar punted out of bounds on the Presbyterian three-yard line. A low pass from center then went astray, and Mercer got two points on a safety.

Mercer 6, Mississippi College 26

Mississippi College defeated Mercer once again in Macon on Homecoming Day before 2,500 as the Choctaws scored in the first minute of the game. Mercer fumbled on the kickoff and recovered on the seventeen-yard line. On the next play Karsznia's punt was blocked on the Mercer eighteen and recovered by Carter Blake for Mississippi College on the Mercer seven-yard line. Lonnie Tadlock sped the seven yards on a reverse for a touchdown. The extra point made the score 7-0.

Mercer scored from the forty-six as Lozar raced forty-six yards around end. Paulk missed the conversion attempt, and the score was 7-6. Thomas intercepted a Mississippi College pass to stop another drive in the second quarter by the visitors. The Choctaws came back with a passing attack to the Mercer seven as the half ended.

In the second half Mississippi College recovered a fumble on the Mercer twenty-six yard line. On the first down Armstrong passed to Fulton for a touchdown and a 13-6 lead. Page passed to O'Quinn on the Mississippi College forty-six, but O'Quinn fumbled and Mississippi College recovered.

Several plays later Karsznia punted sixty-five yards from behind his goal to push the opponents back. On the first play McCleod sped seventy-three yards on a reverse for a touchdown and a 20-6 lead on the conversion. The final points were scored in the fourth quarter when Armstrong went back to pass but found no receivers open and sped fifty-one yards for a touchdown.

Mercer moved with Blaylock getting nineteen yards, then passing for nine more, but Rex McIlvaine's fumble of a pass from Blaylock gave Mississippi College the ball again. Later Blaylock fumbled on the Mercer thirty-three, and the Choctaws recovered again. Mercer made one last drive but lost the ball at the seven-yard line of Mississippi College. The mistakes hurt the Bears severely as the Choctaws were able to get twelve first downs and 452 yards. Mercer had nine first downs and 224 yards in the game.

Mercer 6, Howard 14

Howard defeated Mercer in Macon 14-6 as the Bulldogs scored in the first and fourth quarters on passes. The entire first period was played in Mercer territory with the Bears stopping the first drive at the ten when Richter recovered a fumble. Stager recovered a fumble to halt the Bulldogs at the Mercer eleven-yard line, but Howard came back and scored from the twelve on a pass.

The Mercer drive started from the thirty-eight-yard line. Page passed to

Bill Nee for eighteen-and eight-yard gains. Lazor then passed to Nee again for twenty yards to the four-yard line. Lozar went over on the next down. The conversion was missed, and Howard led 7-6.

Bob Holt recovered a fumble on the Howard forty-three to get Mercer started again. Blaylock passed to Nee for twenty-four yards to the Howard seventeen, but the Bears were unable to score.

Another drive started as Lozar ran for twenty-eight yards around end and then added seven up the middle. A fourth-down pass from Lozar to Heaton was complete to the Howard five on an interference call. In three plays McIlvaine and Lozar moved the ball three yards, but on fourth down Page fumbled.

Howard scored in the fourth quarter after starting from the thirty-eight yard line. Tarrant passed to House for fifty yards to the Mercer twelve-yard line. Tarrant then passed to Goldman for the touchdown.

Mercer 6, Chattanooga 20

Mercer went into the final game of the 1940 season against Chattanooga with a number of men injured. Harry Karsznia was out of action, having sustained a knee injury in the Mississippi College game. Rex McIlvaine was also suffering with a knee injury. Don Spice had bruised kidneys. Horace Richter had an injured hip, while Tony Mason was out with influenza.

Chattanooga picked up four first downs on the way to the first touchdown. Mercer's touchdown came in the second quarter after getting the ball on a fumble at the Moccasin forty, and Yancey scored from the four-yard line. Chattanooga got two final touchdowns in the fourth quarter. Mercer's best drives ended at the seven- and fourteen-yard lines.

The final year of football at Mercer for Lake Russell was a difficult one. The team finished with one win and seven losses for the lowest winning percentage in a number of years. Lake Russell coached at Mercer for twelve years, the longest tenure of any Mercer football coach. His record for the period was forty-three wins, sixty losses, and five ties. His teams scored 1,273 points to 1,265 points for the opposition.

Russell was actually a victim of the times. He came to Mercer during the depression of 1929 and stayed through some financially difficult financial years for the athletic program and for the University. It took a considerable amount of courage to return each year to be faced with the same problems: lack of money, personnel, and support by the fans at the box office.

In 1966 Russell responded with a letter regarding some questions the author asked him about the football situation at Mercer. These statements are presented below.

In response to the question about how many and what type scholarships Mercer offered, Russell wrote:

> They were giving athletic scholarships before I went to Mercer in 1929, but I do not know when they started. Most of my first team (1929) were seniors and were on scholarships, so I imagine they had been receiving help in previous years. These scholarships included board, room, and tuition. The University gave the Athletic Board of Control twenty-four memorial scholarships worth $45.00 each per quarter plus a percentage of the student activity fee which admitted students to all home games. The Athletic Board used the memorial scholarships, student fees, guarantees for games away from home, and home gate receipts to pay for eighteen full board, room, and tuition grants plus six grants of tuition only. These scholarships were a part of the total fiscal budget. Occasionally I begged enough money from alumni and friends to supplement the athletic scholarship fund.

Russell was asked who he regarded as the best football player that he ever had at Mercer and he responded:

> I think that Lester "Swede" Olsson was the best football player I coached at Mercer. He was a 225-pound tackle. He was fast, agile, and very aggressive. After he finished college he played professional football for the Washington Redskins for a few years. He was selected as an All-American professional tackle at least one year. Olsson is now an outstanding high school coach in Ohio.

Russell was asked to pick an all-star team made up of men he coached at Mercer. He responded with these players:

ENDS

Lynwood Mallard	1929
Paul Davis	1938
Nat Reasor	1933
Gene NeSmith	1936
Cotton Harrison	1933
Tom Heaton	1940

TACKLES

Swede Olsson	1933
Frank Wary	1940
Red Camp	1933
Al Gerhardt	1938

Wimpy Jones	1936
Tony Maznek	1940

GUARDS

Bob Sperry	1932
Dick McNabb	1931
Carl Altonen	1933
Gordon Reddick	1933
Roger Dodd	1935
Red Adams	1929
Grady Rainey	1936
Alex Tannas	1938

CENTERS

Bob Smith	1932
Harry Lichter	1933
Harry Lane	1929
Horace Richter	1940

QUARTERBACKS

Jake Trommerhauser	1933
Allen Bloodworth	1936

HALFBACKS

Spec Landrum	1940
Pinky Walden	1931
Al Owen	1937
Joe Pope	1933
Tom Porter	1934
Ernie Zinkowski	1933
Jack Richards	1939
Jody Matt	1930

FULLBACKS

Bill Alderman	1929
John Cimperman	1932
John Mattox	1935
Billy Smith	1938

Russell added several comments regarding his tenure at Mercer, which provide information on conditions that existed in that era:

It is important in evaluating the intercollegiate athletic

program from 1929 to 1940 to be reminded that the big national economic depression was at its worst during those years. It is my recollection that total student enrollment fell to about 300 and was never as much as 500 during these years.

Another feature of the athletic program at Mercer back in that period was that we gave quite a few grants-in-aid to boys from outside the state of Georgia. I received constant criticism for this practice, but I knew I could not compete with the University of Georgia and Georgia Tech for boys who were good enough to make their teams, because the high school players and their coaches, with a few notable exceptions, preferred the bigger school. This was all right with me, but I detested the coaches who pandered their real college material to the prestige schools, and then tried to pressure me into giving grants to second-rate prospects. Consequently, I got any good native boys that would come to Mercer and went elsewhere for additional material that I could subsidize.

I expose a part of my true nature when I say that I have observed with amazement the Trippis, the Bratkowskis and other athletes who left their Yankee homes to become famous stars at Georgia and Georgia Tech since my tenure at Mercer. I do not criticize the two schools for going where the material is located to do their recruiting. I applaud them for it, but it makes me wonder if I could have been a decade ahead of my time when I was coaching at Mercer.

Chapter 7
LAST DOWN

Following the 1940 season, there was considerable discussion among coaches, administrators, alumni, and students on the advisability of Mercer continuing to play football against major college opponents. This high level competition pleased and excited many alumni and students, and also provided large guarantees for team expenses. But the rising cost of fielding a team and numerous unpaid bills from seasons past caused budget-conscious administrators great concern. Quite naturally the athletic staff desired to continue the strong schedule, but recruiting against the major schools was becoming more difficult. Getting athletes who could play a full season against tough opponents like Georgia and Tennessee was almost impossible.

On 3 December 1940 the Mercer board of trustees met and decided that Mercer should get out of big-time football. This marked the first time that the board of trustees entered into the football operation at Mercer in such a significant manner. At the direction of the trustees it was decided that:

- more emphasis should be placed on physical education for all students
- the salaries for the athletic director and the football coaches would be on the same level as professors
- athletic scholarships were to be administered by two committees composed of faculty and trustees
- the budget of the athletic department would be part of the total university budget.

The members of the committee making these carefully considered recommendations were H. P. Fleming, Hamilton Holt, Judge R. C. Bell, and Judge Eugene Cook.

These recommendations met opposition at several quarters. There was some administrative pressure to discontinue football entirely, even after this new direction was established. The athletic department wanted to continue the strong program, while the student body petitioned to keep football on a revised basis. As a result of this rather continued discontent, a second meeting was held on 18 December 1940 where a final decision was made that intercollegiate athletics at Mercer were to continue.

Dr. Spright Dowell, an opponent of big-time football, accepted the recommendations of the committee with some reservations and recommendations. It was recommended that partial scholarships be given on a year-to-year basis, and that the athletic department adhere to authorized budgets. The final stipulation was that a "C" average was required for scholarships.

After the decision was reached that Mercer would continue football on a de-emphasized basis, membership was gained in the South Atlantic Athletic Conference. Other members of the conference were Wofford, Newberry, Presbyterian, Oglethorpe, Stetson, and Rollins.

On 1 January 1941 Bobby Hooks was signed as coach of the Bears. Hooks, the first choice for the position, had been a standout performer at Georgia in 1926, 1927, and 1928. Following his playing career, he coached at Georgia Military College during the 1930 and 1931 seasons, where his team was runner-up as state junior college champion. He then coached at Valdosta High School, winning the 1932 state class B championship. His overall coaching record was eighty-four wins, eighteen losses and five ties. Assisting Hooks at Mercer would be Billy Smith, a former Mercer halfback from Albany, Georgia.

Members of the 1941 squad were Bill Shirley, Holden West, Daniel Morris, James Wary, Frank Mazza, Clarence Boynton, Jr., Eugene Brundage, Lovic Marbury, Bert DeRieux, Holly Mitchell, Earl Bergen, James Dismuke, Wayne Pittman, Louis Blanton, Joseph Dowd, Carlson Phillips, Robert Middleton, Murray Chappell, Hubbard Gray, James Wingate, Harold Shepard, Robert L. Hodges, James Powell, Rodney Blaylock, Earl Harrison, Joseph

Davis, Arthur Yancey, Glenn Ratliff, Raymond Dickey, Tony Page, Knuck McCrary, and Eugene Barwick.

1941

Three mementos of Mercer football glory remain on the campus. One is a helmet trunk that was purchased in 1940, while another is a football that was used in the Mercer-Oglethorpe game in Albany, Georgia, in 1936. The third is two tickets to the Mercer-Georgia game of 1941.

Mercer 0, Georgia 81

The largest crowd in the history of Centennial Stadium was on hand for this game. It was the season opener, and also the first game for former Georgia star and Mercer coach Bobby Hooks. The coach for Georgia was Wallace Butts, a former captain and standout for the Bears.

The 1941 team was composed of thirty-two men, but only nine had seen senior college experience. Georgia proved to be too tough an opponent for the inexperienced Mercer players. The team for Georgia was composed of such standouts as Frank Sinkwich, Lamar "Racehorse" Davis, and George Poschner.

The Bulldogs defeated the Bears by a whopping 81-0 score as six men scored touchdowns with Georgia backs accounting for 428 yards rushing. Fifty years ago the series had started with Georgia winning 50-0. Mercer and Georgia battled twenty-two different times with the Bulldogs winning in each game. Mercer was shut out fourteen times and scored only seventy-one points to Georgia's 740.

Sinkwich started things off with a fourteen-yard touchdown after an eighty-yard drive. Lamar Davis went forty-eight yards on a reverse for the second touchdown. Sinkwich passed to Poschner nine yards for the third score. Allen sped forty-six yards for the fourth touchdown. Costa added the conversion, and the score was 28-0 in the first quarter.

The Bulldogs were just getting warm as Allen passed to Nunnaly for another score. Clyde Ehrhardt went fifteen yards on a pass interception for a counter. Sinkwich scored twice more, and Allen added another. Blanton got one on a thirty-yard run, and Steve Hughes got the final touchdown for the "Varsities" with a forty-yard return of an intercepted pass.

Mercer was no match for the Bulldogs, and the inexperienced Mercer men were unable to stop the scoring even though Georgia substituted freely. Mercer was held to the lowest yardage in history, minus thirty-six yards. The one first down Mercer got resulted from pass interference.

Mercer 25, Georgia Teachers 0

The Bears bounced back with a victory over Georgia Teachers by a score of 25-0. Hodges scored for Mercer from the three-yard line after Yancey ran eighteen yards and Harrison ran fourteen to set up the play. Harrison made nine yards off tackle, and Page scored on a four-yard dash for a 12-0 lead. Yancey capped the first half scoring with an eighty-yard touchdown.

Mercer played poorly in the second half as Knuck McCrary scored from three yards out for the only touchdown. In all, Mercer had eighteen first downs while the Teachers had five. Yancey, Page, McCrary, and Harrison were outstanding for the Bears.

Mercer 20, Wofford 14

The Wofford Terriers provided victory number two for the 1941 edition of the Mercer Bears. The win was not easy, though, for the Terriers led 7-6 at the half. Wofford scored first on a fifty-seven-yard drive with a thirty-four yard pass from Epps to Faust for the touchdown. Hilton added the extra point for a 7-0 lead.

Mercer scored in the second quarter when Earl Harrison punted out of bounds on the Wofford five-yard line. Epps return-punted to the Wofford twenty-yard line. Joe Page then carried the ball to the Wofford six-yard line. On fourth down Carlson Phillips scored, but the point attempt failed and Wofford led 7-6.

On the first play of the second half Jimmy Hilton went fifty-eight yards for a Wofford touchdown and then booted the extra point for a 14-6 lead. Mercer started on the thirty-one yard line, and Blaylock passed to Phillips for sixteen yards on first down. On the next play R. L. Hodges started running with the ball and lateraled to Yancey. Yancey lateraled to Blaylock for a forty-five-yard gain. Page went for four yards and Hodges scored the touchdown. Eugene Brundage booted the point, cutting Wofford's lead to 14-13.

Wofford drove to the Mercer twelve-yard line, but the Bears held. After the attack stalled, Earl Harrison punted the ball sixty-seven yards to the Wofford nineteen-yard line. Wofford punted the ball back, and Hodges went seventy-four yards around left end on the first play for a 20-14 lead.

Joe Dowd blocked a Wofford punt later, and Mercer drove to the Wofford two-yard line but couldn't get across the goal line. Mercer gained 261 yards rushing on thirteen first downs, while Wofford had 135 yards on eight first downs.

Mercer 0, Rollins 52

Rollins College blasted the Bears 52-0 in Orlando, Florida, on 24

October 1941 for their first win after losses to the Bears in 1925, 1926, and 1929. Grady Ray scored five touchdowns for the Tars as they rolled up twenty-two first downs on 316 yards rushing and 112 yards passing. Mercer, with practically no offensive thrust, had minus-sixteen yards rushing and one first down.

Mercer 19, Presbyterian 12

The 1 November 1941 Homecoming game in Macon was successful as Mercer edged Presbyterian College 19-12. Starters for Mercer that day were Robert Middleton, Joe Dowd, James Dismuke, Holly Mitchell, Frank Mazza, James Wray, R. L. Hodges, Rod Blaylock, Arthur Yancey, and Tony Page. Substitutes in the game were Carlson Phillips, Murray Chappell, Louis Blanton, Wayne Pittman, Eugene Brundage, Louis Marbury, Clarence Boynton, Bill Shirley, Harold Shepard, James Powell, Joe Davis, Glenn Ratliff, Earl Harrison, Raymond Dickey, and Daniel Morris.

Presbyterian scored first on a long pass. Blaylock and Yancey led Mercer on a forty-yard drive in the first quarter with a pass play to the thirteen-yard line. On the next play Page rushed around end for the touchdown. Brundage converted for a 7-6 advantage.

Mercer got the ball back on a fumble at the Presbyterian twenty-yard line. Joe Davis passed to Glenn Ratliff for a twenty-yard touchdown. Presbyterian scored again when Rollins passed to Calloway for a touchdown. Hodges blocked the extra point, and Mercer led 13-12. The Bears' final touchdown resulted when Yancey started to his left but got surrounded and lateraled to Blaylock, who went eighty yards for a touchdown.

Mercer 19, Mississippi College 27

Mississippi College defeated the Bears by a close 27-19 score for their fifth victory. Most of the Bear action came on an inspired effort in the second half. Blaylock tossed to Phillips for a twenty-five yard touchdown, but the Choctaws were ahead 13-6 at the half. Tony Page got the second touchdown on a two-yard run. Later Yancey scored on a fifty-five yard run and Hodges converted. For Mercer, Mazza, Dowd, Mitchell, Dismuke, and Phillips were outstanding.

Mercer 13, Newberry 32

Newberry, coached by Billy Laval, defeated the Bears in Newberry, South Carolina, 32-13 as the Flying Fleet registered twenty-four first downs in a big offensive show.

Newberry scored first after driving for sixty-six yards. The Bears couldn't move, and Newberry went to the Mercer twenty-five yard line, where Dowd and Page made the tackle to end the threat. Later in the first quarter Newberry took to the air. After several passes were completed, Randel scored from the Mercer one-yard line for a 13-0 lead. Mercer threatened, but a Blaylock pass was intercepted on the Mercer forty-three. A few plays later Yancey gained sixty-eight yards, but the play was called back. Finally Mercer scored as Yancey, Hodges, and Page drove to the seventeen-yard line. Blaylock then passed to Phillips for seventeen yards and a touchdown. Newberry added another touchdown following the kickoff to lead 20-6 at the half.

Newberry got two touchdowns in the last half. The first came as Randel passed to Holt in the third quarter, and a Mercer fumble led to another score in the fourth quarter. Tony Page scored for Mercer on a return of an intercepted pass for ninety yards. Hodges converted to make the final score 32-13. Bill Shirley was outstanding on defense, and Phillips was a threat both ways.

Mercer 6, Howard 27

Mercer played Howard in Birmingham, and once again the Bulldogs defeated the Bears as the game ended 27-6. Blaylock passed to Phillips for the only Mercer score. The pass and run was good for sixty-one yards. Knuck McCrary led the Bears in the second half.

Mercer 13, Chattanooga 40

The Chattanooga Moccasins and Mercer played for the twenty-fourth and last time in 1941 with Chattanooga winning before 3,988 fans by a score of 40-13. After a 19-0 Chattanooga lead at the half, Mercer came back to score thirteen points. The Moccasins added twenty-one more to clinch the victory.

Knuck McCrary scored for Mercer on a ninety-yard kickoff return, and Yancey went nine yards for the second touchdown. Brundage converted after the touchdown. Yancey was outstanding for the Bears with a thirty-seven yard run on one occasion.

The 1941 season ended with a record of three won and six lost, which gave Hooks about the average season for a Mercer coach. It also could be looked on as a good season in a revised program and a rebuilding year.

Hooks, who had been a highly successful coach and an experienced winner, worked hard at recruiting and in shaping the football future at Mercer. The Board of Athletic Control met many times to iron out problems regarding the forthcoming season. At a meeting in June, Hooks requested the use of freshmen in varsity games for the 1941 season. President Dowell stated that the practice of using freshmen was not permitted by the rules of the Dixie Conference. Although this request was not granted, Hooks was empowered to recruit eight freshmen, and their participation in varsity games was taken under advisement.

At one of the earlier organizational meetings, it had been agreed on by the Mercer trustees and the members of the Athletic Board of Control that nine juniors and nine sophomores would be provided scholarships of $450.00 each for the 1941 season. The coach was also given permission to recruit seven players on scholarships of $200.00 each.

The total budget for the 1941 football and basketball program was set at $14,050.00. Not included in this amount was $2,700.00 for the salary of the coach.

This budget was to be partially met by $4,800.00 from student fees and a $2,000.00 guarantee for the Georgia game. The balance, more than $7,000, was to come from subscriptions and gate receipts.

At another meeting the Board decided that preseason training would not be held, and that the schedule would begin in October and end in November. The game scheduled with Tennessee for September, 1941 was canceled. Ticket prices were set at $5.00 per book for the season. Individual game prices included: Georgia from $2.20 to $.50, Georgia Teachers $.85 and $.50, while Wofford, Rollins and Presbyterian ticket prices ranged from $1.10 to $.50 for each game. The Board also recommended that certain athletes take only two courses, rather than the customary three, during the football season.

The Board met again on 6 October 1941 to discuss the replacement of ten athletes who would graduate at the end of the 1941 season. Dr. Dowell agreed to provide a total of twenty-five scholarships valued at $200.00 each. This was a reduction in scholarship aid from the previous year of $4,500.00. The Board members pushed him for twenty-five scholarships valued at $450.00 each, but money was tight at the University and he refused. At an additional meeting on the subject on 14 October the Board agreed to make up the difference between the $200.00 offered and $450.00 desired for 25 athletes. In other words, the members of tHe Committee underwrote $5,000.00 for athletic scholarships.

It was probably at this point, regarding scholarships, that Dr. Dowell expressed concern and disappointment with the Board of Control and Coach Hooks. Once again the Board was offering scholarships that were not funded and the University stood the chance of being the loser.

In other action the Board recommended that Coach Hooks "supply the Board with a complete account of oral contracts entered into with each individual athlete." Also the motion was made and passed that the "following items be paid immediately; viz., University of Georgia, Mercer Treasurer, printing and advertising bills, Federal Tax, Peeler Hardware Co., preseason meals, and other incidentals connected with the Mercer-Georgia game."

On 1 December 1941 the group met to discuss scheduling the University of Georgia for 1942. The other games suggested by Charlie Hubbard, Mercer's business manager, were Wofford, Presbyterian, Newberry, Georgia Teachers, Rollins, Erskine, and Howard. He reported that Chattanooga did not offer Mercer the Homecoming game for 1942. Hubbard had played a significant role as business manager of athletics as well as business manager of the University for several years. He worked actively in scheduling games, recruiting, paying bills, and handling general business affairs for the athletic department.

The financial management of the Mercer Athletic Department is reflected in a correspondence file of the late 1930s. In this file were found many letters from creditors seeking to collect accounts that were past due. Letters from sporting goods dealers, hotels, ticket companies, and specialty houses were numerous.

One company that sold the Athletic Department some bumper tags tried unsuccessfully for years to collect. Another company retained Charlie Walker, a local lawyer and Mercer graduate, in an attempt to collect an overdue account from the athletic department.

It was the practice among colleges for the athletic departments to be separated financially from the business affairs of the college. They were supposed to be self-supporting, but eventually Mercer would be called upon to bail the athletic department out of trouble. Since funds were continually in short supply, one procedure employed was the use of current money to pay old bills while requisitions were made for items on money yet to be earned. This procedure proved fatal. Often gate receipts were low and at times not even enough to meet individual game expenses.

The coaches also contributed to the problem by ordering supplies, promising scholarships, and making other general expenditures regardless of whether money was available. Prior to 1929, when Lake Russell took over the reins at Mercer, there was a new coach at Mercer every year or two. Each new coach would overspend his budget, then leave to accept another job. The incoming coach would not want to take on the responsibility of paying these bills and the debts grew.

The situation was best summed up in a statement by W. F. Blanks in response to a questionnaire concerning his athletic participation. Blanks, in reflecting on the economic situation, wrote, "It might be pertinent to note that I was at Mercer from the fall of 1934 to the spring of 1939, a time when the Depression was in full swing. Mercer was a very poor school, and its athletic program was one jump ahead of the sheriff."

There is some interesting and unusual correspondence from the athletic business manager's office. It was the practice in the 1930s to farm boys out to junior colleges. Sometimes the junior colleges provided the scholarships, but at other times the Mercer Athletic Department was supposed to provide the funds. Once several boys were sent to South Georgia

College in Douglas for playing experience and to improve their grades. Fred Herndon, a former Mercer player, was the coach at Douglas. Herndon wrote a number of letters trying to collect tuition from the Mercer Athletic Association and eventually the Douglas president wrote Hubbard, and subsequently Dr. Dowell. In reality the Athletic Association was responsible for the debts, and not the University. Dr. Dowell, reflecting on the football situation, noted that his biggest mistake was not putting the Athletic Department under the direct control of the University instead of permitting an athletic board of control to direct the program.

The 15 December 1941 meeting of the Board of Control heard recommendations from Coach Hooks to the following effect:

- make physical education a part of the academic curriculum. This would mean the offering of majors and minors in this area
- maintain a freshman football squad in the 1942 season to the number of fifteen athletes
- maintain a varsity team of twenty-six players. Accordingly, the maintenance of the number of players called for on the two squads would necessitate the raising of funds in the amount of $5,000
- appoint an athletic field man to organize active alumni chapters and to solicit financial support for the athletic program
- purchase a motion picture camera, telescopic lens, projector, and screen. This equipment to cost approximately $300.00
- make a bigger effort than heretofore in procuring a better and more extensive coverage in the press on Mercer's athletic activities.

This recommendation created considerable discussion and a motion was moved and seconded that Chairman Smalley, Secretary Blair, and Coach Hooks confer with President Dowell before further action was taken relative to the above recommendations. Actually, at this point, the athletic department and the administration began to take different views regarding the type of program desirable for Mercer.

No report on the meeting with Dr. Dowell is available and no action was taken on the recommendations. The pressing demands of World War II resulted in the suspension of football at Mercer on 7 January 1942 for the duration.

On 14 February 1946, a special committee for athletics was appointed by Dr. Dowell to consider the resumption of intercollegiate athletics on a non-subsidized basis. Twelve days later a called meeting was held to discuss the recommendations of this special committee. This information had been acquired from:

- Material gathered in light of Mercer University's past experience.
- Opinions and reactions of friends of the institution.
- Data provided by Mr. Blair and Dr. Dixon from institutions visited by them.
- The general views expressed by the presidents of Birmingham Southern, Howard, Mercer, Rollins, and Stetson when they met at Mercer to discuss the matter of intercollegiate athletics.

The special committee consisting of Hugh Hill, Peyton Anderson, Gail Carver, H. P. Fleming, George McCommon, Talmadge Smalley, Earl Timmerman, J. D. Blair, Fred Dixon, and Fred Hattrick presented this recommendation. Resolved:

> That this committee recommend to the Board of Trustees the adoption of an intercollegiate program on a strict non-subsidization basis and that the schedule in football be made with those of like ideals.

The trustees then requested that the recommendation be read in full. Along with the information which aided the committee in making the recommendation were letters of opinion from Dr. Josiah Crudup, A. B. Bell, Wallace Butts, and William Smith, Editor of the *Macon News*. Butts recommended that the University not engage in a program which would be non-subsidized.

Forrest Lanier, chairman of a committee representing the student body, accompanied by Burt Derieux, Pat Stockton, Irving Hall, Emily Sell, and Vallusia Anchors, informed the board that a student body vote of more than 400 to 22 favored resumption of athletics in a subsidized basis. After some discussion, the students expressed objection to the use of student fees to pay off all athletic debts.

John Sammons Bell, co-chairman of an Alumni Athletic Committee, outlined a five-point plan for the resumption of football. Hooks expressed the opinion that athletics were beginning to draw larger crowds, and that amateur teams would not challenge spectators' interest and would not result in favorable publicity for the college.

After more general discussion, H. H. Ware recommended that the board of trustees approve thirty-three tuition scholarships and that sixty days be granted to raise $7,500. It was the general consensus of the group now that an amateur program would not be successful.

Further discussion followed regarding the cost of football and how money could be raised. It was then suggested that $30,000 be granted by the alumni over a four-year period. Other discussion followed but no direction was established. In fact, there was considerable confusion, until H. P. Fleming substituted the following motion: "We recommend that Mercer University re-enter athletics on some form of controlled subsidization and that a committee from the trustees be moved to confer with the Alumni Committee to make out plans to be submitted at the next meeting of the Board of Trustees."

At this point, Dr. Dowell was recognized by the chair and made the following statement: "Gentlemen, if you pass this motion, it will be personally embarrassing to me." Fleming, Holt, and Westberry, in the order named, requested the chairman to table amendments, substitute motions made by them, and those before the board. The chairman so ordered. Dr. Dowell had done extensive work in getting Mercer back into football on a non-scholarship basis and when he saw something other than a non-subsidized program was going to be recommended, he took action to stop the discussion and the voting.

On 27 February 1946, at a meeting on the executive committee of the trustees, President Dowell informed the committee that:

> He felt it was in order for him to clarify his position. He stated that he felt he should go on record before the voting rather than afterwards. He gave as his main reason his feeling that the Baptists of Georgia would not accept the idea of the institution giving more aid to athletes than it would to ministerial or other worthy students. In this connection, he pointed out that ministerial students would get about 50% as much assistance as would athletes under the proposed plan. He called attention to the fact that the athletic program all down the years had incurred financial losses, and that in his opinion no plan had yet been offered which would guarantee against further losses.

Dr. Dowell said that he had hoped that this proposed amateur program would meet the approval of the student body but that the unfavorable response of students and alumni had caused him to decide that such a program would not succeed in football. He did think that basketball, track, tennis, and possibly baseball might prove successful.

In answer to a direct question, President Dowell said that:

> He was undeniably opposed to subsidization in athletics. He stated that his convictions were strong in this matter and despite his personal desire to have some further specific attainments consummated for the institution during his tenure, he would accept retirement if in so doing it would

clear the deck for the satisfactory solution of the athletic problem.

Dr. Dowell's statement created quite a stir among students, alumni, and friends. However, he felt that the decision was logical and right for Mercer University at that time.

Football budgets in this era of college athletics range up to and beyond an expenditure of $2,000,000 annually. In 1971 an eleventh game was added for the additional revenue, and ticket prices advanced to $7.00 a game at most major schools. Subsequently, individual ticket prices were raised to $8.00, $10.00, and then to (currently) $12.00—more than twice the price for a Mercer *season ticket* in 1941. Athletic departments which have budgets in the millions of dollars have to be well organized and some make money. There are, however, many schools playing football that fail to provide enough money through gate receipts and other means to keep the program on a sound financial basis.

The athletic associations of these schools, and particularly at state universities, support themselves. Direction and regulations are formulated by university committees, conference rules, and national organizations.

The Mercer Athletic Association was formed in 1885, and was financed by gate receipts, donations, and subscriptions and was completely responsible for scheduling games, hiring coaches, and paying bills. When this organization was formed, the need for money was not great, but as the program broadened and emphasis began to be placed on college athletics, the need for larger budgets became apparent. Administration of the funds of the association was at the direction of an Athletic Board of Control. This body was composed of faculty members, alumni, and students. The association had little direct relationship with the University and the task of hiring and paying coaches was completely under their control. The salary of the coach remained the responsibility of the association until physical culture became a part of the curriculum. Even then, the salaries of the coaches were supplemented by the association.

Due to the absence of complete records, a thorough account of the financial structure of football from 1892 to 1942 cannot be presented. The accounts for the early years were probably thrown away many years ago, and the records for the final year were lost prior to an audit to determine the 1942 indebtedness. Despite the scarcity of records, it is evident that the Mercer Athletic Association was in financial difficulty since they purchased the first football in 1892.

The earliest available records indicate that the association purchased a tract of four and one-half acres for an athletic park between Boundary and Tindall Old Field for $2,800 in 1903. The Association paid $1,000 down and borrowed the remainder from Mercer. Further financial assistance was sought in 1906 when Mercer loaned the association $400 to prepare for the coming season.

On 25 August 1907, a decision was made to sell the area purchased in 1903 and the property brought $3,450. The money for the land was used to paÿ indebtedness to Mercer.

In subsequent years there were similar problems. In 1911 the association borrowed $7,500 to cover debts and to finance the season. This was followed by loans of $3,000 and $1,185 from the University in 1912.

It became apparent that there was a need for more stability in the athletic program and a need for greater student participation in all forms of athletics. The University thus hired Dr. C. C. Stroud, in conjunction with the Athletic Association, as director of physical culture and associate professor of history at a salary of $1,800 in 1911. Most of his salary was to be paid by the Athletic Association with $300 coming from Mercer.

Students were charged an athletic fee. However, the enrollment was small, and a deficit of $4,184 was recorded for that year. One large item to be paid was a bill for $500 which was due for gymnasium rent to the city. After a successful tenure, Dr. Stroud went to Louisiana State, and was replaced at Mercer by Lewis Hardage. T. A. Robins became the coach in 1914.

Jake Zellars, a former Mercer athlete and Lanier coach, was hired in 1915 for two years. His salary was to be $1,200 for the first year and $1,500 for the second. The total deficit through 1915 was recorded at $14,000.

Following World War I the Athletic Association resumed football and hired W. C. Hunter on 13 February 1919 as athletic director and superintendent of buildings and grounds. Mr. Hunter was experienced in athletics and had also studied architecture at St. Andrews in Scotland. Robert James was the coach for that season.

Hunter was athletic director for one season, then Josh Cody was hired as coach and athletic director for two years at a salary of $2,000. The change in coaches had little effect on expenditures as debts continued to rise. President Weaver got involved in athletics by paying off debts amounting to $4,000 following Cody's tenure.

On 23 May 1923 Stanley L. Robinson signed a five-year contract with Mercer to be professor of physical education and athletic director for a salary of $4,500 with stipulations for a bonus if the athletic program showed a profit. The University took another step in trying to control athletic expenditures by retaining Robinson to instigate better budgeting procedures.

A resumé of the expenditure of the 1923-24 season showed a related athletic deficit of $12,375.81 Part of this indebtedness was approximately $4,000 created by the previous athletic administration, and the new Board of Control thought that the University should assume this responsibility.

Although Robinson's athletic administration made giant strides in reducing debts, the audit in 1924-25 showed a deficit of $1,896.86, not counting unprovided-for scholarships and uncollected accounts on athletes. The deficit in 1924-25 was $5,935.29; 1925-26, $11,146.15; and in 1926-27, $7,073.47.

By 1924 the University was contributing $8,000 from student fees to the athletic program. This was based on an enrollment of between 750 and 850 students. These fees served as a basis for the athletic budget, but additional funds were always necessary. It was a general practice for members of the Board of Control to co-sign notes for the Athletic Association. In 1922 a note was signed for a loan and in 1924 an indebtedness for $700 was still outstanding with the Bibb National Bank. Mercer was eventually forced to pay debts such as this to keep the Board members from being sued.

On 27 November 1925 Robinson submitted his resignation to President Rufus Weaver. In his resignation he stated that when he agreed to come to Mercer that the general conditions were not the most encouraging. He wrote:

> There was no organization of the Athletic Department; the organization of the student body and the Alumni was not of sufficient strength to be of any great value in stabilizing the athletic program. Further, that the facilities for carrying on the work were very limited.
>
> During the past year, certain insidious forces had operated toward the destruction of the genuine loyal cooperation and confidence on the part of the alumni, student body, and faculty toward the athletic administration.

Bernie H. Moore replaced Robinson in 1926, and E. Parker Mosley was named athletic director. Moore was hired at a salary of $4,500 as football and basketball coach. The records for the 1926-27 season showed an income of $25,916.20 with expenses amounting to $28,242.49. In addition to this deficit, there were other items that were not listed on the yearly report by the athletic department. The 3 May 1927 financial report indicated that the University had allowed about thirty scholarships worth $4,478 and only $830 of this amount was repaid.

It was the practice to recruit players on the promise of alumni and friends to provide scholarship money. This practice continued through the years.

In addition to the scholarship debt to the University, the Athletic Association owed $1,464.82 for meals and had other debts to the University amounting to $3,146.36. These figures increased the debt to the University to $9,989.18.

In order to consolidate and supervise the expenditures of the Athletic Association, Dr. Weaver appointed Professor C. B. Wray, a member of the Board of Control, as comptroller of extra-academic affairs. Writing on 29 June 1927 to Mr. Wray, Dr. Weaver stated:

> I am informed that during the past year you notified certain dealers that Mercer University would not be responsible for any purchases which did not bear your signature, and that

> today these certain firms demanded payment of accounts which were irregularly made. Please notify the firms to the effect that in violation of your orders, goods were sold and that we feel no obligation whatever for payment of these goods since the purpose we had in creating this arrangement was to prevent any obligation on the part of Mercer University in the purchase of anything which did not receive your approval.

The main problem with the Athletic Association up to this time was the constant overexpenditure by the coaches and others involved in the athletic program. There was not enough money on hand to provide supplies and equipment at the beginning of each season; therefore, much of the material was bought on credit. It was not uncommon for bills amounting to several thousand dollars to go unpaid for years. This practice resulted in numerous letters from the creditors and sometimes threats of lawsuits.

Bernie Moore was rehired for the 1927-28 season for $4,500 with J. D. Blair as assistant coach for $2,700. At that time Dr. Weaver informed Coach Moore that he would be expected to propose a balanced budget for the coming season.

When the new Board of Control took office in September of 1927, there was a deficit of $3,000. The 1927-28 season began with a cash deficit of $5.01 and with liabilities amounting to $4,170.30. In January 1928 the liabilities had been cut to $2,579.63.

Moore proposed a budget of $24,050 for the 1928-29 football season, which allowed for $2,140.84 to be applied to old debts. At the end of the season Coach Moore took a position with Louisiana State and was replaced by Lake Russell.

On 30 May 1929, at the end of the year there was a deficit of $3,000 and the Athletic Board requested Mercer to put the salaries of the coaches in the University budget. On 1 July 1929, $5,800 was added to the University budget to provide salaries for physical education teachers and coaches. This action helped the Athletic Association. Previously a major part of the budget had been salaries for coaches.

In addition to the financial problems of the Athletic Association, the University was having its own difficulties. Dr. D. B. Ragsdale, treasurer, speaking to the executive committee of Mercer on the proposed University budget for the 1927-28 year, reported a loss of $7,380.86 for the past year. This was added to the prior obligations of the University of $38,563.97 for a total deficit of $45,944.83.

Dr. Ragsdale stated that the chief items of loss grew out of athletics. In order to save the Athletic Board from suits, $2,100 had been advanced by the University to pay pressing debts. He estimated that $4,800 was due to the college from students, whose expenses were guaranteed by alumni and others. Other unpaid accounts of the Athletic Department to the University amounted to $6,100. In addition to university obligations, the Board of Athletic Control had bank notes for $1,600 and other obligations which amounted to $3,000. He concluded his report by relating that the total athletic obligation was over $10,000.

It was agreed by the executive committee of the trustees that the business office of the University take over extra-academic affairs and that no athletic contracts be made by the Athletic Board of Control. S.J.T. Price, business manager of the University, was also named business manager of Athletics, for which he received a salary from the Athletic Association.

This arrangement provided better supervision; however, the report on athletics of 10 July 1930 to 10 May 1931 showed a deficit of $19,639.01 with a loss of $8,348.97 for 1931. This was the height of the depression and the entertainment dollar was lacking in household budgets. As a result the coaches found it more profitable to play games away from Mercer for guarantees. This practice prevailed through the remaining years of football at Mercer.

The proposed athletic budget for 1930-31 included $4,800 from student fees as the enrollment had dropped to around 400 students. Additional income of $15,750 was received as guarantees for road games. Little was expected from the gate as $300 was lost on the Presbyterian game in Macon in 1929, while $930 was lost on the Birmingham Southern game. In addition to possible losses on home games, the Association had agreed to pay guarantees of $4,500 to visiting teams.

In 1932 the Athletic Association received substantial guarantees of $3,500 for the Army game and $3,000 for playing the Naval Academy. The expenses for the trips had to be met, however, and little money was left for the other expenses. It was a practice to provide the contracts for road games as collateral for bank loans to make the trips.

In 1928 Dr. Spright Dowell came to Mercer as president of the University. In 1931 the Athletic Association requested Dr. Dowell to withhold student fees which were designated for the Athletic Association. The money was to be applied to a $3,500 note at the Citizens and Southern National Bank. The request was granted, and withholding continued until the debt was liquidated on 10 June 1934. The loss of student fees during this period forced a curtailment of expenditures to some extent.

Under Dr. Dowell's supervision and leadership and with the cooperation of a new coaching staff, the Athletic Association's 1932 audit showed a net profit of $44.30. The budget had been substantially reduced from the previous year to $18,197.97 and the Association had been able to stay within it. The Association was not out of debt, however, and when the budgets were reduced for 1932 the planned expenditure for baseball was eliminated. It was decided that baseball was too expensive for its overall value at that time. Baseball did not return to the campus on a regular basis until 1947.

On 1 July 1933 an audit showed the Athletic Association owed Mercer $9,688.08. This was the latest cumulative total, and several accounts had been dropped in previous years. The audit in 1934 posted a debit balance of $14,568.54, not counting an old debt for $4,880.46. There was an excess of income over expenses of $2,649.25, the largest seasonal profit in history.

The depression caused Mercer serious financial problems, and it was necessary to borrow approximately $100,000 from the Baptist Holding Commission to repay a loan at a local bank. The money was to be repaid to the Commission in payments of $5,000 a year plus interest. Subsequently, it was necessary to cut expenses as much as possible. The salaries of the faculty members were reduced, and Lake Russell's salary went from $4,200 to $3,070 annually. Most professors were paid around $2,000, and they also had salary reductions.

The 1934 season ended with a deficit of $3,800. The Washington and Jefferson game, which was played in Macon, accounted for most of this as $2,500 was lost at the gate. The reasons for the deficit were that the student body was small, and the citizens of Macon just did not attend the games in sufficient numbers to offset the guarantee promised.

In 1935 the Athletic Association of Mercer and Lanier agreed to light Porter (Centennial) Stadium. Ten percent of the gate receipts were to be applied to the bill until it was liquidated. The Mercer Association was already paying ten percent of the gate receipts at home games as rent on the stadium. The rent bill for the stadium was in arrears on occasion and it became a practice for an official of the city to collect the ten percent at each home game. Originally Mercer donated the land for the stadium and Dr. Weaver, Dr. W. G. Lee, and others spent considerable time and effort in getting the stadium erected. Had it not been for the initiative of Dr. Weaver and the generosity of the board of trustees, it would not have been built as soon as it was.

In 1935 it was reported that the average indebtedness of the Athletic Association for the past ten years was $2,000.00 a year. The number of scholarships was reduced from 21 to 18 in an effort to make ends meet. Paid attendance at home games was still very low during the season as indicated by a loss of $319.90 in a game with Birmingham Southern. In addition to low ticket prices, many free passes were asked for and issued and both of these factors caused small revenues on home games. The highest price ever charged for a ticket was $2.20 for the Mercer-Georgia game in 1941.

When the rent, federal tax, game expense, and guarantees were paid, there was little left to pay bills or provide money for the next game, resulting in constant necessity to borrow money. On 1 June 1937 the Athletic Association's liability to Mercer was $5,175.33, a note to the First National Bank was for $4,500, and other accounts totaled $1,494.46. These items amounted to a total deficit of $11,169.79.

The 1937 season saw the Bears taking to the road again. The game with Chattanooga netted $1,009.96 on a $1,250 guarantee. The Chamber of Commerce in Columbus sponsored a game with Birmingham Southern in Columbus and the Association made $361.50. The 1937 season opened with a game with Georgia Teachers in Macon and lost $202.30. However, $1,819.95 was netted at Georgia, $1,827 at Georgia Tech, $513 at Howard, $392.49 with Oglethorpe at Porter Stadium, $729.90 at Tampa, and $429.61 at Presbyterian. It was definitely more profitable to play on the road than at home.

The financial interest in Mercer football by Macon fans and alumni brought some relief. The records show that contributions amounted to $1,685 in 1936-37. To list the individuals who aided the football program financially through the years would be impossible because of the lack of records. However, it must be recorded that Herbert Smart, once the mayor of Macon, consistently and enthusiastically supported the program for a number of years. W. T. Anderson of the *Macon Telegraph* sponsored a drive to raise $8,000 locally to be matched by state alumni. James H. Porter on one occasion gave $2,544.41 to be used to pay old accounts. H. H. Ware was always a loyal and enthusiastic supporter of the team.

In addition, the Macon Athletic Association was formed on 6 May 1937. The purpose of this organization was to raise and lend money to the Board of Control. The original goal was $25,000 to be available for the seasons in 1937, 1938, and 1939. A subsequent agreement by the Macon group was signed on 27 December 1937 to raise $30,000 to be distributed to the Board of Control in three equal payments.

Mr. Price, the business manager of athletics received from 31 December 1937 to 30 March 1939 $13,900 from H. P. Fleming, the treasurer of the campaign. An additional $5,290 was received by Charles Hubbard, successor to Price, to bring the total amount received through the campaign to $19,910. This money was used to pay various expenses related to the football program.

In 1937 the debt for lighting the stadium had been reduced from $750 to $350 and the athletic deficit as of June 1 was $11,169.79. President Dowell had agreed to take over $16,000 which was on the Mercer books. The Board of Control prevailed on the trustees to cancel an additional debt of $5,000 which the Athletic Association had incurred in the 1936-37 season. This request was refused because of the poor financial condition of the University.

The 1936-37 team, scheduled to play only three home games, opened with Georgia Teachers and lost $94.34 on the game. Financial losses were recorded for the other two home games, as $307.54 was lost on the game with Howard and $575 on Presbyterian. The total indebtedness at the end of 1937 was recorded at $21,333.81. In addition, $2,618.07 which was pledged for individual athletes was never paid.

In 1938 a budget for football of $42,700 was proposed. The University provided $3,000 in scholarships, while student fees brought in $4,700. The Macon Athletic Association contributed $10,600 and the University added an additional $4,930 for the coaches' salaries. Guarantees for six road games brought in $9,250. With the proposing of this larger budget, the number of scholarships was increased to thirty-five with the permission of the board of trustees. The total disbursement for scholarships in 1938 was $18,632.

In 1939 Charles Hubbard succeeded S.J.T. Price as business manager of Mercer and he also took over Price's duties with athletics. In a memorandum to president Dowell on 4 August 1940, Mr. Hubbard pointed out that the athletic deficit to the University had increased since 1 June 1937 when there was a deficit of $16,246.31. There had been some anticipation among athletic officials that this amount would be charged off; however, it was included in the report.

The unpaid tuition for athletics from the fall of 1937 to the spring of 1939 amounted to over $23,000. In addition, there was $2,742.90 on the books for scholarships promised by members of the athletic department and alumni. The total indebtedness as of 4 August 1940 stood at $56,358.97, and this indebtedness did not cover expenditures for supplies which were outstanding.

The final records available are financial results for games played in 1941. Mercer opened the season against Georgia and drew the largest crowd ever at Porter Stadium. The resulting gate receipts were also of record size. The contract between the University of Georgia and Mercer called for an equal division of the income and Mercer's share, $4,079.17, was the most income earned at any Mercer football game.

Georgia Teachers College played the following game in Porter Stadium, and the financial statement showed a net loss of $129.44. Wofford was next and the Athletic Association lost $261.30. This was followed by a game with Rollins in Orlando, Florida, and a profit of $44.30. On 1 November 1941 a game with Presbyterian showed a net loss of $132.56, while a game in Clinton, Mississippi, netted $66.60 on 8 November 1941. There were additional profits of $248.25 with Newberry, $447.15 with Wofford, and $912.10 with Chattanooga. All of these last games were played on the road. An accurate and thorough summation of the expenses for this last year of football, because some records are not available, is not possible. The gate receipts, particularly at home, however, would lead one to believe that the trend of financial deficits did not change.

The final years of football at Mercer were probably the most difficult. The budget had grown to approximately $50,000 a year. This is a modest budget by today's athletic standards, but it was enormous for its time, especially under the difficult financial conditions.

When football was discontinued, there were many outstanding debts and an accurate accounting is impossible. There were bills for laundry, transportation, and supplies. A bill for approximately $4,000 was marked paid by the Peeler Hardware Company. Possibly other bills were treated in a like manner, but there were many that the University had to pay.

The sport which began as a friendly match between Mercer and Georgia had lasted for fifty years. It was fifty years of fun, glory, anguish, and hardship. Football, like no other sport, demands and requires the participation of players, coaches, and fans. Although the end of an era was not a pleasing thought for many, the answer to "Whence Cometh That Bear?" is inscribed in the hearts of those who were there.

EXTRA POINTS

An Afterword

Mercer had eighteen head coaches from 1892 through 1941. Most of these men remained at Mercer only one or two years, but Lake Russell devoted twelve years of his life to Mercer football and Mercer players.

In 1966 I contacted Lake Russell to get information about Mercer football and a list of outstanding players during his tenure here. He was then warden of Brushy Mountain State Prison in Tennessee. In June of 1969 he was appointed Commissioner of the Department of Corrections for the state of Tennessee.

I visited his office to meet and talk with him about football when he was the head coach at Mercer. On entering his office and meeting Lake Russell for the first time, I immediately sensed that here was a man who had a genuine concern for people.

Russell had played football against Mercer in 1922 while a student at Carson-Newman College. He was a standout left tackle on the team which beat Josh Cody's men 12-7. Following his playing days he coached football for seven years at Carson-Newman. Russell later became the only Mercer coach to beat Carson-Newman.

In 1929 he was selected as coach at Mercer from a list of more than twenty-five nominees. Most of these were Mercer graduates. He related that when he accepted the job at Mercer, he went to his bank to take out his money, but the bank was closed. The depression was on. He had actually lost money even before he started to work at Mercer.

Russell was asked by mayor Toole to set up a boxing area in Tattnall Square Park for the youth of the area. Times were difficult, and many youngsters needed something to do.

He helped train Young Stribling for his fight with Max Schmeling in Cleveland Stadium. This was the first athletic contest held in the stadium.

Russell related an unusual incident which occurred during a road game. He stated: "In the game with John Carroll in 1931, the ball floated away from the line of scrimmage on several occasions." This game was played in a pouring rain and thc field was covered with water.

From 1949-55 Russell taught English and coached at Miami Beach High School in Miami, Florida. (He related that he was released from his position as warden because of political expediency and he returned to coaching again.)

In 1933 Russell wanted to fly to New York for the Army game, but the players were reluctant to fly with him. Their parents were apprehensive. He related that he wanted to be first in this method of transportation but could not get the fellows to go with him.

Russell also spoke of the difficulty he had in raising money for the scholarships, how people promised to help but some never did. He did get some help and sincerely appreciated it. Men like George Sparks, Julian "Stick" Roddenberry, Byron Blackburn, Dr. Ralph Newton, and Buddy Tarver were mentioned as having been very helpful. He knew that there were many others, but time has a way of erasing the memory.

Russell stated that "had Earl Lewis had ten more pounds, he would have been a real college player. That boy didn't lack anything in loyalty and courage."

In one of the old programs there was a section devoted to great thrills by former Mercer stars. B. L. "Crook" Smith, great end in the early twenties and former coach at South Georgia Teachers College, states that he received his greatest thrill in the Mercer-Birmingham Southern game of 1921. Big Reese kicked a field goal in the early part of the game to give the Bears a 3-0 lead which was wiped out and the Panthers were ahead by 14-3 in the third quarter. The score remained this way until two minutes before the game ended. From the thirty-yard line Ed Erwin threw Crook a long pass for a touchdown and the extra point was added to bring the score to 14-10. With time almost gone, the reverse pass from left end, Erwin, to right end, Smith, worked again with Crook going over for the winning touchdown. The final score was 17-14. For his great game that day, Crook's teammates gave him a free trip to the dedication of the Vanderbilt stadium the following day in which Vanderbilt and Michigan played.

"Duck" Swann, former outstanding quarterback and later coach and principal at Lanier, said that the most thrilling play he had any part in was in the Mercer-Chattanooga game in 1915. Playing in Chattanooga with the score 0-6 in the Moccasins' favor and but a few minutes left in the game, a ball was kicked to him at safety. He returned it close to the goal line where he received the hardest tackle of his career by the Chattanooga safety man. The ball bounded from his grasp into the arms of Watson Drane, who was following his progress down the field. Drane lugged it over for a touchdown, thus saving the game for the Bears.

Stanley L. Robinson, former head coach at Mercer, gives the following incident as the most outstanding play he saw at Mercer:

> In the Mercer-Furman game the teams fought in midfield all afternoon with one exception, when Furman had succeeded in making a field goal from the thirty-yard line. With the score at three to nothing, the field judge notified the Furman captain that there was three minutes to play and the Furman quarterback launched a forward-pass attack. On one of these passes, Davie Rice intercepted and carried to the twenty-yard line. After three plays, Mercer still had ten yards to go for a first down. Kid Cecil then called "Red Simmons play" in which the ball was passed back to the quarterback who placed the ball behind the knee of the left guard and then ran back as though he was to pass. Cecil's deception was so good that all the Furman team and Tick Tichnor, the referee, followed him as he retreated. This left the opening for Red Simmons to step in behind the guard's knee and take the ball, which he did, and crossed the goal line with practically the entire Furman team rushing Kid Cecil or picking up forward pass receivers. There were but a few seconds left to play and Mercer had won the game by six to three.

Mike Herndon, former stellar guard and coach at South Georgia State, gives as his biggest thrill an incident that is highly ludicrous. Time—1920. Place—Central City Park. Game—Erskine vs. Mercer. Score—6-20. The Bears went on the field to receive Erskine's kickoff with their uniforms excessively patched with towels. Red Welch was back as receiver. He fumbled the ball. In the scramble, Ike Cowart got possession of the ball and with all his 220 pounds started waddling toward the goal some seventy yards distant. On this noteworthy jaunt, the patch in his pants ripped and the towels floated out, resembling Halley's Comet. Eventually Ike covered the distance, arriving about a split second ahead of the towels.

Phoney Smith, considered by many Mercerians to be the greatest halfback in the school's history, says that the greatest thrill he ever received from football was in the Mercer-Georgia game of 1927. Here is his version:

> The greatest thrill I experienced while playing football was in Athens in 1927 when Mercer met Georgia. The Bulldogs, previous to this game, had not had their goal line crossed, and on the kickoff I received the ball on the five-yard line. Falling behind the wedge of the Mercer team, I ran the length of the field, and crossed the Georgia goal standing up without an opposing player laying a hand on me. The thrill was double in that I had done next to the impossible in crossing the goal line of the best Georgia team in its history and that I had been the first man to accomplish the feat. Because of the punishment I had received (including a broken nose), it seemed sweet revenge. Without the fine blocking of my mates, the run would have been impossible.

Wallace Butts, teammate of Phoney Smith and former coach of Georgia, recalls a punt return by Phoney in the Howard game of 1926 as his greatest thrill. Here is his account of the incident:

> Mercer kicked off to Howard and after running one play Bancroft, Howard's star back, punted. The Mercer secondary was in close and Phoney was not over twenty-five yards back of the line of scrimmage. The punt traveled about forty yards and Phoney, running at top speed, took it over his shoulder. (Tris Speaker never made a more sensational catch of a baseball.) Phoney's return of the punt was good for sixty yards to Howard's ten-yard line.

In 1966 Wallace Butts wrote, "Phoney Smith definitely should be in the National Hall of Fame. Bernie Moore should be able to assist. Please get this idea started and count on me for help. At one time *I could have done the job*."

At one time they all could have done the job—and they did, during Mercer's gridiron glory days.

APPENDIXES

A. Mercer Gridiron Record, 1892-1941

Year	Mercer	Opponent		Coach
1892 (Jan)	0	50	Georgia	Dave Beggs
1892 (Feb)	2	20	Savannah Catholic Library Association	(No Coach)
1892	12	6	Georgia Tech	(No Coach)
1894	6	10	Georgia Tech	George Stallings
1896	4	6	Georgia Tech	J. D. Winston
	4	4	Georgia Tech	
	0	46	Auburn	
1897	0	26	Auburn	Gordon Saussy
1903	0	46	Georgia Tech	(No Coach)
1906	0	10	Citadel	E. E. Tarr
	28	5	Gordon	
	0	55	Georgia	
	12	0	Florida	
	0	61	Georgia Tech	
1907	6	0	Florida	H. R. Shencker
	5	0	Gordon	
	0	63	Auburn	
	11	6	Howard	

Year	Mercer	Opponent		Coach
1907	6	26	Georgia	
	0	75	Mississippi A & M	
1908	56	0	Locust Grove	Frank Blake
	0	23	Auburn	
	24	0	Florida	
	6	16	Georgia Tech	
	0	11	Georgia	
	45	0	Howard	
	0	10	Citadel	
1909	5	28	Vanderbilt	Frank Blake
	5	23	Auburn	
	0	35	Georgia Tech	
	10	2	Chattanooga	
	5	3	South Carolina	
	5	6	Howard	
	26	0	Norman Park	
1910	32	0	Locust Grove	C. C. Stroud
	3	0	Clemson	
	22	0	Med. Dept. of Ga.	
	0	46	Georgia Tech	
	13	0	Florida	
	0	22	Georgia	
	0	6	Chattanooga	
	21	0	Citadel	
	28	0	Howard	
1911	25	0	Locust Grove	C. C. Stroud
	20	6	Clemson	
	25	0	Howard	
	12	0	Gordon	
	0	29	Auburn	
	0	17	Georgia Tech	
	0	34	Mississippi	
	0	5	Citadel	
	5	8	Georgia	
	5	6	Columbia	
	6	6	Columbia	
1912	6	0	Stetson	C. C. Stroud
	27	14	Tennessee	
	71	0	Columbia	
	29	6	Gordon	
	0	56	Auburn	
	36	0	Howard	
	13	22	Clemson	
	6	16	Georgia Tech	
	0	0	Florida	

Year	Mercer	Opponent		Coach
1913	44	0	10th District Aggies	Lewis Hardage
	33	0	Alabama Presbyterian	
	0	53	Auburn	
	7	7	Citadel	
	0	52	Clemson	
	0	24	Florida	
	0	33	Georgia Tech	
	6	13	Stetson	
1914	27	7	Kings College	Fred A. Robins
	44	0	Stetson	
	44	0	Gordon	
	39	0	Furman	
	26	0	Georgia Military College	
	0	16	Chattanooga	
	0	105	Georgia Tech	
	0	66	Mississippi A & M	
	0	14	Florida	
1915	6	0	Gordon	John Zellars
	0	52	Georgia Tech	
	13	6	Wofford	
	6	20	Chattanooga	
	14	7	Howard	
	0	45	Auburn	
	20	0	Douglas Aggies	
	32	0	Columbia	
	7	34	Florida	
1916	7	0	Georgia Military College	John Zellars
	0	49	Chattanooga	
	0	93	Auburn	D. R. Peacock
	7	26	Howard	
	0	7	Columbia	
	0	47	South Carolina	
	0	61	Georgia Tech	
1919	0	73	Oglethorpe	Maxwell James
	0	48	Florida	
1920	59	0	Lanier University	Josh Cody
	13	33	Howard	
	0	20	Chattanooga	
	0	30	Florida	
	19	6	Stetson	
	0	14	Gordon	
	0	42	Oglethorpe	
	0	14	Wake Forest	
	6	20	Erskine	

Year	Mercer	Opponent		Coach
1921	0	28	Georgia	Josh Cody
	0	42	Vanderbilt	
	0	7	Florida	
	20	0	Birmingham Southern	
	41	0	Stetson	
	0	37	Furman	
	6	7	Oglethorpe	
	18	0	Chattanooga	
	7	24	Ft. Benning	
1922	24	3	Piedmont	Josh Cody
	0	41	Georgia	
	31	0	North Ga. Aggies	
	17	13	Birmingham Southern	
	7	50	Auburn	
	0	25	Vanderbilt	
	12	0	Maryville	
	6	13	Chattanooga	
	18	10	Oglethorpe	
	7	12	Carson-Newman	
	13	27	Ft. Benning	
1923	0	7	Georgia	Stanley Robinson
	6	3	Furman	
	7	0	Ft. Benning	
	18	3	Chattanooga	
	12	0	Birmingham Southern	
	7	19	Florida	
	6	7	Oglethorpe	
	0	15	Mississippi College	
	0	12	Carson-Newman	
1924	7	24	Georgia	Stanley Robinson
	0	26	Syracuse	
	23	0	Furman	
	33	0	Chattanooga	
	14	5	Howard	
	0	0	Loyola	
	16	0	Wofford	
	10	0	Florida	
	0	25	Oglethorpe	
	7	7	Mississippi College	
1925	0	32	Georgia	Stanley Robinson
	0	24	Florida	
	14	0	Rollins	
	7	12	Chattanooga	
	0	3	North Carolina	
	0	16	Citadel	

Year	Mercer	Opponent		Coach
1925	17	0	Furman	
	21	6	Oglethorpe	
	30	0	Marquette	
1926	0	20	Georgia	Bernie Moore
	7	12	Citadel	
	6	3	Florida	
	3	0	Howard	
	13	21	Ft. Benning	
	13	13	Furman	
	55	0	Rollins	
	31	7	Oglethorpe	
	0	0	Parris Island Marines	
1927	77	0	North Ga. Aggies	Bernie Moore
	6	0	Citadel	
	13	27	Furman	
	26	7	Presbyterian	
	0	14	Howard	
	6	32	Florida	
	21	6	Oglethorpe	
	7	26	Georgia	
	34	0	Wake Forest	
1928	0	52	Georgia	Bernie Moore
	7	0	Citadel	
	0	73	Florida	
	7	15	Howard	
	7	6	Presbyterian	
	14	12	Wake Forest	
	20	20	Birmingham Southern	
	18	38	Duke	
	0	15	Oglethorpe	
1929	0	21	Citadel	Lake Russell
	7	2	Howard	
	0	6	Presbyterian	
	7	7	Chattanooga	
	0	13	Wake Forest	
	7	39	Birmingham Southern	
	6	19	Duke	
	59	0	Rollins	
	0	26	Oglethorpe	
1930	0	51	Georgia	Lake Russell
	7	9	Presbyterian	
	6	8	Chattanooga	
	33	0	Stetson	
	13	6	Birmingham Southern	
	77	0	Georgia Teachers	

Year	Mercer	Opponent		Coach
1930	2	0	Oglethorpe	
	33	0	Florida Southern	
	0	21	Wake Forest	
	6	13	Oglethorpe	
1931	26	0	Citadel	Lake Russell
	20	7	Presbyterian	
	19	27	Chattanooga	
	28	7	Stetson	
	12	0	Birmingham Southern	
	20	6	Erskine	
	25	7	Wofford	
	0	0	John Carroll	
	20	0	Oglethorpe	
	0	3	Centre	
1932	7	20	Vanderbilt	Lake Russell
	21	6	Howard	
	51	0	Presbyterian	
	0	2	Furman	
	57	0	Parris Island Marines	
	8	0	Centre	
	25	0	Chattanooga	
	7	6	Oglethorpe	
	42	0	Erskine	
1933	44	3	Spring Hill	Lake Russell
	6	19	Army	
	6	25	Navy	
	0	0	Birmingham Southern	
	12	13	Georgia	
	6	6	Furman	
	7	0	Chattanooga	
	13	0	Clemson	
	31	0	Oglethorpe	
1934	6	7	Presbyterian	Lake Russell
	0	21	Loyola	
	0	14	Birmingham Southern	
	3	9	Furman	
	6	0	Stetson	
	30	7	Washington and Jefferson	
	13	13	Chattanooga	
	0	32	Clemson	
	13	16	Centre	
	7	6	Oglethorpe	
1935	0	31	Georgia	Lake Russell
	0	27	Navy	
	14	0	Birmingham Southern	

Year	Mercer	Opponent		Coach
1935	14	7	Presbyterian	
	0	13	Clemson	
	7	12	Chattanooga	
	21	7	Troy State	
	19	0	Oglethorpe	
	0	32	Furman	
1936	40	0	Georgia Teachers	Lake Russell
	6	15	Georgia	
	20	6	Oglethorpe	
	0	6	Birmingham Southern	
	9	20	Furman	
	0	13	Miami	
	20	6	Presbyterian	
	0	32	Mississippi State	
	0	0	Howard	
1937	77	0	Georgia Teachers	Lake Russell
	0	28	Georgia Tech	
	0	7	Howard	
	0	7	Birmingham Southern	
	0	19	Georgia	
	13	6	Oglethorpe	
	25	13	Presbyterian	
	20	0	Tampa	
	7	19	Chattanooga	
1938	15	0	Wofford	Lake Russell
	0	19	Georgia Tech	
	0	7	Birmingham Southern	
	19	28	Georgia	
	0	51	Tulane	
	33	7	Oglethorpe	
	28	0	Presbyterian	
	21	26	Mississippi College	
	7	9	Chattanooga	
1939	12	0	Wofford	Lake Russell
	0	7	Presbyterian	
	7	0	Carson-Newman	
	0	20	Alabama	
	10	0	Birmingham Southern	
	0	17	Tennessee	
	9	16	Georgia	
	0	15	Mississippi College	
	3	7	Howard	
	18	21	Chattanooga	
1940	0	49	Tennessee	Lake Russell
	0	20	Alabama	

Year	Mercer	Opponent		Coach
1940	0	20	Louisiana State	
	45	0	Erskine	
	2	3	Presbyterian	
	6	26	Mississippi College	
	6	14	Howard	
	6	20	Chattanooga	
1941	0	81	Georgia	Bobby Hooks
	25	0	Georgia Teachers	
	20	14	Wofford	
	0	52	Rollins	
	19	12	Presbyterian	
	19	27	Mississippi College	
	13	32	Newberry	
	6	27	Howard	
	13	40	Chattanooga	

B. Mercer Gridiron Record, by Opponents

Alabama

1939	0	20
1940	0	20

Alabama Presbyterian

1913	33	0

Alabama Teachers

1935	21	7

Army

1933	6	19

Auburn

1896	0	46
1897	0	26
1907	0	63
1908	0	23
1909	5	23
1911	0	29
1912	0	56
1913	0	53
1915	0	45
1916	0	93
1922	7	50

Birmingham Southern

1921	20	0
1922	17	13
1923	12	0
1928	20	20
1929	7	39
1930	13	6
1931	12	0
1933	0	0
1934	0	14
1935	14	0
1936	0	6
1937	0	7
1938	0	7
1939	10	0

Carson-Newman

1922	7	12
1923	0	12
1930	6	13
1939	7	0

Centre

1931	0	3
1932	8	0
1936	13	16

Chattanooga

1909	10	2
1910	0	6
1914	0	16
1915	6	20
1916	0	49
1920	0	20
1921	18	0
1922	6	13
1923	18	3
1924	33	0
1925	7	12
1929	7	7
1930	6	8
1931	19	27
1932	25	0
1933	7	0
1934	13	13
1935	7	12
1936	0	6
1937	7	19
1938	7	9
1939	18	21
1940	6	20
1941	13	40

Citadel

1906	0	10
1908	0	10
1910	21	0
1911	0	5
1913	7	7
1925	0	16
1926	7	12
1927	6	0
1928	7	0
1929	0	21
1931	26	0

Clemson

1910	3	0
1911	20	6
1912	13	22
1913	0	52
1933	13	0
1934	0	32
1935	0	13

Columbia College

1911	5	6
1911	6	6
1912	71	0
1915	32	0
1916	0	7

Douglas Aggies

1915	20	0

Duke

1928	18	38
1929	6	19

Erskine

1920	6	20
1931	20	6
1932	42	0
1940	45	0

Florida

1906	12	0
1907	6	0
1908	24	0
1910	13	0
1912	0	0
1913	0	24
1914	0	14
1915	7	34
1919	0	48
1920	0	30
1921	0	7
1923	7	19
1924	10	0
1925	0	24
1926	6	3
1927	6	32
1928	0	73

Florida Southern

1930	33	0

Ft. Benning

1921	7	24
1922	13	27
1923	7	0
1926	13	21

Furman

1914	39	0
1921	0	37
1923	6	3
1924	23	0
1925	17	0
1926	13	13
1927	13	27
1932	0	2
1933	6	6
1934	3	9
1935	0	32
1936	9	20

Georgia

1892	0	50
1906	0	55
1907	6	26
1908	0	11
1910	0	22
1911	5	8
1921	0	28
1922	0	41
1923	0	7
1924	7	26
1925	0	32
1926	0	20
1927	7	26
1928	0	52
1930	0	51
1933	12	13
1935	0	31
1936	6	15
1937	0	19
1938	19	28
1939	9	16
1941	0	81

Georgia Military College

1914	26	0
1916	7	0

Georgia Tech

1892	12	6
1894	6	10
1896	4	6
1896	4	4
1903	0	46
1906	0	68
1908	6	16
1909	0	35
1910	0	48
1911	0	17
1912	6	16
1913	0	33
1914	0	105
1915	0	52

Gordon

1906	5	28
1907	5	0
1911	12	0
1912	29	6
1914	44	0
1915	6	0
1920	0	14

Howard

1907	11	6
1908	45	0
1909	5	6
1910	28	0
1911	25	0
1912	36	0
1915	14	7
1916	7	26
1920	13	33
1924	14	5
1926	3	0
1927	0	14
1928	7	15
1929	7	2
1932	21	6
1936	0	0
1937	0	13
1939	3	7
1940	6	14
1941	6	27

John Carroll

1931	0	0

Kings College

1914	27	7

Lanier University of Atlanta

1920	59	0

Locust Grove Institute

1908	56	0
1910	32	0
1911	25	0

Louisiana State University

1940	0	20

Loyola, New Orleans

1924	0	0
1934	0	21

Marquette

1925	0	30

Maryville

1922	0	30

Medical Department of Georgia

1910	22	0

Miami, Florida

1936	0	13

Mississippi

1911	0	34

Mississippi College

1923	0	15
1924	7	7
1938	21	26
1939	0	15
1940	6	26
1941	19	27

Mississippi State (formerly Mississippi A&M—1907 and 1914)

1907	0	75
1914	0	66
1936	0	32

Navy

1933	6	25
1935	0	27

Newberry

1941	13	32

Norman Park

1909 26 0

North Carolina

1925 0 3

North Georgia Aggies

1922 31 0
1927 77 0

Oglethorpe

1919 0 73
1920 0 42
1921 6 7
1922 18 10
1923 6 7
1924 0 25
1925 21 6
1926 31 7
1927 21 6
1928 0 15
1929 0 26
1930 2 0
1931 20 0
1932 7 6
1933 31 0
1934 7 6
1935 19 0
1936 20 6
1937 13 6
1938 33 7

Parris Island Marines

1926 0 0
1932 57 0

Piedmont

1922 24 3

Presbyterian

1927 26 7
1928 7 6
1929 0 6
1930 7 9
1931 20 7
1932 51 0
1934 6 7
1935 14 7
1936 19 6
1937 25 13
1938 28 0
1939 0 7
1940 2 3
1941 19 12

Rollins

1925 14 0
1926 55 0
1929 59 0
1941 0 52

Savannah Library Association

1892 2 20

South Carolina

1909 5 3
1916 0 47

South Georgia Teachers College

1930 77 0
1936 40 0
1937 77 0
1941 25 0

Spring Hill

1933 44 3

Stetson

1912 6 0
1913 6 13
1914 44 0
1920 19 6
1921 41 0
1930 33 0
1931 28 7
1934 6 0

Syracuse

1924 0 26

Tampa

1937 20 0

Tennessee

1912 27 14
1939 0 17
1940 0 49

10th District Aggies

1913 44 0

Tulane

1938 0 51

Vanderbilt

1921	0	42
1922	0	25
1929	6	28
1932	7	20

Wake Forest

1920	0	14
1928	14	12
1930	0	21

Washington-Jefferson

1934	30	7

Wofford

1915	13	6
1924	16	0
1931	25	7
1938	14	0
1939	12	0
1941	20	14

C. Football Scoring Leaders for the Mercer Bears

Name	Years*	TD	FG	EP	Total
Joseph F. "Phoney" Smith	1925-27	24	3	23	176
Roy "Pinky" Walden	1930-32	21			126
Allan Bloodworth	1934-36	13	2	18	102
Ernie Zinkowski	1931-33	15			90
Bill Alderman	1927-29	11		22	88
Al Owen	1935-37	14		1	85
Johnny Cimperman	1930-32	11		2	68
Art Wright	1927-28	11			66
Frank Norman	1910-12	11		2	62
Jody Matt	1928-29	10			60
A. J. Swann	1914-15	10			60
Wright Bazemore	1936-37	8		11	59
E. B. "Crook" Smith	1921-24	9		2	56
H. S. Irwin	1911-12	6	5	9	55
G. H. "Skipper" Cochran	1912-14	9			54
James "Spec" Landrum	1937-39	8			48
Clay Binion	1908-10	7	2	6	47
Houston "Kid" Cecil	1921-24	7		1	43
Neufville "Shorty" Poore	1921-24	7			42
Ralph Skelton	1925	6		1	37
Henry Allen	1933-35	6			36
Norman Felder	1922-23	6			36
Tom Porter	1933-35	6			36
Dave Rice	1922-24	6			36
John T. "Jake" Zellars	1910-11	7			35
Art Pledger	1938-39	6			34
Willie Parker	1913-14	4			32
Bill Foxworth	1910-12	5			31
John Jasonis	1931-32	5			30
Robert E. "Bob" Lee	1932-34	5			30
Joe Pope	1932-33	5			30
B. Frank Sammons	1914-15	5			30
Arthur Yancey	1940-41	5			30
Seth Weekly	1915-20	4		4	28

*Indicates years the scores were made.
All scores were based on available records.

Name	Years	TD	FG	EP	Total
S. R. McDaniel	1910	5		1	26
Neal Allen	1937-38	4			24
Paul Davis	1938	4			24
P. E. Garrison	1920	4			24
Jimmy Glover	1924	4			24
Gerald McQuaig	1933	4			24
Anthony Page	1941	4			24
Carlso Phillips	1941	4			24
Jake Trommerhauser	1931	4			24
E. R. Welch	1921	4			24
Bob Sperry	1930-32	1		17	23
F. A. Sams	1912-13	3		4	22
R. L. Hodges	1941	3		2	20
Elder Hollingsworth	1929-31	1		14	20
Bob Poole	1909-10	4			20
S. T. "Little" Reese	1922-23	3	1		19
Rod Blaylock	1940-41	3			18
Henry Lawrence	1923-24		3	9	18
Tony Long	1931	3			18
Johnny Mattox	1937-38	3			18
Hugh Mills	1913	3			18
Billy Smith	1936	3			18
Edwin Varner	1934-36	3			18
Leon McKnight	1911-12	3			16
J. A. Scoggin	1907-09	3			15
Sid Ellison	1920-24	2		2	14
George Harmon	1921-22	2		2	14
John Westmoreland	1913	2		2	14
Bill Bruner	1926	2		1	13
Herschel "Big Boy" Forrester	1912-13	2			12
Jim Harbin	1921	2			12
Dick Hawes	1914	2			12
Bill Howland	1938	2			12
Buchanan "Buck" Loser	1928	2			12
Leo Lozar	1940	2			12
W. M. "Knuck" McCrary	1941	2			12
Jack Morris	1936	2			12
John Parks	1925	2			12
A. B. Phillips	1912	2			12

Name	Years	TD	FG	EP	Total
Carl Stager	1940	2			12
Jarred "Red" Simmons	1922-23	2			12
F. M. White	1920	2			12
E. S. Whitehead	1920	2			12
J. W. Jacobs	1909	2			10
Tom Rentz	1920	1		4	10
Ike Cowart	1920	1		3	9
Ed Irwin	1921-22			8	8
Roscoe Cline	1937-38	1		1	7
W. H. Drane	1916	1		1	7
Veo Yon	1938	1		1	7
R. B. "Red" Adams	1924	1			6
Bob Alley	1938	1			6
Tarzan Bowling	1923	1			6
Frank Branch	1930	1			6
Red Camp	1933	1			6
Brewer Corbin	1929	1			6
Al Davino	1934	1			6
R. C. Dorsey	1915	1			6
Bob Dutton	1939	1			6
Denver Fleming	1924	1			6
Al Gerhardt	1938	1			6
Harry Karsznia	1939	1			6
Bob Hendry	1939	1			6
W. Holman	1912	1			6
Brad Lamson	1929	1			6
Lynwood "Baggy" Mallard	1928	1			6
Jimmy Matthews	1927	1			6
Gene NeSmith	1934	1			6
Lehmon "Frog" Newsome	1928	1			6
J. R. Newton	1916	1			6
Lester "Swede" Olsson	1931	1			6
Raymond O'Quinn	1940	1			6
Charlton "Bit" Pierce	1925	1			6
E. H. "Bubber" Pope	1922	1			6
Glenn Ratliff	1941	1			6
Nat Reasor	1932	1			6
Jack Richards	1939	1			6
Don Spice	1940	1			6

Name	Years	TD	FG	EP	Total
Wilbur Smith	1927	1			6
Kay Tipton	1924	1			6
Rod Tuach	1937	1			6
Tom Veasey	1930	1			6
Eugene Brundage	1941			5	5
Donald Powell	1911	1			5
H. P. Bell	1932-33			3	3
Bowie Gray	1933			3	3
Bob Smith	1930			3	3
Wally Byrom	1935			2	2
Ellis Paulk	1940			2	2
Lamar Plunkett	1940			1	1
Grady Gillon	1938			1	1
Don Lockert	1935			1	1

D. Mercer University Athletic Hall of Fame

1971*
Wright Bazemore '38
James Wallace Butts '28
James M. Cowan (C) 1946-1956
Malcolm Lawrence Green '27
William Green Lee '99
Carl Lester Olsson '39
Julien Bostwick Roddenbery '13
Lake Fern Russell (C) 1929-1940
James Arthur Scoggin '09
Jarred Alexander Simmons '26
Bryon Lambert Smith '25
Joseph Farrar Smith '28
William Arthur Stone '24
Zebulon Baird Vance (C) 1942-1971
Glenn Newton Wilkes '50

1972
Wilton Byron Alderman '30
Allan Rabun Bloodworth '37
Luther Usrie Bloodworth '18
William Lamar Clements '51
George Hugh Cochran '14
Charles C. Morgan '17
John Richardson Parks '27
Charlton Louian Pierce '28
Robert Boyd Reeder '51
Claude Duane Smith (C) 1943 -1977
Albert Jernigan Swann '16
John Lenoir Westmoreland '14

1973
Norman King Carter, Jr. '60
James Clayton Clements '17
Herschel Forester '15
Walter Jasper Grace '15
George F. Harmon '25
Ernest Lynwood Mallard '30
William Robert Pinkston '26
Thomas Joseph Porter '36
Richard Francis Reid '54
Robert Monroe Smith '33

1974
Glenn E. Cassell '52
Josh Cody (C) 1920-1923
Robert Mann Gamble '22
Franklin Lee Hunt '15
Carl Erastus Lancaster '23
Robert Edward Lee, Jr. '35
Harold Lichter '36
Arthur Thomas Mixon '55
Robert Ellis Wilder '52 (C) 1957-1970

1975
Charles E. Dewberry '15
C. Bradley Hogg '11
James D. Landrum '40
Ernest F. Zinkowski '34
Robert F. Sperry '33
F. Manly McWilliams '24
H. Alton Owen '38
Joe Pope '34
Nat H. Reasor '34
Thomas H. Rentz '22
Bert D. Schwartz '54

1976
Neal Allen '41
Jimmy J. Carnes '56
Sidney H. Ellison '25
George C. Gibson '14
Dan W. Hammack '23
Oscar L. Long '26
Neufville Poore '25
Charles R. Dorsey '17

1977
W. Mayes Dobbins '50
J. King Dunn '25
Ferrol A. Sams '14
John V. Skinner '27
William C. Smith '38
Erie O. Sinclair '20

*Year indicates year of induction.
(C) indicates coach.

1978
Steve Moody '67
Emmett H. "Bubber" Pope '25
Tommy Day Wilcox '65
I. Giddens Wilkes '23

1979
Sybil A. Blalock '75
Mike E. Herndon '24
Henry M. Melton '09
Woodrow W. Richardson, Jr. '58
Judson R. Roberts '69
Virginia Williamson '37

1980
Robert Houston Reeves '66
Walter Ravenelle Salter '28
Donald Glenn Veal '61

1981
Robert E. Belloir '70
Walter L. Moore, Jr. '57

1982
James C. Hearn '64
Bela A. Lancaster '26